Jesus of History,
Christ of Faith

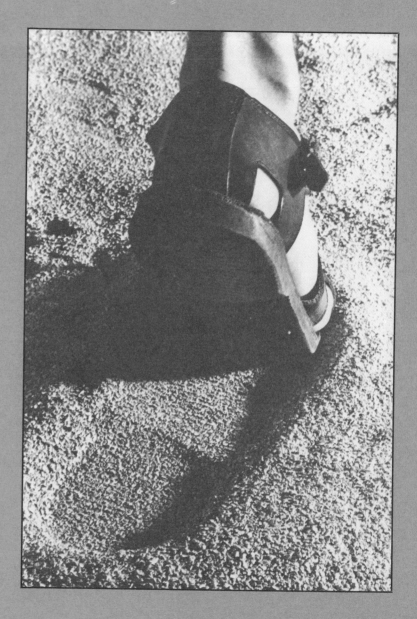

Jesus of History, Christ of Faith

A Gospel Portrait for Young People

by Thomas Zanzig

Saint Mary's Press
Christian Brothers Publications
Winona, Minnesota

Nihil Obstat: Msgr. Roy E. Literski, PhD, STL
Censor Deputatus
February 20, 1982
Imprimatur: †Loras J. Watters, DD
Bishop of Winona
February 20, 1982

The special consultants for this course book were
Donald Gary, PhD
Donald Senior, CP

The development of this course book has been made possible through a special grant to the Christian Brothers by Mrs. Rose Totino.

Scriptural excerpt on page 195 is from the *New American Bible,* copyright © 1970, by the Confraternity of Christian Doctrine, Washington, D.C. Used by permission of the copyright holder. All rights reserved.

Other scriptural excerpts used in this work are from *The Jerusalem Bible,* copyright © 1966 by Darton, Longman & Todd, Ltd., and Doubleday & Company, Inc. Used by permission of the publisher.

Drawings on pages 64-65, 67, and 154-155 are from *Jesus and the Four Gospels* by John Drane, copyright © 1979 by John W. Drane. Reprinted by permission of Harper & Row, Publishers, Inc.

The acknowledgments continue on page 204.

Printed in the United States of America

Printing: 14 13 12 11 10 9 8
Year: 1995 94 93 92 91 90 89

Library of Congress card catalog number 81-86361
ISBN 0-88489-145-3

Contents

Maps, Charts, and Illustrations

Introduction: "Who Do You Say I Am?"

Now one day when he was praying alone in the presence of his disciples he put this question to them, "Who do the crowds say I am?" And they answered, "John the Baptist; others Elijah; and others say one of the ancient prophets come back to life." "But you," he said, "who do you say I am?" It was Peter who spoke up. "The Christ of God," he said. But he gave them strict orders not to tell anyone anything about this (Luke 9:18-21).

1) A Humble Beginning to a Great Story

Nearly two thousand years ago he was born in poverty. The magnificent paintings of his birth by countless artists, the inspiring sound of Christmas carols sung by choirs, and brightly wrapped presents under decorated trees tend to mask the fact that his real "birth-day" was very humble.

He was raised in an obscure Galilean village in Palestine, a small country no bigger than New Jersey. The names perhaps sound remote, strange, distant—Galilee, Palestine—as do so many names of towns and villages which would someday become famous chiefly because of their association with him: Bethlehem, Cana, Bethany, Capernaum.

He was the son of a carpenter. Today television's constant harping about the glories of Craftsman power tools and Black and Decker Workmate benches and "the friendly hardware man" have blurred our understanding and appreciation of the particular joys and challenges of carpentry two thousand years ago. How much we think we know of him; how little we really do.

We know very little about his early life, and most of what we claim to know about his childhood and young adulthood is drawn from our understanding of his Jewish roots, our knowledge of the historical circumstances of his time, and from the recollections of people upon whom he made a powerful and lasting impact. We can only speculate on what he looked like, the types of people he

associated with as he grew, the kind of education he attained. Yet our strong impression is that we know him well. His face is, after all, recognizable in literally thousands of paintings, films, and statues—all bearing different images, of course, and yet all looking vaguely similar. The stories of his encounters with people have become as familiar as reruns of old favorites on TV. Many even think that his profound ideas came easily to him—certainly without a need for any formal education. Somehow his having to go to school strikes us as almost humorous, even ridiculous. How much we think we know of him; how little we really do.

So we know little about his early "hidden years." And we have only a brief and somewhat confusing record of what would come to be called his "public life," starting from about the time he was 30 years old. He almost seems to come out of nowhere, taking the people of his time by surprise. His people, the Jews, had waited a long time for someone who would claim what he was to claim—that he was "the one sent by God" who was to free them from their oppression. And yet when he came among them, many rejected him. He was so unlike what they had hoped for and expected.

His public life seems in some respects to be as cloudy and vague as his early life. He may have been a public figure, for instance, for as little as six months or for as long as three years. The few written records we have of his life and work—what we call "gospels"—seem so often to conflict with each other on the details of his actions and words that some people choose to reject them as unreliable, even as fables and fairy tales.

Matters of life and death.

In his own time he was most often called simply a teacher, yet one whose "classroom" varied from the formal setting of Jewish houses of prayer and worship to crowded and dusty streets, from peaceful lakeshores to rolling hillsides. His basic message as he delivered it might well fill only a small pamphlet, yet library shelves today groan under the weight of thousands of books that have attempted to "simplify" and to explain the message he felt was so simple that even children—perhaps only children—could quickly understand it. It was a message about a good God and a proclamation of unlimited love, of generosity, of a world of peace, of brotherhood and sisterhood. It was a message of hope in the midst of despair, of joy beneath the tears and hunger, of freedom from the chains of oppression, of life in the face of death. And the man who preached that message of unbounded hope, of unquenchable joy, of profound liberation and abundant life was savagely executed on a cross by people he had somehow frightened. The glorious vision he offered had become for some people a horror show. His words of love and joy and peace had become for some a threat, even a curse. How could this happen? How much we think we know of him; how little we really do.

Like so many great leaders throughout history, he was fully appreciated and understood only *after* his brutal death. That in itself is not unusual. We humans often seem to appreciate wonderful gifts only when they have been taken from us, to experience deep love when the one we love is absent, to recognize great people when death snatches them from us. John Kennedy, Martin Luther King, and John Lennon were all young men when assassins' bullets brought them down. Our human inclination in such cases is not only to mourn the loss of what once was, but also to ache for what might have been—the promise that was never fulfilled, the talent left untapped, the wisdom never shared, and the music that would never be sung. But with *this* young man, this man from Nazareth nearly two thousand years ago, the response was strangely, mysteriously different. Following his death there was barely time for grief and no time to write obituaries. All the talk of "what might have been" had just begun when a completely shocking message rang out across the land. "The one whom you have crucified has been raised by God and is now alive!" Incredible! Stupendous! If true, it was a reality that almost shook the world at its foundations! And yet in cathedrals and churches across the world today, that message of joy is often received with a yawn, with boredom, with apathy. We have, after all, heard it all before. How much we think we know of him; how little we really do.

Nearly two thousand years have passed since the days when "the carpenter's son" walked the roads of Palestine, and still we must ask, "Who is this man?" He was called by many names during his earthly life—teacher, rabbi, the Nazarene, a prophet—and still we must ask, "Who is this man?" We need to constantly seek out new answers to that question primarily because of what people claimed about him *after* his death and after the event that some claimed was his Resurrection from the dead. The titles he then received come so easily to us now that we lose touch with what they mean—we forget that many people throughout history have endured torture and execution with these words on their lips and joy in their hearts. We fail to realize how haltingly these titles must have been uttered by those who first spoke them: Lord, Redeemer, Savior, Son of God, the Christ of God. How many throughout history have fallen to their knees with the overwhelming realization: "My God . . . he's God!" Yet how many today find those titles nearly meaningless? How many "put on" their faith in him with the same sense of routine as putting on a well-worn shirt? "Do you believe he was God, I mean, *really* God?" "Me? Oh, yeah, I suppose so. But let's talk about more exciting things . . . like food." How much we think we know about him; how little we really do.

Could we have your attention, please?

This is a course about that man from long ago, the son of the carpenter from Nazareth, the one called simply "Jesus" in his own time, the one now recognized by a quarter of all the people in the world as "the Christ," the one sent by God. The name and the title are perhaps *too* familiar. They fall too easily from the lips of some people, at times as a curse when life gets rough, perhaps as an expression of surprise, and even occasionally as a sigh of disgust. "Oh, Jesus!" "Christ Almighty!" But listen to what one of his followers, St. Paul, said long ago about Jesus and about that title:

> His state was divine, yet he did not cling to his equality with God but emptied himself to assume the condition of a slave, and became as men are; and being as all men are, he was humbler yet, even to accepting death, death on a cross. But God raised him high and gave him the name which is above all other names so that all beings in the heavens, on earth and in the underworld, should bend the knee at the name of Jesus and that every tongue should acclaim Jesus Christ as Lord, to the glory of God the Father (Philippians 2:6-11).

Hardly a routine statement! The point is this: For many of us, our lives have been filled with stories about Jesus and with explanations of his message that the Church—that community of people gathered in his name—has developed through the years. And there is a chance, even a likelihood, that after awhile it all becomes so routine that we lose the sense of joyous surprise that should be a part of our experience of Jesus. It is important that we at least acknowledge that possibility early in this course and that we try to identify why so many of us feel that way about Jesus, about religion courses, about Christian faith.

This is certainly not to say that *all* people find religious discussions boring. Many people throughout the world continue to demonstrate a sincere excitement about and a deep commitment to Jesus and his message. But at times those people themselves become the objects of scorn and ridicule from their peers and others, labelled "religious freaks" or "holy rollers" or worse. Why is this so? What causes so many of us to find our religious traditions and beliefs so unappealing, even boring? Or, to view the question from another angle, what is it that happens in the lives of those people who find great meaning and significance in their Christian faith, people for whom Jesus and his message of love are the very center of their lives? And what about you? Upon what foundation or basis are you to make judgments or decisions about Jesus? For the greater part of your life, Christian faith has probably been simply a given, something that was "just there," a reality about which you had to make no choices or personal decisions. But there comes a time in each of our lives when we must freely choose those values, ideals, and beliefs upon which we will base our lives. How will you decide?

2) This Course and You

The question before us, then, is the same one posed by Jesus years ago and ever since: "Who do *you* say I am?" We want to commit ourselves to the discovery of an answer to that question that is honest, mature, and based on truth. But, looking back to the passage that began this introduction, note the way in which Jesus asked the question of his disciples. His first question was, "Who do the *crowds* say I am?" In other words, what have all the other people been saying about me? The disciples tell him they've heard many answers: John the Baptist, Elijah, one of the ancient prophets. And then Jesus makes the question more personal, more to the point: "All right, that's what everyone else has been telling you, but now what about you—you as a free individual, you as an adult who can think for yourself—who do *you* say I am?"

For perhaps sixteen or more years, you have been hearing what "the crowds" have to say about Jesus—from your parents, from the pulpit in your parish, from teachers. In many cases you have been asked to accept their conclusions without being told how they arrived at them. When you asked, "Who is Jesus?", you might have been told that he is God's Son and that he died for our sins. You may have been told that he was a great miracle-worker and a teacher of marvelous truths. When you were a child that may have been enough for you. But what about now? Are there not new questions to be asked and new answers to be discovered about this man Jesus? Can you make a mature decision about Jesus and his message on the information you have received up to this point? Or isn't it perhaps time to stand back, gather all the facts you can, and make your own decisions about him?

What will this course offer you?

This course is an attempt to offer you the facts about Jesus as clearly and directly as possible. It doesn't begin with the conclusions about Jesus that the Church has reached after two thousand years of study, reflection, prayer, and historical experience. Rather in this course we are going to begin at the beginning, starting our discussion of Jesus with the earliest sources we have for understanding him, and then learning how our present teachings have evolved from those early foundations. But if any of that information is going to be of value to you, we must begin with you—with your experience of Christian faith and the questions you may be confronting at this stage of your life. That is the purpose of chapter 1, in which we will discuss in a very general way the manner in which the Catholic faith is often passed on from one generation to another, and how we as individuals often grow from a religious heritage offered to us by parents and the Church to a faith that is personally and freely chosen—or rejected—by us as mature persons. From that initial discussion, then, we will move on to the following content:

In chapters 2 through 5 we will discuss the various sources we have available for information about Jesus and offer some important background on the geographical, religious, and political world in which he was born, grew, preached his message, and eventually died by crucifixion. Without this kind of background, it is virtually impossible to understand what Jesus was all about and why the world reacted to him as it did.

In chapters 6 through 9 we will take a close look at the message Jesus proclaimed to the world and the ways in which he proclaimed it—the words that he spoke and the things that he did that often spoke more loudly than words. Was Jesus proclaiming a message about himself or rather about his vision of God and of life? The answer to that question is central to our understanding of Jesus and of what it means to follow him.

In chapters 10 through 12 we will discuss those factors that have made Jesus the most widely proclaimed figure in history—his death and its meaning, the proclamation of his Resurrection from the dead, and the developing understanding of Jesus through the years by those, the members of the

Church, who profess to follow him. It is only at these latter stages of this course that we will deal directly with many of the issues and teachings about Jesus with which you may be most familiar—the Church's convictions about his nature as God, the development of the doctrines and official teachings about him that we recite regularly in the creeds at Mass, and so on. It is hoped that, by that point in this course, most if not all of these teachings will make more sense because they will be firmly rooted in an understanding of the history which led to their development.

In addition to all the information provided in this book, your teacher will supplement this course on Jesus with numerous strategies, exercises, and activities during your actual class time which, it is hoped, will make the course even more personally meaningful and enjoyable for you.

What can you offer this course?

In the opening pages of this book, there was a sentence that was repeated several times. It was this: "How much we think we know of him; how little we really do." That was not meant to be a put-down or a criticism of our background as Catholic Christians or an accusation of total ignorance on our parts as individuals. Certainly we *have* learned a great deal about Jesus through the parents, priests, religious sisters and brothers, and other teachers who have shared their convictions about him with us. The intent of that repeated sentence, however, was to call to our minds the fact that there is always so much more to learn about Jesus, so much to be clarified as we grow, so much new information that is only today being discovered by those who spend their entire lives studying the life, times, and message of Jesus. The greatest gift you can offer this course is an openness to that reality, a willingness to put aside possible prejudices about religion courses, and to involve yourself in this course with an open mind and an attitude of honest searching and sharing.

This course assumes that kind of attitude on your part. Intentionally challenging, at times difficult, it may sometimes raise doubts in your mind rather than offer clear-cut, simple answers to difficult and complex issues. Because it is an honest course, it cannot be an easy one. It is not only designed to affirm or reinforce the faith of a child but also to challenge us to grow to more mature understandings about our Christian faith. If you can participate in that search with an openness to truth and a willingness to share your own convictions about it, this can be a most rewarding course indeed.

As is true in most courses you take, you will be asked during this course on Jesus to read, to reflect, to discuss, to argue, and to participate in numerous classroom activities. We would also ask that you do all these things with an attitude of prayerful consideration of the material offered. The message of Jesus touches not just the mind but the heart as well. And the heart often needs silence, times of quiet reflection, in order to "hear" the message offered it. If you can take that kind of time to reflect on what we are about to pursue, the course will be even that much richer for you. With that invitation in mind, let's begin.

1
Growing as Christians: The Journey of a Lifetime

When I was a child, I used to talk like a child, and think like a child, and argue like a child, but now I am a man, all childish ways are put behind me. Now we are seeing a dim reflection in a mirror; but then we shall be seeing face to face. The knowledge that I have now is imperfect; but then I shall know as fully as I am known (1 Corinthians 13:11-12).

1) Looking Back Can Be a Step Forward

In the introduction we indicated that a person's interest in and response to Jesus is not a static, unchanging, once-and-for-all kind of reality. Rather, if one is to grow as a Christian, there will be an almost constant development in faith from childhood through adolescence and adulthood until death. It is precisely this kind of continual growth and development that can make living as Christians so challenging, exciting, and fulfilling.

To get an idea of what you might be experiencing at this stage in your life, let's take a look at a so-called average Catholic as he or she is gradually introduced to Christian faith as a child and then grows and matures through adolescence and into adulthood. It must be quickly admitted, of course, that what one person calls average another would recognize as unique and even strange. There is no attempt here to say "all normal people" will develop in the way described here—only that many have demonstrated characteristics similar to these. Also, these characteristics are so general that they may apply as well to persons raised in other religious denominations or faiths.

From birth to age 4: Taking care of the basics.

The first years of our lives are spent taking care of some pretty basic business—like survival! It is a time when the needs we experience are the most obvious and perhaps the most easily fulfilled: the empty stomach that literally cries out to be filled, the wet diaper that needs to be changed, the sense of fear that needs to be calmed by the warm touch of a loving parent or by an older brother or sister. As these needs are consistently met and the child experiences healthy growth, there is a gradual development of some sense of independence, the initial experience by the child of being a person apart from the others upon whom it has depended so totally. This sense of growing separation and independence is most clearly expressed during the so-called terrible twos, the discovery of the word *no* by the toddler, and what the psychologists often call the "first stage of negativity." For the parent with a good sense of humor, this stage can be cute; for others, it can be a real pain!

It's hard to imagine what we would normally term *religious development* during these early years, but even at this stage some foundations for later religious and spiritual growth are being constructed. In many Christian homes, for instance, the child will be introduced to religious symbols during this time: pictures of Jesus on the walls, the crucifix above the bed, and prayers recited by parents and others before meals. Young children will often have their first taste of church life as well: the strange goings on at Mass as the 3-year-old struggles free of its parents and attempts to scale the pew, tries to throw the missalette at the lady in the next pew, or shouts down the priest during his homily. All of these experiences—and the way parents and others react to them—have perhaps a far greater impact on us than we might imagine.

It should also be noted that some psychologists claim that the first three years of life are among the most critical in terms of the development of our self-image, our sense of being loved, and therefore of our gradual ability to reach out to others in love as we grow. The child whose needs are tenderly met at this age will often grow with a sense of security and openness to life. The children tragically subjected to abuse and cruelty in these very early years will often grow to be suspicious, closed, bitter adults who, sadly, often become the kind of parents who will someday abuse their own children. When one recalls the qualities so often described as central to Christian life—love, joy, peace, kindness, and so on—it is clear that even at this very early stage in development, we all experience things that will greatly affect our religious attitudes later in life.

Ages 4-10: Gaining control of things.

Following the development of some basic survival skills (feeding oneself, being toilet trained, learning to walk), the child begins a process of gaining further control of the world about him or her. This is primarily a matter of achieving some mastery or control over the world of things more than people, and the child accomplishes this through the gradual and continuing development of language and body skills.

Every parent remembers the thrill of the first words a child speaks—not just the emotional kick of hearing the "mama" and "dada" of the toddler, but that magical time when the child truly discovers the wonderful world of words and their meaning. All of a sudden there is an explosion of curiosity and delight as the child begins to understand the world by naming it and therefore gaining some control over it. The constant questions it seems are two: "whaaizzdat?" (the child's version of "what is that?") and "why?" . . . over and over and over again. These are usually followed by "meedodat," baby talk for "let *me* do that now!" All of life takes on new meaning, including the child's relationship with others. He or she can now meet people on different ground, in simple conversation, in the discovery of different personalities, and so on. As language skills progress through early childhood, they are enhanced gradually by the ability to read, and life becomes even more fascinating. Bedtime stories read by parents at night gradually evolve to quiet times alone, losing oneself in books from the library, in comic books, in books at school that begin to reveal the meaning of the world through words and pictures. A mind is being awakened, and it is a glorious and wondrous time.

It is also during this stage that one begins to master the world of things through the development of body skills. This is expressed in all kinds of ways. The 5-year-old child creates forty "masterpieces" a day with crayons and paper, and a milestone is reached when the page out of the coloring book can be completed without "going outside the lines." The 8-year-old catches thirty football passes in a row in the backyard and wins that first big race in the park against all the neighborhood kids. The memorable day arrives when we move from the tricycle to the "two-wheeler." Similar moments are repeated over and over again, from generation to generation, from family to family, across the world. Yet each time they seem somehow very special, because for each of us as individuals, they *are* special. It is the first time *I* colored the page perfectly, the first time *I* caught the pass and won the race, the first time *I* rode the bike without training wheels. And because of that, these are all special, even unforgettable, moments for each of us.

Religious development of children.

What about our religious development during this stage? It too can be a time of discovery, a time of gaining control, a time of mastering the world of religious *things*. And again this is accomplished through the same gradually developing language and body skills. We begin to learn what religious words mean. The priest says, "The Lord be with you," and we learn how to answer him. Some important prayers are memorized, and there is a great sense of pride when we can say the "Our Father" while standing next to our parents at Mass. Slowly the stories about Jesus and his message are learned, many of them sounding at first like the delightful fairy tales and fables told at our bedside at night. We learn how to perform physically as well. The sign of the cross is one day made correctly during the mealtime prayer and everyone at the table applauds and offers congratulations. We learn to genuflect and when to sit, stand, and kneel during Mass.

It is usually during this stage that two particularly sacred events occur: First Penance—what we now call the Sacrament of Reconciliation—and First Communion. Many high school students, when asked to identify the moment in their lives when they felt closest to God, when they most sensed the sacred in their lives, will recall their experience of "receiving my first Holy Communion." In many homes the event is celebrated with parties and special new clothes, and commemorated with photos for the family album. Years later, when we stumble across those photos, there is often a sense of sadness along with the fond memory, a sense, perhaps, of having lost the innocent kind of faith represented by the pictures—the slightly embarrassed smile, the fancy clothes, and the parent's arm placed with pride around our shoulders.

One of the frequent religious recollections from childhood is the feeling that, when we are young children, religion seems to provide a lot of answers to questions. It offers occasions when we feel very special and even holy. It may even be enjoyable to attend religion classes where we can learn about God. But for many, those feelings of enjoyment and interest don't last. For some people, the answers that religion once provided now only raise more difficult questions. For some, the feelings of being special and the experiences of "holiness" turn into long periods of loneliness and confusion. For many, it seems, courses in religion become the least interesting part of their education. Why does this happen? Where is the process of development taking us?

2) Adolescent Faith Development

Adolescence: No longer just "the teen years."

It used to be common to define the stage of development we call adolescence as lasting from about age 12 to age 20, that is, the teen years. There has been a lot of study of this stage of development over the years, and many psychologists now recognize that the "developmental tasks" of adolescents—those things we have to confront and deal with on our way to healthy, mature adulthood—are far too complex to resolve in seven or eight short years. Therefore, some now consider adolescence to last from about age 10 to as late as age 30 and beyond, and to consist of many different stages and processes rather than, for example, simply achieving physical maturity and leaving home. This certainly seems to be a refreshing and helpful change in our attitudes, at least from the point of view of eliminating the frightening feeling that we are somehow magically to become full-fledged adults on our eighteenth or twenty-first birthdays! On the other hand, it may be a bit disconcerting to think that we have to deal with the difficult chores of adolescence for eighteen years or more! In any case, let's take a look at what psychologists are saying about adolescent development these days, and in particular note the implications of this stage for our religious development and our attitudes about faith. We stated earlier that one of the chief purposes of this course is to help us answer that central question posed by Jesus: "Who do you say I am?" That is a question, however, that cannot be fully answered by us until we discover *our own* identities, the answer to the question, "Who am I?" Discovering the answer to *that* question is a major challenge of adolescence.

Ages 10-12: A physical and emotional upheaval.

Adolescence begins with a tremendous surge in physical and emotional development called puberty. This is not the place to detail what occurs at this time and why, but it's fair to summarize it by saying that the body over which one had just begun to gain control goes haywire. There is generally a period of rapid growth that will continue for several years with consequences that can drive parents crazy: new shoes are outgrown in months, food bills skyrocket with the child's appetite, hours are spent locked in the bathroom trying to make oneself presentable to the public.

This kind of physical change can't help but have strong emotional implications: the horror and self-consciousness that increase with each new pimple; the embarrassment of the kid—a great athlete at age 8—who suddenly finds it difficult to walk on a sidewalk without tripping on each crack; the strong attraction to the person of the opposite sex (who could hardly be tolerated just a few years earlier). Some of these things may one day be looked back upon with a grin and a sense of humor. But at the same time many adults continue to live with permanent emotional scars from this period of their own development—memories of being laughed at, for instance, the strong recollection of being unlovable, the continual fear of rejection by one's peers. It doesn't eliminate all the pain and heartache to tell people these are feelings shared by each of us, but it can make the pain more bearable.

There seem to be two major religious reactions during this stage of early adolescence. **Some people turn to religion in a more serious way, perhaps as a possible solution to the problems they are encountering.** A few may even seriously consider the religious life at this time—that is, becoming a priest or a religious brother or sister. Religion can also take on an increasing sense of superstition as well, when we begin to bargain with God or to perform religious practices in the hope of forcing God to take care of our problems.

Prayer becomes a more serious affair for some. At a younger age prayer was often primarily a matter of saying prayers at the appropriate times and places. During this stage, however, we may experience prayer as a time for almost begging God to help us out, and perhaps offering some sacrifice as our end of the bargain: "If I pass this test, God, I'll become a priest." "God, if this guy just asks me to go to the dance, I'll go to church every day for a year." "If only my parents don't find out what happened, God, I'll give up candy for six years." There is nothing wrong with this kind of religious attitude, certainly, at least not when experienced by a person in sixth or seventh grade. The problem occurs when people never outgrow this stage and continue to bargain this way with God when they are 50 years old.

The second religious reaction to early adolescence may simply be a lack of interest in religion at all. The personal tasks of dealing with new physical and emotional experiences can be so important that everything else—including religion—can take a back seat for a while. For persons like this, going to Mass seems to be the time for doing some of their most creative daydreaming. Religion classes have all the excitement of a math test. This isn't always a case of being turned off or negative about religion in the sense of actively complaining about it either. It's simply a matter of not really thinking about it at all. There are too many "important" things in life to deal with. Again, this is neither a good nor a bad attitude necessarily. It's just the way it is. But it will likely not stay that way for long.

Ages 13-15: Clearing the way for people.

Remember our comments about the stage from ages 4 to 10 when the challenge of life was primarily one of gaining control over the world of things through language and body skills? During this stage of development—from ages 13 to 15—that task almost seems to be reversed. All of a sudden the world of things becomes boring. Hobbies that used to hold our attention for hours now no longer even appeal to us. The common cry is "there's nothing to do around here!"—a claim which parents often have a hard time understanding and accepting. ("What do you mean, nothing to do? Take out the garbage!") What the young person is actually saying, however, is that none of the things that could be done are attractive or exciting anymore.

Speaking of parents, the relationship with them often changes radically during this time. During our early childhood our parents were probably the most

important people in the world to us. It didn't make much difference what others thought of us as long as our parents still cared. Now that changes. It now seems that our friends become more important to us than our parents, at least in the sense that we'll often risk our parents' anger rather than our friends' rejection of us. Now it seems that no matter what our parents say to us and about us, if people our own age don't accept us, we hurt—badly. We find ourselves lashing out at our parents, saying things to them that we would never have dreamed of saying earlier, and then suffering great feelings of guilt because we truly love our parents—even if we can't tell them that.

All of the experiences that began with puberty—the physical changes, the developing emotions, the self-consciousness—all of these deepen during this stage of development. We begin to grow away from the gang mentality that seems so common with grade school children, when we had twenty-five "best friends" and there was always something happening. During the junior high school years we start developing more exclusive friendships, deeper, stronger friendships with just one or two people. Though we may often lack compassion at this age (eighth graders, for example, can be extremely cruel to each other), it seems now that when we hurt someone's feelings we almost seem to hurt ourselves as well—we feel a bit guilty, and we would like to apologize but still find it hard, if not impossible, to do that.

Time to move on.

Some psychologists call this stage of adolescent development a time of "negative discovery of self." That's pretty scientific language, but the idea it expresses is fairly understandable. **At some time in our lives each of us has to begin to move away from the simple world of children and from the** parents upon whom we have depended totally in order to prepare to live our lives as unique, individual, free, mature persons. That is essentially what is happening here. During roughly the junior high school years, about seventh through ninth grades, we begin to reject the world of children and all that we associate with it—kids' games, dependency upon adults, sometimes school, and so on. This is expressed well by another common cry of young people at this age: "I'm not a kid anymore!" The problem is that, at this stage, we are not yet adults either. We are caught between two worlds—childhood and adulthood—and at times it can seem that we are being pulled apart from both sides. It can be rough, no question about it. It can also be exciting, exhilarating, and just plain fun. In any case, it is clearly one of the most important of all stages of development, and the way we handle the challenges of this stage will often have great impact on what kind of adults we eventually become.

What about our religious attitudes at this time? It seems that, for many, religion can appear to be another of those "kids' games" that we react against and perhaps temporarily reject during this stage of development. Earlier in our development we may have simply been bored by religion and religious practices. That boredom may now turn to anger for some people. The religious training and practices that we once accepted and even enjoyed as children now become things from our past that no longer appeal to us. In earlier adolescence maybe we just didn't think about religion all that much. Now we may begin to actively question it: Why am I supposed to believe all that stuff? What gives other people the right to tell me what's right or wrong? Why do I have to go to church? Why should I listen to what people were saying thousands of years ago? Why should I believe that Jesus was anything more than just a good man? What does all this have to do with my life right now?

It should be clearly stated that this process of gradually rejecting the world of children is as necessary in terms of religion as it is in every other area in our lives. It is just as unhealthy to blindly and unthinkingly accept all religious traditions and teachings as it would be to refuse to grow up, to never leave the homes of our parents, or to refuse to take charge of our lives as mature persons. The hope, in the latter case, is that after breaking free from childish dependency upon parents we can eventually grow to meet them on common ground as equals, as friends. This often occurs in young adulthood when we begin to have our own careers and families and thereby gain a whole new appreciation for and love of our parents. The same kind of growth is required if we are to gain religious maturity. In rejecting our childish understandings of religion, we should open ourselves to a more mature and free and conscious personal faith relationship with God. That process can and should begin at the next stage.

Ages 16-20: A time for weaving dreams.

One of the most encouraging things to say about the process of negative discovery of self we just discussed is that it doesn't last. For some the process of throwing off childhood and the pain that accompanies that process is deep and intense but perhaps completed in a year or less. For others it may be a relatively simple matter and one that just happens with little difficulty or suffering. In either case, there comes a time for moving beyond the possible anger and negativity of early adolescence and getting on with the business of building fulfilling lives for ourselves. That next step often involves one of the most exciting and enjoyable phases of personal development, a stage of growth that many will look back upon years later as among the fondest memories in their lives. It is a time of experiencing great potential in our lives, for building visions of exciting futures, a time when we perhaps "fall in love" for the first time, and a time, it is hoped, when faith and religion can take on a whole new character and appeal.

During our senior high school years—particularly the eleventh and twelfth grades—young people often experience a time of renewed hope and optimism about life in general and about their own lives in particular. **This has been characterized by some as a period of "discovering the spirit world." It can be a time for discovering all those realities that touch the interior spirit of each of us.** It can be, for instance, a time for experiencing a real sense of brotherhood and sisterhood with all peoples of the world. Ideals like truth, beauty, justice, and peace become more important to us. Many young people will fall in love during this time, but in a way that is much more mature and real than the simple "puppy love" of children. They will discover the wonder of another human being, the delight of feeling at one with another's heart and mind, the exhilarating feeling of being loved for what one truly is as a person. It is a time when all forms of art can be more appreciated and when many young people turn with a new interest to music, to poetry, to film. People begin to come to terms with their future, often by sorting out career opportunities and imagining the nearly unlimited ways in which to direct their talents. This is sometimes a period when people become more reflective, more able to be alone for extended periods of time, occasionally even yearning for some distance from the people they so recently wanted and needed to be with all the time. Admitting that for some young people the difficult tasks and pains of earlier adolescence continue during this stage, it is still true that for many others this stage of adolescence is one during which they can experience in a new way the wonder and awe of simply being human.

Discovering "the spirit world."

The implications of this stage for our religious development are perhaps more clear and direct than for any of the earlier stages we have discussed. For many people the "discovery of the spirit world" *does* include a powerful and even profound new appreciation of their personal relationship with God. In some cases this will come about through deep personal experiences—the death of a loved one, the experience of falling in love when the

whole world seems to take on new meaning, and so on. For others the new religious awakening might be the result of a good retreat experience like those offered to young people in many parts of the country: SEARCH retreats, for example, or TEC retreats. For still others this discovery may be the result of simply growing up a bit, taking a new and more mature look at life and its possibilities and challenges.

Regardless of the causes of this new openness to religion and religious experiences, the results are commonly the same—a richer sense of the presence of God in our lives, a greater ability and need to pray, a much deeper sense of compassion for others, or a desire to reach out to others in loving service. **In other words our faith as Christians becomes more truly a part of who we are as persons rather than simply another series of beliefs and practices accepted blindly by us as children.**

It should be understood, however, that this re-

newed sense of interest in the spirit world seldom if ever entails a return to the childlike acceptance of religious traditions and practices we discussed earlier. In fact, just the opposite often happens. For some, the discovery of a more personal relationship with God can lead to even greater frustration, anger, or boredom with formal, institutional religion. A common example of this would be the case of the young person who feels a deep desire to pray but who also feels that prayer can be more enriching and fulfilling when experienced during a walk in the woods than while sitting in church on a Sunday morning. And parents are often confused and even offended by young people who return from a retreat experience with great religious fervor but who, at the same time, continue to argue with them about their religious practices and beliefs. This is a complex issue, but our main point here is clear: During this stage of development, it is not uncommon for a young person to experience a renewed sense of

interest in personal faith while at the same time continuing to have real problems accepting the formal religion he or she was raised with.

Not the end of the process.

We cannot take the time or space here to continue our discussion of faith development as it normally proceeds throughout adulthood. Perhaps this will be further discussed as part of your classroom activities. It is important to note here, however, that the process is one that does in fact continue throughout our lives until death. As we enter young adulthood, there is normally a renewed openness to institutional expressions of religion as we strive to live out our personal faith-lives in community with others. Adulthood holds many challenges, not the least of which is the experience of personal, professional, and even physical limitations that each of us must eventually encounter and learn to accept. And ultimately, of course, each of us must deal with the most profound and difficult limitation we will ever face—death. Each of these steps along the path of human development offers both challenges and opportunities for growth in our relationships with Jesus and the God he reveals to us.

As we mentioned earlier, a major goal of this course is to provide you with the facts about Jesus. How you react to that information, however, will be in part dictated by the stage of religious development in which you now find yourself. If you are dealing with the adolescent task of reacting against

3) What Does This Have to Do with Jesus?

We have spent quite a bit of time discussing the process of human growth and development and how it affects our growth as persons of faith. It can now reasonably be asked, what does all this have to do with a course on Jesus? The answer in a word—everything.

First, it is very important to recognize that being a person of Christian faith is not simply a matter of accepting a series of religious teachings and practices received in childhood. Rather we have seen that the process of developing a personal and mature faith-life is a lifelong, changing, and always challenging adventure, one that literally continues to the point of death and beyond. If Christian faith could be learned and lived in full by a child, it could easily be agreed that there is little reason to continually study and attempt to apply it in new ways at each stage of our lives. If, on the other hand, Christian faith is a continually developing relationship with a God whose love for us is infinite and unlimited, then the ongoing concern for and nurturing of that relationship is not only vitally important to us but incredibly exciting—or at least it should be. At every stage of our lives our experience of Christian faith offers us new invitations to grow as persons, and provides us with the insights and inspiration we need as we move from infancy to maturity and ultimately to death. Our faith in Jesus, therefore, and in the God whom he reveals to us, should always be new and fresh to us because we are always new, changing each day of our lives.

and perhaps rejecting many of the things of childhood, we ask you to remember that Jesus and the Good News he shared with us are anything but "kids' stuff." Though some of the topics we discuss will no doubt be familiar to you, we are going to challenge you to view these realities with new eyes, the eyes of a young adult rather than those of a child. That change in your own perspective can have a radical effect on your understanding of Jesus and his message. If, on the other hand, you are experiencing a sense of renewed idealism and a surge of excitement about life and all the possibilities it holds for you, we ask that you look to Jesus as one who has set hearts and minds afire with hope and love for nearly two thousand years. No one in history has ever shared a more glorious dream than his or offered a stronger example of what it takes to make one's dream a reality. In other words, regardless of what your own particular religious attitudes and convictions may be at this time in your life, our discussion of Jesus in this course can offer significant and even profound help to you.

Second, the reason we offer a course on Jesus at *this* particular stage in your life is that at no other time perhaps will you be experiencing such rapid and dramatic changes as you will during your high school years. And, as we have seen, among the many physical, emotional, intellectual, and social changes you are experiencing, you are also likely encountering some changing perceptions and attitudes regarding religion and faith.

Perhaps you are in the process of reacting against and rejecting the childish images and understandings about God and faith that were a part of your life before now. Maybe you've moved beyond that process and are now experiencing a new openness to a more mature relationship with God in your life. In either case it is important that your reactions and decisions regarding faith be based on solid information, on the facts, on truth. Many people before you have rejected a meaningful relationship with God on the basis of hang-ups left over from childhood. Many others have desired to grow in their relationship with God but have been misled or confused in their efforts by false information, by good people who offered apparently contradictory messages, or by dishonest people—like the leaders of religious cults—who often take advantage of adolescent confusion about religion.

Where do we go from here?

To what sources do we turn for reliable information about Jesus? There are so many people saying so many different things about him, about the message he proclaimed, and about what he calls his followers to. How can we make mature judgments about him given all this confusing information? The answer to that important question is the subject of the next chapter.

Review questions and activities:

1) Why do psychologists claim that the first three years of life are among the most critical in terms of human development? What are the implications of this fact for the development of religious attitudes?

2) What are two basic skills developed during childhood which allow us to "gain control of the world of things"? How are these skills used in introducing us to the world of religious "things"?

3) What is the major shift we have recently witnessed in our understanding of the stage of development we call "adolescence"?

4) For each of the phases of adolescent development listed below, describe the common religious characteristics and attitudes:
   a) ages 10-12: physical and emotional upheaval
   b) ages 13-15: clearing the way for people
   c) ages 16-20: weaving dreams

Exercise for personal reflection:

Using the insights provided in this chapter, reflect upon what you feel to be the common religious characteristics of most people your age. Are they primarily positive or negative about religion and what it can offer? Are most people your age involved in reacting against their childhood experience of religion, or are they involved in developing a more personal understanding of their faith? And, finally, how would you describe your own attitudes toward faith and religion at this time in your life?

2
Knowing and Learning About Jesus

This disciple is the one who vouches for these things and has written them down, and we know that his testimony is true. There were many other things that Jesus did; if it all were written down, the world itself, I suppose, would not hold all the books that would have to be written (John 21:24-25).

1) What Do We "Know" About Other People?

Sometimes seeing is believing.

It is quite possible to know a great deal *about* a person but never truly *know* him or her. The opposite is perhaps less obvious but just as true: it is possible to *know* a person well but yet know very little *about* him or her. Perhaps a couple of examples will help to clarify this point, one that is central to our entire discussion about Jesus.

You and a friend are sharing a pizza one night, and she tells you that she knows a boy she thinks you would enjoy meeting. You ask for a description. Your friend begins with the obvious information—what school the boy is from, how she met him, and what he looks like. You may ask your friend why she thinks you would enjoy meeting the boy, and she might then tell you about his less obvious characteristics—about his personality, his interests, his sense of humor, and so on. You begin to build a mental image of the boy, perhaps aided by a photo of him supplied by your friend. And it's likely that you have already begun to construct an image of him that goes beyond his physical characteristics, perhaps even to the point of initially deciding whether or not you would like the boy as much as your friend promises. If you never actually meet the boy, however, you will likely not move beyond this point.

But let's say that one night you actually meet the boy at a party. From the first word of the conversation you realize how far off your image of him has been. Maybe he doesn't even look like his picture, but perhaps more remarkable than that is how different his personality is from what you had anticipated. You spend a lot of time talking that night, just getting to know each other. As you leave the party with your friend, she asks what you thought about the boy. Did meeting him just confirm everything she had already told you about him? Or was he totally different from what you had expected? It is likely that you can answer yes to both questions. You probably found that everything your friend had told you made more sense now that you had actually met the boy, but also that you now understood what she was saying in a completely different way—a deeper, more personal way. Perhaps before, the boy was nothing more than a series of descriptive phrases, some recollections of your friend, and a photograph. Now he is a real person, another human being with whom you have been able to share some enjoyable time and conversation. Everything has changed, and you may now be on your way toward developing a true and deep friendship with the boy.

Sometimes believing is "seeing."

Another example. There have been few television shows that have had the staying power and continual appeal of the series,

M.A.S.H. A documentary has even been made about the show, trying to explain how it has been able to maintain its remarkable popularity in both prime time and reruns. A central quality of the show is the fact that we as an audience are allowed to "get inside" the characters, to gradually develop a real understanding of and even affection for them as persons, despite the fact that we never learn much about their backgrounds outside of the context of their work together during the war.

In one episode of the show, a news correspondent is seen doing a film story on life at the M.A.S.H. unit. The episode consists of a series of interviews with each of the main characters. A consistent comment in the interviews is that the characters have a deep love and respect for each other despite the lack of many opportunities we often think are necessary for love to develop. They don't often join in recreation, they never actually meet one another's family members and relatives, there is very little talk about their backgrounds, what schools they attended, or about mutual acquaintances. But they live and work together under some brutal circumstances and out of that, love grows. Hawkeye Pierce speaks of his admiration and affection for B. J. Hunicutt. Margaret Houlihan says she can't stand all the things those two guys do and say but she loves them anyway. Colonel Potter grows teary-eyed just thinking about Radar O'Reilly. Somehow they all managed to truly *know* each other without really ever getting to know much *about* one another. One can only imagine how delightful it would be if one day B. J. and the wife he loves so deeply could actually visit Hawkeye at his little hometown of Crabapple

Cove, or if Sherman Potter could walk through the fields with Radar at his parents' farm. In any case, one of the truly magical things about human relationships is how profoundly close we can feel to some people after only a brief meeting, and how deeply we can care for a person even when we have limited facts about him or her.

Knowing by heart and by head.

So what does all this have to do with our discussion about Jesus? A great deal, really, for these insights into human relationships are at the very core of what it means to truly know Jesus. As in the case of our first example, it is very possible to know a great deal *about* Jesus, to know all kinds of facts about his life, the message he preached, the historical and religious conditions of his time, and so on, and yet never truly "meet" him, never actually get

beyond the random details *about* him to the point of developing some kind of a personal response to him and his message. In such cases Christian faith may appear to be simply a series of teachings, religious principles, traditions, and perhaps meaningless practices and rituals.

If, on the other hand, we have all that information about Jesus as a foundation, and then actually meet him in a personal way through a particular life experience, all the cold, hard facts *about* him take on new meaning, new power in our lives. What before were just descriptive phrases and some recollections by others now touch us more deeply, more profoundly, in our hearts rather than just in our minds. And, perhaps, we begin to develop a true and deep response to Jesus, a relationship of love in and through faith.

Think also of our second example and its relationship to Jesus. Just as is true for the characters in *M.A.S.H.* and their relationships with one another, it is very possible to develop a sincere and even profound love for Jesus and all he stands for while actually knowing very little *about* him. Maybe we are touched by the infectious strength of another believer—a parent or close friend deeply committed to Jesus, for example. Perhaps we experience a tremendous surge of peace in our hearts as we sit quietly in a darkened church, and we know of a depth of God's true presence that we could never describe or explain to anyone in words. Maybe we have a powerful experience of a loving community of friends—as often happens on good retreats—and we know in our hearts that Christ is real even if all we can say about the experience is, "You had to be there to understand what I mean." In these cases we may say that we know Jesus "by heart" long before we know all that much *about* him, that we in fact love Jesus even before we can logically explain why we do.

Therefore, a strange kind of reality now becomes more clear to us. It is possible to be a deeply faith-filled Christian, a believer, without taking a lot of courses in Christian theology and philosophy. It is also possible to have a thorough grasp of Christian teaching and history and to know Catholic beliefs to the point of teaching them in the halls of great universities but remain an unbeliever, even an atheist, one who truly accepts none of it. Christian faith, therefore, is as much a matter of the *heart* as it is of the *head*. In selecting his Apostles, Jesus did not recruit people on the basis of their intellectual abilities. He looked, rather, into the hearts of simple and honest people, and he touched them there. This should be a great consolation to those of us who find religion courses difficult and even overwhelming. God will never judge us—thank God —on the basis of our grade point average or the score on our last religion test.

Love hungers for knowledge.

Having said this, however, it is important to add two more brief comments about knowing and learning about Jesus that have a direct bearing on the intent and design of this course. **First, even though it is possible to love Jesus without knowing a great deal about him, it is equally true that *real* love always causes a great hunger to discover more about the person loved.** It is unimaginable to think of falling in love with a person but having no great desire to learn anything more about him or her. Just the opposite is always true. There is a deep yearning for more information, for knowledge about the person's past, for discovering in a continually growing way all the details that must be hidden within the life of the person we have already accepted in our heart. Therefore, for the person who already feels certain of his or her love for and commitment to Jesus, there is a real need to plunge more deeply into that relationship and to discover even greater richness in it.

That may not always be a comforting experience, however. We may find, for example, that the image of Jesus we had when we initially invited him into our hearts is not a totally accurate one, that "our Jesus" may be too middle-class, too White, or too easily accepted because his message as we had understood it was not all that demanding. In such cases, even believers may be challenged by what they discover in the search for a deeper understanding about Jesus, but they will find also that a more mature and accurate understanding of him ultimately strengthens and confirms their love for him rather than weakens or threatens it.

Secondly, for those who have not yet come to know Jesus "by heart" in the sense of having made a personal decision to accept him, it is worth recalling a reality alluded to in the first chapter. **Often we fail to find Christian faith appealing and exciting and attractive, not because of any lack of effort or openness on our part but rather because we have simply never heard the message of Jesus effectively proclaimed and explained.** Perhaps we have not yet shared in the journey of a truly faith-filled person. Maybe we have not yet reached a stage of development that permitted or called for a mature response on our part to the Christian faith. It is not the purpose of this course to be a means of conversion, at least not in the sense of trying to force or trick someone into accepting faith in Jesus against their will. Not only would such an attempt in itself be un-Christian, it would also be impossible. One cannot be forced or tricked into accepting and loving another. What this course can offer, however, is solid information about Jesus upon which the person in doubt may someday make a free and personal decision, and one based not on the immature images of childhood but rather on the facts, on truth. With these important preliminary thoughts as an introduction, we turn now to a discussion of how we can learn about Jesus, where we get our information about him, and how we can determine if that information is accurate and honest.

2) Where Did It All Come From?

How do we learn about Jesus? At first this may seem like a fairly easy question with an obvious answer, but the fact is that this initial question in our search for a mature understanding of Jesus is about as basic and critical as we can encounter. If the foundations of our understanding are shaky and questionable, then everything we build upon them on our way to some ultimate decisions about Jesus will be uncertain, unsettled, and easily disproved or uprooted. If these initial foundations are solidly and clearly constructed, however, we will be able to pursue our understanding of Jesus with confidence, self-assurance, and conviction.

It had to start somewhere.

As we've seen in chapter 1, we initially learn about Jesus normally from our parents and others close to us. But how did *they* learn about him, and what makes their understanding acceptable and reasonable? They probably learned from their parents, of course, and also from parish communities and their leaders—from pastors and other priests, from teachers, from other lay people, and so on. But have you ever stopped to think where all those pastors of all those parishes and all those teachers and others got *their* information? A few seconds of reflection and we come up with a good answer: The parishes and their leaders receive their information from the bishops and the pope. But where did the bishops and the popes over the last two thousand years or so in the Church get all *their* information, and how do we know that all the things they have taught about Jesus are reliable and worthy of our acceptance as truth? That is a pretty tough question, but after some thought we come up with a good response: The popes and bishops through the years have based their teachings on the Apostles and the early followers of Jesus. Now we are clearly getting close to the roots of the matter.

Only one question seems to remain: How did the Apostles and those who walked with, listened to, and learned directly from Jesus accurately pass on the information about him to the early members of the Church and then preserve its accuracy through the last two thousand years of history? In other words, how can I *today* get in touch with that very early teaching about Jesus and compare my own understanding to it? How do I find out if my own understanding of Jesus is one with the understanding of himself he wished to offer us? **On what solid foundation of information can I reasonably build an understanding of Jesus, an understanding upon which I can eventually make a mature, rational, solidly based decision about him?** There is, it seems, only one real answer—the same foundation upon which all the popes, bishops, teachers, and other believers through the years have ultimately been called to base their own understanding of Jesus and their faith in him—the gospels.

Maybe we know more than we think.

Many Christians—particularly Catholic Christians—feel they know little more about the gospels than that there are four of them (Matthew, Mark, Luke, and John) and that we hear the gospels read at each Mass. Even in these cases, however, it is likely that the average Catholic knows more about the gospels than she or he thinks, simply because these sacred writings are in fact central to every-thing we know and believe about Jesus. Try this exercise either in class or on your own to gain a sense of this fact: Take any one of the four gospels and, with your eyes closed, thumb through it for a few pages and then stop randomly at any point. Place your finger anywhere on the page and then open your eyes and read the passage indicated by your finger. Have you ever heard that passage before? Is there a chance you could even guess what the next verse or sentence is going to be without looking ahead to it? Repeat this exercise ten times using each of the four gospels. It is very likely that most of what you read will be familiar to you, even though you may feel that you don't know the gospels at all.

The chief source of just about everything the Church teaches about Jesus is grounded in the gospels, and the gospels in turn must serve as the scale or test of truth and authenticity for everything the Church proclaims about him. The Christian Scriptures—what we often call the New Testament—and more specifically and directly the four gospels which are part of those sacred writings, are *the* link between Jesus of Nazareth and the people of every age through history who claim to be his followers. To truly know, and know about, Jesus in the clearest and fullest sense, and to do so in a way that is free of our perhaps childish images as well as from the complex and often cloudy historical development of our understanding of him, we have to return to those early and very special sources, the gospels. It is from the gospels and commentaries upon them that the vast majority of the information contained in this course is drawn, and we must begin by gaining a very clear sense of just what the gospels are in order that we might fully appreciate what they offer us in our search for Jesus.

But the gospels are not our only source.

As a brief aside here, before discussing the gospels as our chief source of information about Jesus, we should note that they are not our *only* sources. This is an important point to consider because, as we will see in a moment, the gospels were written by people who already believed in Jesus and the message he proclaimed about God. They are therefore personal accounts rather than the objective kind of reporting we might expect, say, of newspaper and television reporters. How can we be sure that these people didn't just "create" Jesus out of their own imaginations? How can we be sure that he even actually existed?

There are several non-biblical and non-Christian references to Jesus available which prove that he actually did exist as a historical person. A Jewish historian named Josephus mentions Jesus in his writings about the years A.D. 93-94, roughly sixty years after Jesus' death. As a Jew, and later as a member of the Roman imperial court, Josephus would have no reason to accept the historical reality of Jesus unless there was some sound basis for it. In one of his works Josephus discusses disturbances that were caused by the Jews during the time Pontius Pilate was procurator of Judea (A.D. 26-36):

> About this time arose Jesus, a wise man, *if indeed it be lawful to call him a man.* For he was a doer of wonderful deeds, and a teacher of men who gladly receive the truth. He drew to himself many both of the Jews and of the Gentiles. *He was the Christ;* and when Pilate, on the indictment of the principal men among us, had condemned him to the cross, those who had loved him at first did not cease to do so, *for he appeared to them again alive on the third day, the divine prophets having fore___ ___ these and ten thousand other wonderful things about him.* And even to this day the race of Christians, who are named from him, has not died out.

Some scholars seriously question that the italicized words from this quote were actually written by Josephus, because it seems hard to believe that he would have recognized Jesus as "the Christ" (a title we will discuss more in a moment) or that he would have accepted him as a teacher of truth and one who rose from the dead. At the very least, however, it seems clear that Josephus certainly understood Jesus to be a historical person who had profound impact upon the people he encountered.

Christianity—horrible and shameful?

There are several references to Jesus by Roman authors as well. Suetonius, a Roman historian and lawyer, compiled biographies of several Roman emperors around the year A.D. 120. In a discussion of the Emperor Claudius, he says, "(Claudius) expelled the Jews from Rome, on account of the riots in which they were constantly indulging, at the instigation of the Chrestus." Though there is some debate on this, it is generally agreed that "the Chrestus" refers to "the Christ." Note also that at this time, Christians were still commonly regarded as a Jewish sect, a point that will become clearer later in this course.

Another Roman historian, Tacitus, also refers to Jesus in his writings. He writes of a fire that burned Rome in A.D. 64, for which the Emperor Nero blamed the Christians. Though Tacitus was apparently skeptical about Nero's claim, he obviously had no great love himself for that strange group of people called Christians:

They got their name from Christ, who was executed by a sentence of the procurator Pontius Pilate in the reign of Tiberius. That checked the pernicious superstition for a short time, but it broke out once more, not only in Judea, where the plague first arose, but in Rome itself, where all the horrible and shameful things in the world collect and find a home.

Nero's hideous torture of the Christians reflected not only his own sick mind but also the extent to which many early followers of Jesus would go rather than deny faith in him:

. . . (the Christians) were covered with wild beasts' skins and torn to death by dogs; or they were fastened on crosses and, when daylight failed, were burned to serve as lamps by night.

Another Roman source, a man named Pliny the Younger, was governor of one of the Roman provinces in Asia Minor. About the year 110, he wrote to the Emperor Trajan for advice on what to do about the Christians. The Roman state was always concerned about the growth of any political or religious sect, and the Christian communities clearly baffled them. Though Pliny mentions Jesus, he offers no new information about him.

Our point in briefly mentioning these sources is not to claim that they offer us more information about Jesus than we can find in the gospels. On the contrary, without the gospels we would have only vague and confusing references to Jesus in the records of history. Without the gospels, Jesus would be little more than a rumor out of the past. But these non-Christian and non-biblical sources do demonstrate that their authors simply presumed the historical existence of Jesus and found the movement which was based on his life and teachings—Christianity—worthy of at least brief mention in their writings. But the fact remains, if we want to know about Jesus to any reasonable degree, we must turn to the Christian Scriptures and—more specifically—to the gospels which proclaim him and the Good News he shared.

3) The Christian Scriptures

It is becoming more common in our day to refer to the Bible in terms of the "Hebrew Scriptures" and the "Christian Scriptures" rather than as the "Old Testament" and the "New Testament." Some feel—and we agree—that the use of the terms *old* and *new* could be viewed as insulting to our Jewish friends whose sacred writings are certainly not old to them in the sense of being outdated or surpassed in value by later writings. There is also a tendency on the part of Christians to lose sight of the value of the Hebrew Scriptures in their search for understanding their own faith. After all, the term *old* is seldom one we use to describe things of lasting and current value. Therefore, out of respect for our Jewish friends and in the hope of renewing our own interest in their sacred writings, we will refer in this book to the Hebrew and Christian Scriptures rather than to the Old and New Testaments.

The Christian Scriptures contain a variety of materials representing not only different authors but also different styles or types of writings. There are personal letters, homilies or sermons from early liturgical or worship services, some highly symbolic and imaginative writings, and, of course, the four gospels. Try this revealing exercise: Pick up a copy of the entire Bible and note the point of division between the Hebrew and Christian Scriptures. Compare the size of the two collections of writings. Then find the four gospels of Matthew, Mark, Luke, and John and hold just those pages between your fingers. That slim collection of writings is the only source we have for any basic information about the life history and teaching of the person Jesus. The other Christian Scriptures—the epistles of St. Paul, for example—offer us little information about Jesus himself. They concentrate, instead, on the impact of his life and message on those who followed him. They are, in that sense, more discussions about Christians and their lives than they are about Jesus and his life. None of the authors of the Christian Scriptures other than those of the gospels offers us anything like a portrait of Jesus.

The gospels are not biographies of Jesus.

We must be clear, however, that the gospels are not themselves biographies or life stories of Jesus in the same sense that we would view that kind of writing today. We will completely misunderstand the purpose and meaning of the gospels if we view them as detailed descriptions of the life and work of Jesus. They simply do not offer us that kind of information. As we indicated earlier in this book, we know very little about Jesus' infancy and childhood. We can't give a precise date for his birth, nor can we provide anything like a complete description of the personalities of his parents, Mary and Joseph. Though we have probably arrived at certain mental images of his appearance, we actually have no idea now tall or short he was, whether he was handsome or unattractive, or whether he was formally educated or not. In short, we lack a great deal of the kind of information we would simply assume to be provided in an accurate biography of a person.

If the gospels are not biographies of Jesus, then what are they? A clue can be found in the very word *gospel* itself. Our word is derived from the Middle English word *godspell,* which means "good news" or "glad tidings." That word in turn was a translation of the Greek word *evangelion,* also meaning the proclamation or announcement of good news. So the first verse in Mark's gospel identifies clearly what he is about: "The beginning of the Good News about Jesus Christ, the Son of God." We learn from the very word *gospel* itself that the purpose of these writings is to announce or proclaim a message of faith in Jesus. They are, in other words, *testimonies of faith* written by people who are totally convinced that Jesus was and is the Messiah. Note also that we call the authors of the gospels "evangelists" based on that Greek word, *evangelion;* they are, literally, "proclaimers of the good news."

Perhaps the most effective way to understand the nature and purpose of the gospels, however, is to describe how they came to be written. Scholars who have studied the Christian Scriptures have identified at least three major steps or stages in their development:

1) the life and works of Jesus and their effects on his disciples;

2) the experience of the disciples and the early Church after the death and Resurrection of Jesus; and

3) the actual writing of the gospels by the evangelists who likely served as editors or collectors of material that had gradually developed through the years.

Because so much of this course and your understanding of it depends on the gospels, we will make an effort here to discuss their development clearly and completely.

Stage 1: Jesus of Nazareth and his disciples.

It seems that it would go without saying that the gospels are based upon the words and works of Jesus of Nazareth, a historical figure from Palestine some two thousand years ago. However, the recognition and acceptance of this truth is central to our understanding and appreciation of the gospels. For if they are not based upon historical realities and events that truly happened, then all that they teach and call us to would be little more than flights of fancy or idealistic visions that we would have no reason to accept, much less live by. This does not necessarily mean that every incident recorded in the gospels is described exactly as it happened historically. As we will see in a moment, the intent of the gospels was not to record events minute by minute, as if with movie cameras and tape recorders. They were intended, rather, to convey the *meaning* of those events for the persons of that time and, through them, for us as well. Nevertheless, it is essential that we recognize that the source and foundation of the events *and their meaning* as recorded in the gospels is Jesus of Nazareth, a man, a historical person, one whose blood flowed through flesh as truly as does our own. This is precisely what is meant by the first phrase in the title of this book. When we talk about Jesus, we are definitely talking about the "Jesus of History."

What can we say about this Jesus of History that can be accepted even by those who do *not* accept him as the Son of God, the Messiah, the Christ? From the gospels and other sources we know that he was born a Jew sometime around the year 5 B.C., "in the Bethlehem of Judea in the reign of Herod the king" (Matthew 2:1). He was raised in

Nazareth of the northern province of Galilee. (All of these dates, locations, and persons will be discussed more thoroughly later in this book.) He learned and practiced the trade of carpentry. At about age 30 he began a public career of preaching and teaching, proclaiming the beginning of a new era, a new "Kingdom of God" as he called it. He apparently demonstrated some unusual powers and was referred to by historians of his day as a worker of wonderful deeds. His preaching and actions stirred great interest among the Jewish people, leading some to proclaim him as a great prophet and others to reject him as a sorcerer, a magician, a blasphemer, and a threat to the Roman state. Those in power eventually brought him to trial, found him guilty of crimes under Roman law, and had him executed by crucifixion sometime around the year A.D. 30. This much virtually all people of any religious persuasion or belief could accept simply by being open to the available historical records. But the early Christians—those who followed this man Jesus and the others who would eventually write about him in the gospels—clearly believed him to be much more than just a man, more than just Jesus of Nazareth, more than simply the Jesus of History. What is this "more than"? What is the extra dimension that has made the historical Jesus of two thousand years ago so consistently influential and powerful in the lives of countless people up to and including those of our own day?

It all rises or falls with this.

The factor upon which all Christianity rises or falls, almost literally, is the event that the followers of Jesus claim to have experienced *after* his death, an event that completely and radically changed their understanding of everything he had said and done *while* he had walked the dusty roads of Palestine. For the followers of Jesus claimed that he did not remain dead, but rather that they had experienced him alive again and present among them some three days after he had been savagely executed on a cross. This became the identifying mark of all those who claim Jesus as their Lord and Savior—belief in the event we call his "Resurrection." So central to the lives of Christians is the conviction in Jesus' living presence after death that one of the most influential of all early Christians, Paul, was led to say, ". . . if Christ has not been raised then our preaching is useless and your believing is useless" (1 Corinthians 15:14).

We will discuss the Resurrection in more detail later in this book, but the point here is that the first stage in the development of the gospels was the experience by Jesus' disciples not only of his earthly existence, his message, and his actions, but also of his rising from the dead, an event which made all that he said and did prior to that believable and acceptable as truth. Without the Resurrection the followers of Jesus would likely have dispersed in fear of their own execution. But with the experience of the Risen Jesus, they burst forth from their places of hiding and began proclaiming the Good News that "God has made this Jesus whom you crucified both Lord and Christ" by raising him from

the dead (Acts 2:36). Some immediately rejected that proclamation as foolhardy, ridiculous, insane. For them the Jesus of History would always remain only the carpenter's son who preached a radical message and paid for it with his life. But others were nearly overwhelmed by the conviction that this proclamation was true, that Jesus was in fact raised by God from death itself, and that he truly was and is forever Lord and Savior. For these people, the Jesus of History was clearly much more than that, a fact represented in the second phrase in the title of this book. For these "Christ-ians," the Jesus of History was also truly "the Christ of Faith."

We have come to think of the title "Christ" as simply a kind of last name or family name for Jesus. But, in fact, he was never known by that name during his earthly life. The name *Jesus* was a common one for Jewish boys, meaning literally "Yahweh (God) saves" or "Yahweh (God) is salvation." But the title *the Christ* means literally "the anointed one." It is based on the Greek word, *Christos,* which is itself a translation of the Hebrew word, *messiah.* The Jewish people, as we will discuss in more detail later, had long awaited the Messiah, "one sent from God," one who would save them from all oppression. For those Jews who accepted Jesus as this Messiah after his Resurrection, he became known as "Jesus *the* Christ," which in turn became rather quickly shortened to what we now know as a single name: Jesus Christ. This development may have been an unfortunate one, for it clouds to some degree our recognition of a tremendous reality—that the Jesus of History is truly the Christ of Faith. It was this realization that overwhelmed the disciples of Jesus after his death and Resurrection, and the experience by them of this reality formed the first stage in the development of the gospels.

Stage 2: The disciples and the early Church.

Try to place yourself in the position of the early disciples of Jesus. You, along with them, walk with Jesus, you hear his inspiring message proclaimed from the synagogues and hillsides, you touch him and are touched by him, and you witness the marvelous impact he makes on everyone he meets. Gradually you find yourself falling in love with this man. You find in him the answer to all your hopes and dreams, and you are certain that in this man from Nazareth you have discovered true freedom, joy, peace, love, and the fullness of life. And then you witness the horror of Calvary, the man you love so deeply stretched out against the sky, nailed to a beam of wood, carrying all your dreams and hopes along with him to his death. You and so many who had believed in him run away in fear, shattered, hopeless, convinced that all he promised was a sham, a lie, or at the very least a terrible mistake.

But then comes Easter. Suddenly you have the overwhelming experience of him present again, alive, as truly with you—in fact, even more truly with you than he had been before. He is risen! Even death is conquered in this man! Incredible joy and peace surge into your heart, and you run from your place of hiding shouting the Good News from the rooftops: "He's alive. Everything he told us is true!"

Now what would you do next? At the risk of sounding a bit sarcastic perhaps, it is doubtful that you would immediately sit down and begin to write an essay on what you had experienced. This would be even less likely for the people of Jesus' time who believed that his death and Resurrection meant the almost certain end of the world in a short time. They truly believed that he was coming back again very soon and that people had little time to make up their minds about him. Either they would turn from their past ways, repent of their sins, and accept Jesus as Lord and Savior or they would perish. We learn from the Christian Scriptures that some early Christians even advised against marriage and some refused to take jobs, feeling these were silly considerations when the end of the world was right around the corner!

Spreading the word about Jesus.

So what do you do? What did the early Christians do? Rather than write about their experiences with Jesus, they began an intense missionary campaign to proclaim the life, death, and Resurrection of Jesus to all people. In a matter of decades, the proclamation of the Good News of Jesus spread like wildfire throughout the Roman Empire, from Palestine where it had begun out to Egypt, Syria, Greece, Mesopotamia, Asia Minor, and ultimately into the capital city of Rome itself.

Though it was clear to these Christians that preserving their message for the future was not necessary—there was, after all, no "future" expected—they did not lose any of their love for the past. In fact it was only in terms of their long and difficult history as a people that the Jews could understand Jesus. They began to see how so much of what he said and did took on meaning only in light of the events and ideas contained in their own Hebrew Scriptures, what we often call the Old Testament. As St. Paul was to say to his fellow Jews, "We have come here to tell you the Good News. It was to our ancestors that God made the promise but it is to us, their children, that he has fulfilled it, by raising Jesus from the dead" (Acts 13:32-33). This pattern of the promises of God fulfilled in Jesus became a fundamental part of the preaching of the early Christians as they spread the word across the land.

It was within the context of preaching the Good News throughout the land that the process of picking and choosing what to remember about Jesus was begun. Incidents from his life and teaching would be used to instruct people who were interested in joining the community of faith. Reflections on his life in terms of the Hebrew Scriptures became part of Christian worship services. Words of Jesus were not only recalled but applied to the lived experience of the early Christians as they began to share and celebrate and live out his message in their daily lives. In other words, Jesus' life and words and works were never recorded in a logical, day-by-day, biographical fashion. Not all of the available information about Jesus was preserved but only those events and words and teachings that had particularly profound impact on the early Christians, the members of the early Church. In many cases this meant eliminating confusing or unnecessary details from certain accounts. When we look at the miracle stories, for example, we find only the briefest descriptions, often making them seem stark and unreal. Or sometimes the words of Jesus as they are recorded in the gospels seem so direct, so straight to the point, that they almost seem brutal or cruel. It is on the basis of these carefully selected and highly polished recollections and applications to the Church's experience that the gospels would eventually be written.

Many examples from the gospels will be used throughout this course to provide an understanding of Jesus and the message he proclaimed. It is important in pursuing that understanding that we don't lose sight of this stage in their development.

Stage 3: The early Church and the evangelists.

Jesus died around the year A.D. 30. The process of proclaiming the Good News about his death and Resurrection and of selecting and polishing recollections of his words and actions for use in preaching and worship continued for at least forty years before the first gospel was written. It was then decided that the kind of free-floating stories and words and teachings of Jesus being passed on orally or by "word of mouth" should be collected into organized and permanent records by the editors we call evangelists. It is generally held that the first gospel written was Mark's, about the year A.D. 70 or some forty years after the death of Jesus. Matthew and Luke were perhaps written during the early eighties, and John's gospel not until as late as A.D. 90-95. We will say more about these editors and their unique gospels in a moment, but first a more basic question: Why were the gospels developed at all? There seem to be at least two answers:

1) **By the latter half of the first century, it was becoming clear that the Church would probably be around for a long time.** The early expectations of an immediate return by Jesus and the certain end of the world gradually faded with the passing years.

4) The Four Gospels

With the realization that the Church did indeed have a future, it became necessary to find a means for preserving its teachings and for passing them on to future generations. This was certainly one of the motives for developing the gospels as we now have them.

2) Yet the preservation of the message of Jesus for future generations was not the only reason for collecting the available material about him into gospels. There was also a continued need to instruct and inspire the already existing communities of faith that had been formed throughout the Empire during the previous decades of missionary activity. **Each of the gospel writers gathered all the traditions about Jesus into a coherent story in such a way as to respond to the needs of a particular audience in a particular location at a particular time.** This accounts for the fact that each of the gospels is unique and that certain activities and words of Jesus recorded in one of the gospels appear to be described or expressed differently in another. No one gospel, therefore, provides a completely accurate understanding of Jesus. And, again, we cannot look to the gospels as detailed life stories or biographies of Jesus. Rather we must seek an understanding of the *common threads of meaning* that run through the gospels and try to understand their meaning and significance for us today by studying their roots and implications in the historical, religious, and cultural times in which they were written.

We can see now that the gospels were not simply the result of four individuals named Matthew, Mark, Luke, and John sitting down independently and writing life histories about Jesus based on their own personal recollections of him. Rather each evangelist had a wealth of material available to him—stories about Jesus told over and over again in community worship, the words of Jesus recalled day after day in prayer and then applied to life experiences, insights drawn by preachers into the relationship between the life and message of Jesus and the history of Israel, and so on. Each also had a particular audience in mind when he began to collect this material into a coherent and understandable whole. It is even doubtful that any *one* person was responsible for the total development of any of the gospels. It seems instead that the work was done by at least several people, perhaps friends or followers of the evangelists who honored them by attributing the work totally to them as individuals. Finally, it should be noted that today scholars are constantly studying and arriving at new speculations about the identities of the gospel authors, their purposes in writing, and about the dates when they wrote their accounts of the Good News of Jesus. What we offer here are very brief summaries of the most commonly held judgments about these issues, recognizing full well that, for each point mentioned here, scholars could be found who disagree. This fact can make the study and discussion of Scripture a bit confusing, perhaps, but also as fascinating and challenging as trying to grasp the plot of a well-written mystery story.

Mark's gospel.

Who wrote it? Mark was a common name during the time of Jesus, and the Mark credited with writing the first gospel could literally have been almost anyone. None of the gospels actually names its author directly, and the names we attach to each one represent the opinions of the early Church about the authors. The author of Mark is at times associated with a certain John Mark who is mentioned in the Acts of the Apostles (Acts 12:12). A group of Christians regularly met at John Mark's mother's house for prayer. Some believe this John Mark to be the author of this gospel.

For whom was it written? It is traditionally accepted that Mark's gospel was written in Rome for the Church there and that it was intended for non-Jewish readers. Jewish customs that would be readily understood by Jews themselves, for instance, are explained in Mark's gospel in a way that indicates they are not familiar to its readers.

When was it written? There is general agreement that Mark was written sometime between A.D. 65 and 70, that is, thirty-five to forty years after the death of Jesus. There is a heavy sense of suffering in Mark with many references to trials and persecutions. Some suggest this reflects the persecution of the Christians by the Roman Emperor Nero, who as we mentioned earlier blamed the Christians for the burning of Rome in the year A.D. 64. Or, as we will discuss in a later chapter, the Jews revolted against the Romans in a violent conflict between A.D. 66 and 70, and many scholars feel Mark reflects awareness of that period. For our purposes, we will settle on the year 70 as roughly the date of writing.

Why was it written? Mark's gospel stresses the human suffering of Jesus in his passion and death, perhaps as an encouragement to the Christians who were suffering terrible persecution at the time. It is almost as if the central point of his entire gospel is to describe the death of Jesus, and everything else that precedes it is by way of introduction. It seems certain, then, that one of Mark's intentions was to explain to the members of the early Church how suffering is an essential part of Christian life and to give them the courage to endure it as Jesus had. There is also a heavy concentration on the humanity of Jesus in Mark's gospel, in which we see Jesus expressing strong emotions, for example. Some suggest that Mark was trying to counter the claim of some during his day that Jesus was not truly human but only divine and had simply pretended to be a man. Mark's account makes it very clear that Jesus was truly a human being.

Luke's gospel.

Who wrote it? The gospel of Luke is actually the first part of a two-volume history of early Christianity. The second part is the Acts of the Apostles. There has been a persistent tradition in the Church that the author of Luke and Acts was a physician, a well-educated Gentile convert to Christianity. A certain Luke was identified by St. Paul as a doctor, and some have pointed out parts of the gospel that seem to indicate a certain medical knowledge. This point has probably been exaggerated, given the limited evidence. Luke is mentioned three times in the Christian Scriptures and on each occasion he is said to be a companion of Paul. At one point Paul says that Luke was not a Jew. If this is true, then the author of Luke and Acts is probably the only non-Jewish writer of the Christian Scriptures.

When was it written? It is difficult to date the writing of Luke's gospel. It seems clear that he had Mark's gospel available to him when he was writing since he uses some of the material directly from that gospel. Therefore we know that Luke wrote after Mark's gospel was in circulation, which means sometime after A.D. 70. Admitting the limits of our knowledge, for our purposes we will say that Luke was written sometime during the eighties.

Why was it written? There is great debate over the intent of Luke in writing his gospel, and we will simply summarize the more important suggestions here. First, at the very beginning of his gospel Luke tells a certain Theophilus, to whom he is addressing his gospel, that he is writing "so that you will learn how well-founded the teaching is that you have received" (Luke 1:4). Luke claims that he had studied all the available accounts and wanted to offer his own "ordered account." So it seems that Luke was writing to offer those who were already Christians help in better understanding their faith and its roots. He sets out early to demonstrate the continuity of Christianity with the Judaism of the Hebrew Scriptures. And throughout his gospel Luke emphasizes the central role of the Holy Spirit in Jesus' life. He even closes his gospel by stressing the continuing presence of Jesus through his Spirit after his death and Resurrection, perhaps trying to support those readers who were discouraged that Jesus had not yet returned. Another major feature of Luke's gospel is its emphasis on the fact that the Christian message is for everyone—Jews and Gentiles, men and women, rich and poor. And there is a continuing reminder of the joy that is shared by those who experience God's forgiving love in Jesus. The gospel of Luke, therefore, clearly depicts a Jesus who deeply loves all men and women.

The Development of the Gospels

10 B.C.	0	A.D. 10	20	30	40	50	60	70	80	90	100

		Stage One	Stage Two		Stage Three	

| Birth of Jesus | "Hidden years" in Nazareth | Public life, death, and Resurrection | Early Church; missionary activity; stories and sayings of Jesus recalled, shared, and collected | Mark's gospel: first one written | Matthew and Luke gradually develop | John's gospel: last one written |

Matthew's gospel.

Who wrote it and when? There is no clear agreement on either the author or the date for Matthew's gospel. Rather early in the history of the Church, tradition had it that the author was Matthew, a disciple of Jesus and therefore an eyewitness to his life and work. However, the author seems to have used almost all of Mark's gospel and has much in common with Luke's account as well. It would be strange that an eyewitness of these events would rely so heavily upon other sources. Regarding the date of writing, the majority of scholars would opt for a date anywhere between A.D. 80 and 100. Certainly these questions are not all that essential to us. What is of interest, however, is the fact that Matthew's gospel is so thorough, contains so much of Mark and Luke, and is so well organized that it quickly became the most popular and widely used of all the gospels in the life of the early Church, one reason why it appears first in our Christian Scriptures today.

Why was it written? Matthew's gospel is very different in structure from Mark or Luke. It is very well organized, and in the past some scholars have suggested that its pattern copies that of the first five books of the Hebrew Scriptures, indicating a desire by the author to show the Jews particularly that Jesus was clearly the Messiah they had awaited. There is a special emphasis on demonstrating that all of Jesus' life was a fulfillment of the promises made by God to Israel. Jesus, for example, is presented as a true teacher of the Jewish Law. Matthew also shows interest in the Church itself, which may provide a clue to his intent in writing. The gospel contains Jesus' teaching in a clear and thorough way so that it could serve well in instructing new converts to the faith. His sensitivity to the continuity between Christianity and Judaism also made the gospel valuable for Jews who were inquiring about the faith. For all these reasons, as we have noted, Matthew's gospel soon became the most widely used of the four gospels.

John's gospel.

Different from the other three. Matthew, Mark, and Luke are similar in so many respects that they are often referred to as the "synoptic gospels." The word *synoptic* (sin-op'-tik) indicates that they can only be fully understood when seen or looked at together or side by side. We have already alluded to this fact by mentioning how the authors of the first three gospels seemed so often to be using either the same sources or one another's work in writing their gospels. John's gospel, on the other hand, is very unique, a fact that can be experienced if not fully understood with just a quick reading of sections of it. Almost everything about this gospel—its author, the date it was written, and the audience for whom it was intended—has been debated and argued for years. We can only offer the briefest comments here about these very complex issues.

Who wrote it and when? There is wide disagreement over the author of the fourth gospel and we may never resolve the question. Church tradition for years suggested that the author was John the Apostle, who, it was believed, wrote the gospel at the end of a very long life after much prayer, reflection, and personal experience actually living out his faith in Jesus. This would account for the very reflective, prayerful, and thoughtful style of the gospel. But many feel that the gospel was not written until the year A.D. 90 at the earliest, which would make it highly unlikely if not impossible for a disciple of Jesus to have written it. We also know that John the Apostle was martyred, while it appears from John 21:23 that the author of this gospel was not. Again, these are questions of more interest and importance to scholars than to us.

Why was it written? The late date of writing for the gospel of John helps us to gain an understanding of its unique style and the purposes for which it was written. Many years had passed since Jesus of Nazareth had walked among the people of Palestine, years during which there was a continually deepening understanding of his true identity—of who he truly was. As we noted earlier, it was only after his Resurrection that Jesus was fully recognized as "the Christ," "the Messiah," and even later as "the Son of God." The more time people had to reflect on these realities and their implications, the more central to their teaching and preaching did they become. Therefore, in John's gospel we see a much stronger attempt to present a profound and prayerful understanding of Jesus as the divine Son of God than we find in the synoptic gospels of Matthew, Mark, and Luke. **For this reason, many scholars feel that if we are to attempt an accurate historical portrait of Jesus as he lived and taught in Palestine, we should rely more heavily on the synoptics than on John.** This does not mean that John's gospel is not truthful, but rather that the truths it attempts to share are more deeply theological and reflective than in the other gospels. On the other hand, the almost poetically prayerful nature of John's gospel and its familiar and treasured imagery of Jesus as "the light of the world," "the bread of life," and "the Good Shepherd" have made this gospel a favorite source for meditation on the divine significance of Jesus' life.

5) Searching for the "Jesus of History"

Before concluding our discussion of the sources of our information about Jesus, we must deal with a question that has haunted many people through the years who have worked toward making a sound decision about Jesus and his message. The question is, given the nature of the gospels as testimonies of faith by people who already believed in Jesus, is it possible to attain an objective and unbiased account of his life and message? Can we ever truly discover the Jesus of History so that we can make up our own minds on whether he was and is in fact the Christ of Faith? How can we be sure that the Jesus portrayed in the gospels is accurately presented? Must we simply take somebody else's word on these critical issues? As is true with many of the questions dealing with faith, our answer will be neither easy nor, perhaps, totally satisfying.

One possible answer to these questions—or, at least, the hint of an answer—can be found in more clearly understanding the nature of what we call *history*. History can be viewed as the simple recording of observable facts and events, as if these events were captured accurately by movie cameras and tape recorders and then transcribed in words by a reporter. This is a simplistic and naive understanding of history, however, because life is too complex for this kind of objective description. To demonstrate this point, choose one event that happened in the world today and compare the reports of that event as given by two television stations and two newspapers. There will obviously be some basic similarities in all these news stories, but sometimes the differences in reporting can be truly

startling. Besides the possible discrepancies that might appear in the basic details of the reports, there will often be various understandings and opinions presented on the *meaning* of the event as well. **In other words, what we normally call "history" is not simply the objective reporting of facts and events but almost always includes the meaning and significance of those events as seen through the eyes and perspectives of the person doing the reporting.** This is precisely why people are so often urged to read more than one paper or watch more than one news program, in order to gain a more balanced and true understanding of the events in the world.

What does it all mean?

This insight into the nature of history helps to clarify our question about the reliability of the gospel portraits of Jesus. First, it must be admitted that we will never attain a totally objective and detailed understanding of Jesus and his message as he actually lived and preached some two thousand years ago in Palestine. Nor, for that matter, can we do so with any other figure of history, whether it be Caesar, Cleopatra, the Buddha, Abraham Lincoln, or any other historical person. **What we *can* attain, however, are not only some basic facts about Jesus and his message but, far more importantly, the *meaning, significance,* and *impact* of Jesus upon the people and events of his time—and upon us as well.** Ultimately is this not of far greater importance to us than mere facts? Hearing a person's words firsthand is valuable, but *understanding the meaning* of those words is far more important. Witnessing an event in person is valuable, but *understanding the meaning* of the event is far more

Christ as a Young Man, an oil painting on wood, by Rembrandt, dated about 1600

important. What the gospels, and the Church as a whole, offer us is an understanding of the meaning and significance in our own lives of the Jesus of History, the one whom Christians believe to be the Christ of Faith.

A final word.

Many people today live with the illusion that it would be so much easier to believe in Jesus if only we could see him, touch him, hear his voice, walk with him. Some seem to think that those who actually experienced Jesus during his earthly life in Palestine had a much easier time understanding and accepting him than we do today. The facts, however, don't support that notion. If it were in fact so easy to recognize and accept Jesus in his own day, why did so many have such a hard time doing so? If the message of Jesus was so understandable for those who heard it firsthand, why did so many reject it? The fact is, we who live today have the benefit of nearly two thousand years of historical experience with the person and message of Jesus. So much is known today that was not known in

his day. History has recorded the profound impact of his vision on the world and, despite the shortcomings of Christian people throughout the years who have failed to live his message fully, it has still been verified as the most powerful and life-changing vision ever offered to humanity. **And, finally, for those who profess faith in Jesus as Lord, we can experience him in his fullness as Risen Lord today and, in that sense, know him far more truly and perfectly than could those who actually walked with him.**

So we *can* know Jesus—both by heart and through deepening our intellectual understanding of him. In the next few chapters particularly, we will be discussing different dimensions of Jesus' life and times that can help us a great deal in understanding the meaning, impact, and significance of the message he proclaimed. We will be discussing his social, cultural, and religious background as a Jew of his day and also presenting some insights into the historical setting in which he presented his vision of God. These insights can help us dramatically in gaining a full understanding of the one called Jesus the Christ.

1) Explain the difference between "knowing about" a person and truly knowing him or her. What are the implications of this distinction for understanding what it means to "know Jesus"?

2) In what sense are the gospels "the scale or test of truth and authenticity for everything the Church proclaims about Jesus"?

3) Give two non-Christian sources which prove the historical existence of Jesus.

4) Why is it not accurate to refer to the gospels as "biographies of Jesus"?

5) What are the three major steps or stages in the development of the gospels? Briefly describe each stage.

6) Explain both the distinction and the relationship between the terms "Jesus of History" and "Christ of Faith."

7) What does the author mean when he says that belief in the Resurrection of Jesus became "the identifying mark of all who claimed Jesus as Lord and Savior"?

8) For each of the four gospels, give the following information:
   a) the author as generally accepted by tradition
   b) an approximate date of writing or compilation
   c) the basic intent or purpose of the author in writing his gospel

9) Can we truly discover "the Jesus of History"? Explain your answer.

Terms to identify and remember:

gospel	Christ
evangelist	synoptic
Jesus	

Exercise for personal reflection:

Try to imagine having to write a letter introducing your best friend to someone who has never met him or her. That person's only source of information about your friend will be your letter. On a piece of scrap paper list all those things you would want to include in your letter. For example, would you include much information about what your friend looks like—height, weight, color of hair, and so on? Would you want to discuss certain personality characteristics about your friend—his or her sense of humor, for example—or particular talents? Do you think you would need to do a lot of story-telling, sharing recollections of good and bad times you experienced with your friend? Finally, reflect on what this exercise can teach about the evangelists and their attempt to share Jesus with us.

3
Jesus' Roots: The People of the Covenant

He came to Nazareth, where he had been brought up, and went into the synagogue on the sabbath day as he usually did. He stood up to read, and they handed him the scroll of the prophet Isaiah. Unrolling the scroll he found the place where it is written:

"The Spirit of the Lord has been given to me, for he has anointed me. He has sent me to bring the good news to the poor, to proclaim liberty to captives and to the blind new sight, to set the downtrodden free, to proclaim the Lord's year of favour."

He then rolled up the scroll, gave it back to the assistant and sat down. And all eyes in the synagogue were fixed on him. Then he began to speak to them, "This text is being fulfilled today even as you listen." And he won the approval of all, and they were astonished by the gracious words that came from his lips (Luke 4:16-22).

1) Jesus the Jew

If we are to understand and fully appreciate both Jesus and the message he proclaimed, we must never forget or lose touch with a most basic fact about him: he was a deeply faith-filled and profoundly committed Jew of his day. In a startling and highly disturbing interview, the television host Phil Donahue one day confronted a major leader of the Ku Klux Klan with this fact. With an icy stare and hate-filled conviction, the man strongly denied that Jesus could have ever been a Jew, claiming with an almost incredible lack of understanding that Jesus was, rather, "the first Christian." For most people, of course, the lack of sensitivity to the Jewish roots and religious experience of Jesus is not motivated by such prejudice. But the fact is, unfortunately, that many of us in our Christian education and upbringing have not clearly grasped the tremendous importance of having a solid background in Jewish religious, social, and political history in order to truly understand Jesus Christ.

As an illustration of this fact, take another look at the Scripture passage that introduces this chapter. This is perhaps one of the most popular and frequently quoted of all passages from the Christian

49

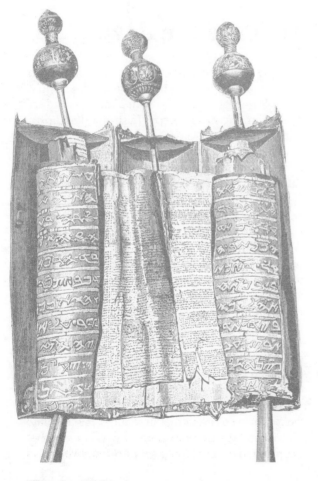

Scriptures, one often used in prayer services because of its dramatic presentation of the mission of Jesus. But note the number of insights and lessons here that can only be recognized and comprehended within the context of the history of Israel: *Jesus went into the synagogue* (what is a synagogue?) *on the sabbath day* (what's so special about that day?) *as he usually did* (it must have been an important practice to him if he did it repeatedly). *He stood up to read* (what gave him the right to do that?) *from the scroll of the prophet Isaiah* (who is Isaiah, and what is the scroll all about?). Jesus then read a beautiful passage, one clearly not created by him. It was, rather, a very old and sacred passage from the Hebrew Scriptures, one that Jesus felt identified both who he was and what he was all about because, as he said, the text was being fulfilled that very day in him.

The point of this example, it is hoped, is clear: **We simply cannot understand Jesus and his message outside the context of his Jewish heritage.** We are going to make a strong effort in this book to recognize and respond to this conviction. In this chapter we will offer some insights into the basic history of the Jews and briefly discuss several of the central Jewish religious concepts, practices, and groups of people that flow out of that history and shape the gospels. In chapter 4 we will look at the land and daily life of the Jewish people of Jesus' time. Though perhaps not as essential to our faith-understanding of Jesus as is the religious history of the Jews, this information about the basic lifestyle of the people—the homes they lived in, the food they ate, the nature of their family life, and so on—can make the Jesus of History much more real and personal to us. Then, in chapter 5, we will close this part of our discussion with a brief overview of the political history of the Jews at the time of Jesus, in which we will gain a perhaps new understanding of the personalities and religious factions that are so much a part of the gospels—people like Herod the Great and Pontius Pilate, for example, and groups like the Sadducees and the Pharisees. This kind of background can make the reading of the gospels not only more understandable but, because of that, more enjoyable and personally enriching.

The nature of religious experiences.

So Jesus was a devout Jew, steeped in the history, religious traditions, and rich prayer life of the Jewish people. In order to gain a sense of the impact of this on him, consider for a moment the many ways in which our own religious heritage as Catholic Christians touches all dimensions of our lives. Even for those of us who do not practice our faith in a truly committed way, the withdrawal of even a modest part of our routine religious experience would leave us feeling a certain emptiness, a void in our lives. Try to imagine, for example, how your life and that of your family would be affected by the following:

- **if all Catholic churches in every part of the world locked their doors for one year so that you and your family could not celebrate communal worship.**

- **if Christmas and everything surrounding it—the worship, the carols, the gift-giving and manger scenes, the family traditions—were all dropped for one year.**

- **if Easter and all the joyous events that surround it were not allowed.**

- **if every religious symbol and expression in your home—from religious pictures on the wall to family prayer before meals—were taken away from you.**

- **if you could personally be controlled in such a way that you were unable to pray even privately for one year, never able to turn to God in your moments of need.**

- **if every Bible in every home, church, and school were confiscated and locked away for a year.**

Granted this is hard to imagine, but perhaps that is precisely the point. It *is* very difficult to imagine a world in which those things that touch us very personally and perhaps even unconsciously are simply eliminated, taken away. The purpose of this exercise is simply this: For each of us—and particularly for those of us who are religiously devout and committed—our religious traditions are part of our very identities, a part of who we are as persons, not simply realities that are in some artificial way attached to us and therefore easily discarded. Many of our religious impulses arise from within us—as in our need to reach out to God in prayer at certain moments in our lives or in the yearning to celebrate great and joyous events in communion with other people. The more deeply we become involved in communal religious experiences—as in celebrating the Mass with people we love, for example—the more these communal experiences too become a deeper part of us, personally valuable and life-giving experiences.

A deeply religious man.

We should strive to be sensitive to this kind of inner religious experience in Jesus as well, aware of his personal identification with the Jewish community's rich heritage. In this chapter we will very quickly mention names, events, and various religious buildings and celebrations. **We must realize that these realities touched Jesus deeply in his heart and mind, influencing to a profound degree all his hopes and dreams.** This is the only way we can understand, for example, why Jesus would "weep over Jerusalem," or why his cleansing of the Temple was such a striking event both for those who witnessed his powerful religious convictions and for himself as well. This is the only way we can hope to comprehend the drama of a scene like the one which introduces this chapter when Jesus stood up before a hushed crowd, his heart pounding and hands trembling as he unrolled that very sacred scroll, and proclaimed for himself a role that would eventually lead him to the cross. So in a spirit of respect and with a desire to comprehend with both our hearts and our minds, let us begin our review of Jesus' roots as a Jew.

2) A Brief History of the Jewish People

It is likely by this time in your Catholic Christian education you have acquired a fairly good sense of the basic history of the Jewish people. We will therefore offer only the most central highlights of that history as a kind of quick review or thumbnail sketch for you. Your teacher will be able to flesh this out with greater detail if necessary.

The story begins: The patriarchs.

Sometime between the years 1900 B.C. and 1750 B.C.—nearly two thousand years before the time of Jesus—Hebrew history began. It started with the profound religious experience of a man named Abram. Abram experienced a single loving God in an age when people believed in countless gods, few of whom entered into any kind of friendly relationship with people. This God of Abram called him into a very special kind of personal relationship, one called a "covenant." As we discover it recorded in the book of Genesis from the Hebrew Scriptures, God appeared to Abram and said:

> Bear yourself blameless in my presence, and I will make a Covenant between myself and you, and increase your numbers greatly. . . . Here now is my Covenant with you: you shall become the father of a multitude of nations. You shall no longer be called Abram; your name shall be Abraham, for I make you father of a multitude of nations. I will make you most fruitful. I will make you into nations, and your issue shall be kings. I will establish my Covenant . . . to be

your God and the God of your descendants after you. . . . You shall circumcize your foreskin, and this shall be the sign of the Covenant between myself and you. When they are eight days old all your male children must be circumcized (Genesis 17:2-24 abbreviated).

This was the first covenant experience between God and the Hebrew people, an experience in which God entered into a profound, personal, loving relationship with people through Abraham. Abraham and the people, in turn, were called to follow that God loyally and lovingly.

Though very old, Abraham and his wife Sarah had a son named Isaac. It was revealed to Abraham that he had to sacrifice Isaac as a sign of his loyalty to God. But God then withdrew that command, recognizing that Abraham's willingness to sacrifice his son was testimony enough to the strength of the covenant. Isaac and his wife Rebekah later gave birth to a son named Jacob. The covenant was renewed with Jacob when, in a dream, God told him, "Be sure that I am with you; I will keep you safe wherever you go, and bring you back to this land, for I will not desert you before I have done all that I have promised you" (Genesis 32:26-29). Jacob eventually fathered twelve sons and later, like Abraham before him, was given a new name as a sign of his special relationship with God—"Israel."

Settlement in Egypt.

One of Jacob's twelve sons was named Joseph and, because he was Jacob's favorite, all his brothers were jealous of him. The depth of their jealousy became apparent when they sold Joseph as a slave to some merchants who were on their way to Egypt. But Joseph ended up serving as a steward in a rich Egyptian's house and eventually worked his way up to the position of prime minister of the country. From that position of authority he invited his father, Jacob, and all his brothers, whom he had long since forgiven, to join him and live in Egypt. After Jacob died—about the year 1650 B.C.—the Hebrews went on to prosperity in Egypt. This ended what is known as the **patriarchal period** of Hebrew history, that phase of their history dominated by the three patriarchs—or "fathers" if you will—Abraham, Isaac, and Jacob. **The reference to the God of Israel as "the God of Abraham, Isaac, and Jacob" is a recurring one in the Christian Scriptures and refers to this period.** And, incidentally, because Jacob had been given the name Israel by God, the people were known as "the Israelites" during the period of Hebrew history which centers around his story and that of his sons.

The prosperity of the Israelites in Egypt did not last. After about one hundred fifty years of living under kind pharaohs who came from a people related to their own, the Israelites came to be dominated by Egyptian pharaohs who enslaved them, giving them the backbreaking jobs of brickmaking and of constructing public buildings. As a people who had always been free, this enslavement was miserable for the Israelites and they dreamed of being liberated. The one who would lead them to freedom would be born to them hundreds of years later.

The Mediterranean Lands

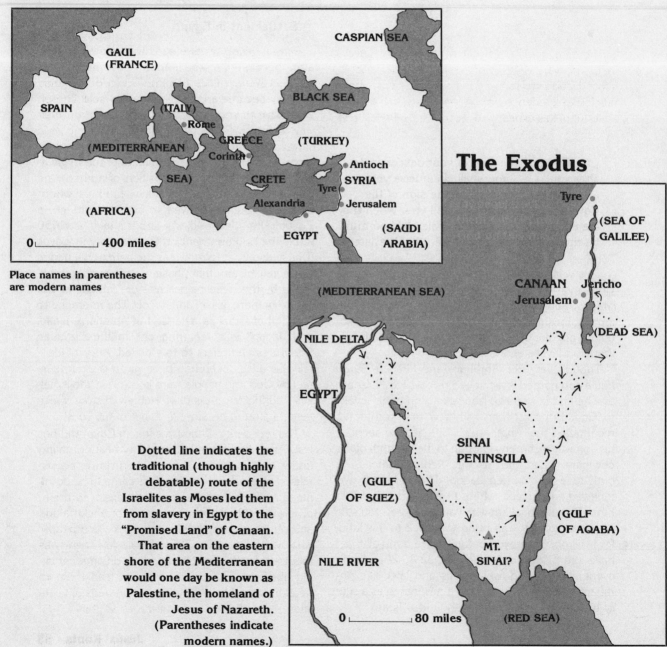

CASPIAN SEA

GAUL
(FRANCE)

SPAIN

BLACK SEA

(ITALY)
Rome

(MEDITERRANEAN

GREECE

(TURKEY)

Corinth

SEA)

CRETE

Antioch

SYRIA

Tyre

Alexandria

Jerusalem

(AFRICA)

0 _____ 400 miles

EGYPT

(SAUDI
ARABIA)

Place names in parentheses
are modern names

The Exodus

Tyre

(SEA OF
GALILEE)

CANAAN   Jericho

(MEDITERRANEAN SEA)

Jerusalem

(DEAD SEA)

NILE DELTA

EGYPT

SINAI
PENINSULA

(GULF
OF SUEZ)

(GULF
OF AQABA)

MT.
SINAI?

NILE RIVER

Dotted line indicates the
traditional (though highly
debatable) route of the
Israelites as Moses led them
from slavery in Egypt to the
"Promised Land" of Canaan.
That area on the eastern
shore of the Mediterranean
would one day be known as
Palestine, the homeland of
Jesus of Nazareth.
(Parentheses indicate
modern names.)

0 _____ 80 miles

(RED SEA)

The story of Moses: 1300 B.C.

The man called to free the Israelites from slavery in Egypt was the powerful figure, Moses. Moses sensed God's call to this mission during a profound religious experience. In the words of the biblical account of this experience, Yahweh tells Moses that

> . . . the cry of the sons of Israel has come to me, and I have witnessed the way in which the Egyptians have oppressed them, so come, I send you to Pharaoh to bring the sons of Israel, my people, out of Egypt . . . After you have led them out of Egypt, you are to offer worship to God on this mountain (Exodus 3:9-12).

It was at this point that God did something truly startling, something that we can understand only if we have a firm sense of the Hebrew mentality— God revealed his name to Moses. This reality is expressed through the biblical imagery of the Book of Exodus:

> Then Moses said to God, "I am to go, then, to the sons of Israel and say to them, 'The God of your fathers has sent me to you.' But if they ask me what his name is, what am I to tell them?" And God said to Moses, "I Am who I Am. This," he added, "is what you must say to the sons of Israel: 'I Am has sent me to you.' " And God also said to Moses, "You are to say to the sons of Israel: 'Yahweh, the God of your fathers, the God of Abraham, the God of Isaac, and the God of Jacob, has sent me to you.' This is my name for all time; by this name I shall be invoked for all generations to come" (Exodus 3:13-15).

It is not entirely accurate to call *Yahweh* simply "the name of God" revealed to the Hebrew people. Actually in the Hebrew Scriptures we find only the letters **Y-H-V-H**—those four letters offering a *symbolic* name for God. When translating into English, we have become accustomed to adding the vowels *a* and *e*, and changing the *v* to our *w* so that we are able to pronounce the word given our speech patterns. But the Hebrews themselves would never think of uttering the actual name of God, for it was their belief that knowing the name of something gave one power over that thing. **To call God by name would have been the greatest sacrilege; it would have implied that people had control over God.** Therefore the Hebrews, and later the Jews, would actually skip over the symbol Y-H-V-H when reading, and replace it orally with the word *Adonai*, meaning "Lord." In an effort again to demonstrate a greater sensitivity to Jewish religious beliefs, some writers today do not use the word *Yahweh* but rather *LORD*, using all capital letters to indicate the reference to the symbolic Hebrew word. Because of common practice, however, we will continue to use *Yahweh* as the Hebrew name for God in this book.

What does the name *Yahweh* mean?

Scholars have argued for years over the meaning of the name *Yahweh* and, in part because of the symbolic nature of the word, we may never arrive at a generally accepted translation. There *is* general agreement that the word is based on the verb *to be*. Various translations include "I am who am," "I am the one who is present," or "I bring into existence all that is." One translation for Yahweh currently gaining popularity is "I will always be present for you." Rather than actually defining God, the word seems more to hint at his nature, at who he truly is, namely, a God who loves people enough to always be with them.

We realize that discussions such as these may

appear to be "nitpicking" by some, too much concern about something apparently "simple." **The fact is that we are dealing here with the Hebrew people's very perception and understanding of and relationship to their God, an understanding that would be developed and passed on from generation to generation and ultimately to one particular Jewish boy in an obscure village in northern Palestine—Jesus of Nazareth.** As we will see later, Jesus himself would grapple with this understanding of his God, the God of Abraham, Isaac, and Jacob, and would offer his own startling and profound insights into God's very nature. Jesus would, in fact, even offer a new name for God, a fact that must have not only astounded but deeply angered the loyal Jews who heard him speak.

A special religious feast is born.

Now let's get back to our story of the history of the Hebrew people. Moses was sent by God to try to convince Pharaoh to free the Israelite people from bondage. But Pharaoh was not easily persuaded to free the Israelites, and God had to provide a great deal of help to Moses if he hoped to accomplish his mission. Pharaoh's hand was forced when a series of ten plagues revealed God's dominating power over the lives of people. The tenth plague—the one that ultimately freed the Israelites from Pharaoh's grip—was one that also resulted in key religious rituals which to this very day highlight the spiritual lives of the Jewish people. It was revealed that the first-born of all the families in Egypt were to be killed. But God gave the Israelites a sign that would protect them, and them alone, from this disaster.

They were to slaughter either sheep or goats from their flocks, and take some of the blood from the slaughter and put it on the doorposts and above the doors of their homes. The flesh of the slaughtered animals was then to be eaten along with unleavened bread and bitter herbs. As the first-born children in all of Egypt were then killed, God "passed over" the homes on which the blood had been poured, saving the Israelites and convincing the Egyptians to let them go. And God revealed to them that "This day (Passover) is to be a day of remembrance for you, and you must celebrate it as a feast in my honor. For all generations you are to declare it a day of festival, forever" (Exodus 12:14). We will return to a discussion of key Jewish feasts—including Passover—later.

The covenant of Mount Sinai.

Following their miraculous escape from Egypt, the Israelites roamed for fifty days in the desert. Then God ratified his covenant with them in one of the most important events recorded in all of Scripture. In a dramatic encounter (see Exodus 19-20), Yahweh called Moses to the mountain top and there said to him, "Say this to the House of Jacob, declare this to the sons of Israel, 'You yourselves have seen what I did with the Egyptians, how I carried you on eagle's wings and brought you to myself. From this you know that now, if you obey my voice and hold fast to my covenant, you of all nations shall be my very own for all the earth is mine. I will count you a kingdom of priests, a consecrated nation.' Those are the words you are to speak to the sons of Israel" (Exodus 19:3-7). So God now extended his offer of the covenant to an entire people, the implications of which we will see in a moment.

An Egyptian wall painting from the tomb of a pharaoh

But a covenant is a two-way kind of relationship, and something was expected of the people by God. **Their end of the bargain was the elaborate system of Jewish Law, the cornerstone of which was the Ten Commandments.** The Law of the Jewish people would one day be misused and would be a stumbling block between Jesus and his own people. But at this point in their history, it was recognized for what it truly was—a wonderful gift, establishing in a very unique way a relationship of love between Yahweh and his people.

As we have said, the covenant of Sinai was one of the central events in all of Scripture and in the history of the Jews. God had transformed a crowd of poor slaves into a nation—his own special people. Until this point he had spoken only to individuals (Abraham and Jacob, for example) and these were at most only leaders of small clans of people. On Sinai the "People of God" were born, with the special name of Israel. So this was now a covenant *community,* and it is only in terms of that community that we will come to understand the Jews and, for that matter, our own community of faith, the Church.

Following these marvelous events, the Israelites roamed the desert for forty difficult years. But Yahweh, their God, remained firm in his commitment to this covenant community. He was indeed their God, and they his people—though, as we shall see, not always a faithful people.

Life in the Promised Land.

Following the death of Moses, the Israelites crossed the Jordon River into the land that had been promised them by Yahweh—"the Promised Land" of Canaan. The next few hundred years, however, were brutal ones, with many wars and seemingly endless turmoil for Israel. During this time men called "judges"—great warriors rather than judges in our sense of the term—were periodically appointed to fight and defeat Israel's enemies. **As land was gradually conquered, it was divided among "the twelve tribes of Israel," one tribe descending from each of the twelve sons of Jacob.**

Nearly two hundred years after Israel began the conquest of the land of Canaan (about 1050 B.C.), they confronted a new enemy—the Philistines. With new weapons, and fighting a now divided Israel, the Philistines proved to be too strong for the Israelites. They captured the treasured Ark of the Covenant in which Moses' written version of the Ten Commandments was stored and honored. If the Israelites were to survive, they needed to be unified against their enemies. In desperation they appointed their first king, a man named Saul.

The kingdom of Israel: Saul, David, and Solomon (1000 B.C.).

Saul, the first king of Israel, was actually more a warrior than a king in our sense, and though he was a brave man in battle, he was a weak man personally. He was very jealous of a young man named David, one of the leaders in his army, who had gained public acclaim for leading the people in some of their victories over the Philistines.

By this time the twelve tribes of Israel had divided into two main groups—ten tribes in the north who retained the name of Israel and two tribes in the south called Judah. These major groups were separated by the city of Jerusalem. After the death of Saul, the kingdom of Judah recognized David as the king while Israel to the north recognized one of Saul's own sons. That son was a weak leader and was murdered after just two years on the throne. The people then turned to David as their only king. He was 37 when he united all the people of Israel, around the year 1000 B.C., and he led Israel in defeating the Philistines and conquering much of the surrounding territory.

Jerusalem became known as "the city of David" where he built a palace and desired to build a great Temple in which the reclaimed Ark of the Covenant could be kept and honored. Jerusalem therefore became the center of not only the political but also the religious life of the people of Israel. **David is still recognized as the greatest of all the kings of Israel.** Before his death he saw to it that his son, Solomon, was publicly crowned as his successor.

Solomon served as king for some forty years. It was a period of great building, increased trade, and prosperity. Solomon built the magnificent Temple that David had dreamed of, but he had to resort to heavily taxing the people and drafting ten thousand men a month to complete that and his other building projects. Though the Temple was beautiful and attracted the people to worship, Solomon himself turned to idolatry, building pagan shrines and worshipping their idols.

The kingdom divided: Israel and Judah.

After the death of Solomon, his son was proclaimed king of Judah in the south. However, to be accepted as king of the northern tribes, he had to go there for his coronation. The people of the north wanted relief from their taxes and the labor draft, but the king refused and alienated them all. The ten tribes in the north therefore refused to accept him as their king and instead formed themselves into a new kingdom of Israel, thereby destroying the unified kingdom of David.

What followed was a history of weak kings and religious disgrace. **Great prophets arose, men who** tried to call the people of Israel back to the coven-ant. But the people of the northern kingdom of Israel continued to weaken and eventually were destroyed by the Assyrians in 721 B.C. Judah, the southern kingdom composed of just two of the original twelve tribes, also had its great prophets, chief among them a man named Isaiah. The king-dom of Judah was able to last about a century longer than the northern kingdom because its leaders, successors of David, were somewhat more loyal to the covenant with Yahweh than were the kings of the north. Isaiah, however, recognized that one day the southern kingdom too would be de-stroyed. But he made a prediction. Comparing the royal family to a tree that is cut down, Isaiah said that only a stump would be left to represent the family which had started with David's father, Jesse (thus the familiar religious term, "the Jesse tree"). However, said Isaiah, from this stump would come a shoot, a new branch—and that future king of David's line would be someone powerful and good, someone who would bring peace. (See Isaiah 11:1-9.) Christians, of course, would much later recognize that someone in the person of Jesus, "one born from the line of David."

In 598 B.C. Jerusalem was overrun by the Babylonians, and the leading citizens of the country were carried off as captives into Babylon. The southern kingdom had been destroyed, just as Isaiah had predicted. Another prophet, however, by the name of Jeremiah, wrote to the captives in Babylon and urged them to settle as permanent residents there, promising that someday Yahweh would return them to their home.

Back in Jerusalem everything worsened, and in 587 B.C. the city of Jerusalem was destroyed and thousands of captives were led off into exile. Many

The Kingdoms of Israel and Judah

After the death of Solomon, the kingdom of the Hebrews split into the northern kingdom of Israel and the southern kingdom of Judah. Note the double dashed line which identifies the point of separation between the two kingdoms. Other unnamed regions indicate areas inhabited by other peoples of that time. (Parentheses indicate modern names.)

of the people left the country for places along the Mediterranean Sea where small colonies of the faithful began to grow. **These people made up a group called the "Diaspora," the name given all those groups of Jews who lived outside the central area of Palestine.** Through the voice of the prophet Jeremiah, however, Yahweh refused again to turn aside from his people. " 'Behold the days are coming,' says the Lord, 'when I will make a new covenant with the house of Israel and the house of Judah . . . I will put my law within them, and I will write it upon their hearts. Then I will be their God, and they will be my people' " (Jeremiah 31:31-33).

Renewal of the covenant community.

Somehow the experience of being in exile, with Jerusalem destroyed, led many of the people to a renewed appreciation for their faith. Certainly many of those held in Babylon gave up in hopelessness, and the time of the captivity was perhaps the saddest in all of Jewish history. But a certain number of these people—called "the remnant"—began to live much more closely to Yahweh than ever before. The Exile was seen not just as a punishment by God for what they had done, but rather as God's way of bringing his people back to a recognition of him.

In 539 B.C. the Persians overcame the Babylonians, and their leader allowed all the exiles in the new Persian Empire to return to their native lands with freedom of worship. This had been predicted by perhaps the greatest of all the prophets, one whose name we have never even known. His writings were added to those of the prophet Isaiah, and so we have come to call this prophet Second Isaiah.

He wrote some of the most beautiful passages in all of Scripture, including the famous "Suffering Servant passages," which speak of a great servant of God who would one day save his people through his own suffering and death rather than through military conquest. (See especially Isaiah 53:1-12.) To us, as Christians of the twentieth century, this makes sense. To those exiles who first heard it in the middle of the sixth century before Christ, it was a bewildering kind of talk. They were a people who expected victory by fighting for it. The thought of gaining victory by suffering willingly was apparent nonsense.

By 537 B.C. the first Jews to return to Palestine— "the remnant"—began arriving in caravans. They worked on rebuilding the Temple, a project completed in 515 B.C. **They were no longer a political nation under a king, but rather a religious community under a new form of leader—the high priest.** Because these people were a remnant from the southern kingdom of Judah, it is at this point in this long history that we can begin to speak of *Judaism* as we use it today, and it is also from this term that we have derived the word *Jew* for those who follow this faith. Gradually two main classes of leaders developed among the Jews—the priests, who were responsible for offering sacrifices in the Temple, and those called scribes, who were responsible for teaching the Law of Moses.

The story is not completed.

We are going to pause in our discussion of the history of the Jewish people at this point, returning

Summary of Hebrew History: 1800-500 B.C.

Key persons and events indicated by capitalization

2000 B.C.		1000	

THE PATRIARCHAL PERIOD: About 1800 years before Jesus (B.C.), Hebrew history begins with ABRAHAM in the land of Canaan. Abraham and Sarah give birth to ISAAC. Isaac and Rebekah have two sons, one of whom is JACOB. Jacob has twelve sons, from whom the "twelve tribes of Israel" are derived. One of the twelve sons is JOSEPH, who settles in Egypt where he is later joined by his brothers. One hundred fifty years of prosperity follow.

1750

From about 1550-1300 Israelites suffer SLAVERY in Egypt.

1500

From 1300-1250 B.C. MOSES leads Israelites out of Egypt (the EXODUS) and experiences the SINAI COVENANT with Yahweh. Israelites then settle in "the Promised Land" of Canaan. From 1200-1000 the JUDGES lead the Israelites against their enemies.

1250

The kingdom of Israel formed. SAUL is the first king, followed by DAVID (1000-961 B.C.) who is the greatest of all the kings. It is David who establishes Jerusalem as the central city of his people. He is followed by SOLOMON (961-922) who builds the original TEMPLE. The kingdom splits following Solomon, into the northern kingdom of ISRAEL and the southern kingdom of JUDAH.

750

Northern kingdom is DESTROYED BY ASSYRIANS in 721 B.C. Southern kingdom of Judah survives until 598 B.C. when its leading citizens are taken into CAPTIVITY IN BABYLON. In 587 Jerusalem is destroyed and thousands more led into captivity (the EXILE).

In 539 the PERSIANS DEFEAT THE BABYLONIANS and the people of Judah are allowed to return to Jerusalem. From this point on they are known as "JEWS" (from "Judah"). The TEMPLE IS REBUILT by 515 B.C.

500

in chapter 5 to a discussion of the occupation of Palestine by the Romans and how that political situation directly confronted and was challenged by Jesus. There is always a degree of hesitation in a book of this kind to deal at any length with discussions of history for two reasons chiefly:

1) History is itself so complex and involved that an adequate discussion of it takes a library of books rather than just a few pages out of one. There is no question, for example, that our "thumbnail sketch" has greatly oversimplified the profound and incredibly moving history of the people of faith we now call Jews.

2) Our second reason for avoiding long historical discussions is an even less acceptable one, however. Many today, for whatever reasons, find history plainly and simply boring. However, it is only in the study and appreciation of our history that we can ever hope to understand our own identities. And, in the case of our discussion of Jesus, this is no less the case. **Every moment of Jesus' earthly life grew out of, was touched by, and spoke directly to the Jewish community of his time.** Without understanding that, as we said before, we cannot understand him.

As an illustration of this critical point, we will close this chapter with a concise listing of some basic and essential features of Jewish religious conviction, lifestyle, and communal custom that literally fill the pages of the gospels. Try to be sensitive to and conscious of these characteristics of Jewish religious life as you read the gospels and as we pursue our study of Jesus. In doing so you will discover a new sense of richness and insight into the life and message of the Jesus of History who is called, by one quarter of the world's people, the Christ.

3) Major Features of Judaism

Jerusalem: The city of David.

Jerusalem is clearly a unique and central city for the Jews. It is the capital of the country, but in a much richer sense than our contemporary understanding of capital cities would lead us to understand. It is geographically central in Palestine, which made it ideal as a capital, a fortress, and a center of marketing. But much more importantly than that, it is a "holy city," and it had been recognized as such for ten centuries before Jesus' time. Every Jew who lived outside Palestine cherished the dream of one day seeing its many beautiful gates, walking its bustling streets, and most importantly, setting his or her tear-filled eyes on the Temple there, that wondrous building which expressed and celebrated and symbolized the Jews' entire history as a people of faith. To tread the soil of Jerusalem was, for the Jew, to walk on holy ground.

During Jesus' time, Herod the Great, a master builder, added the last beautiful touches to the Jerusalem that the remnant had begun to rebuild five hundred years earlier. He even started to rebuild the Temple to the majesty it knew when Solomon had originally built it. The present Wailing Wall in Jerusalem, in fact, is all that remains of Herod's efforts. At the time of Jesus, Jerusalem was a major city of some 150,000 people, but that number could swell almost incredibly to 500,000 during the great religious feasts we will discuss later. It is of this central and holy Jewish city that Jesus could cry out:

Jerusalem in
modern times,
the Old Wall
in foreground

Jerusalem, Jerusalem . . . how often I have
longed to gather your children, as a hen gathers
her chicks under her wings (Matthew
23:37-38).

The Temple.

The Temple, as we have seen, was at the very
center of the life of the people of God. As mentioned above, the Temple that Jesus knew was the
one that Herod was building. Construction had
begun about fifteen years before Jesus' birth and
was not completed until nearly thirty-five years after
his death, only to be totally destroyed by the Romans a short time after its completion. It is difficult
to gain a visual sense of its splendor. Thirteen gates
opened into the Temple proper, and one of them—
the Nicanor Gate—was made entirely of bronze
and was so large that it took twenty men just to
open it! It was the sound of this gate opening that
signaled the beginning of the day for the people of
Jerusalem.

Sacrifices were offered at the Temple, of course,
and particularly important ones accompanied all
major feasts. Lesser sacrifices were offered as signs
of thanksgiving or by those seeking forgiveness for
their sins. Though such rituals were officially
recognized by the Jews as just exterior or outward
signs of what was supposed to be an honest and
interior personal religious attitude, many of the
people actually viewed these sacrifices as having
almost magical power.

The Temple was a center of prayer as well as
sacrifice, with the famous story of the Pharisee and
the publican in Luke 18 an illustration of this fact. It
was also the seat of the religious, political, and
judicial body of the Jews called the Sanhedrin,
which will be discussed in a later chapter. The
Temple was so large that it could contain literally
thousands of priests and tens of thousands of believers at once. It is only when we know the cen-
trality of the Temple to the religious life of the Jews
that we can begin to appreciate their reaction when
Jesus stormed into the Temple, enraged by the way

Herod's Temple

The Holy of Holies, divided from
the Holy Place by a curtain
which Matthew's gospel says split
from top to bottom when Jesus died.
The Ark of the Covenant stood here
in Solomon's day but no longer existed
in Jesus' time

The Holy Place, where the
priests regularly burnt incense

A bowl
for ritual
washings

The altar
where animals
were sacrificed.
Jesus was described
by John the Baptist
as being "the lamb of God
that takes away the sin
of the world"

The court of the Gentiles.
This was the only part in
which non-Jews were allowed.
The traders and money-changers
worked here and were turned
out by Jesus

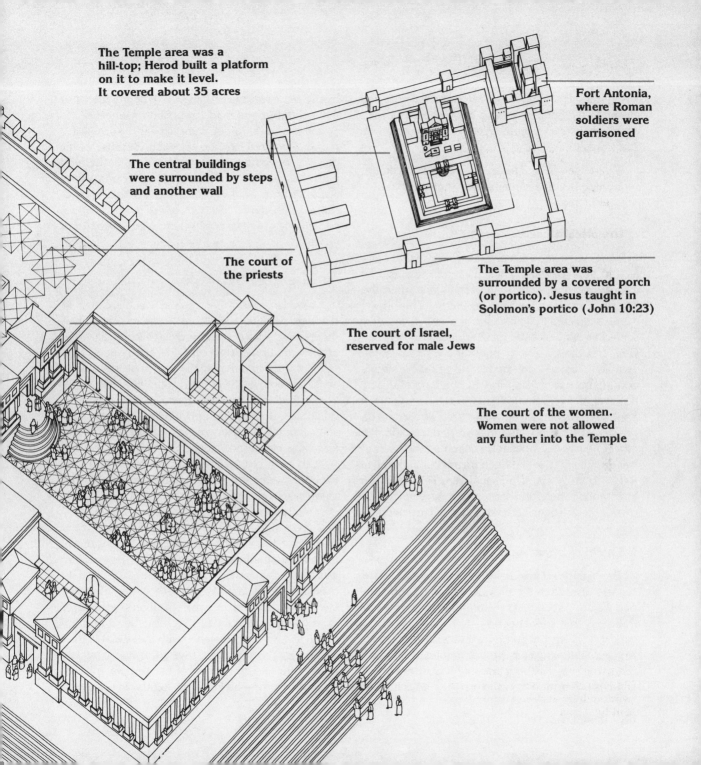

The Temple area was a hill-top; Herod built a platform on it to make it level. It covered about 35 acres

Fort Antonia, where Roman soldiers were garrisoned

The central buildings were surrounded by steps and another wall

The court of the priests

The Temple area was surrounded by a covered porch (or portico). Jesus taught in Solomon's portico (John 10:23)

The court of Israel, reserved for male Jews

The court of the women. Women were not allowed any further into the Temple the money changers had been desecrating it and cheating the people. Turning over tables and scattering chairs and pigeons alike, he shouted out with the words of Scripture:

My house will be a house of prayer. But you are turning it into a robbers' den (Luke 19:46).

The priestly caste.

Priests were known in Hebrew history as far back as the time of Moses, but they took on special importance during the time of the kings when the Temple became a national institution. The priests were considered the guardians of worship, and they served as go-betweens or intermediaries between God and the people in offering sacrifices in the Temple. Originally one became a priest by simply coming from a certain tribe. By the time of Jesus, however, the powerful officials of the Temple—the Sanhedrin mentioned above—chose who would be priests from among the many members of that tribe. They were supposedly chosen on the basis of "respectability," but that often meant that only those with wealth or social prestige were selected. The priesthood, therefore, became a very exclusive class, and one often hated by the common people.

The high priesthood.

The high priest was the head of the priestly caste. He was also often the president of the Sanhedrin, and we will discuss his role further in the context of that body in a later chapter. The high priest held a very special kind of authority that went beyond his role as spiritual leader. He was anointed in much the same way as the kings of his day, lived in a lavish palace, and dressed in very colorful and highly recognizable clothing. The appointment of the high priest was made by political masters of the country, and a lot of intrigue—and sometimes money—entered into the selection. Because of his position as spiritual leader of his people, the high priest had so much influence that politicians always wanted to stay on his good side. All of this helps to explain the role of the high priest in the gospels, particularly when we see him involved in the trial of Jesus.

Synagogues.

As we have seen, the Temple was the center of religious sacrifice and also a house of prayer. But the Temple was eventually destroyed for all time, and it was the existence of the synagogues as a place of worship that held the Jewish people together as a community of faith after its destruction. Some traditions say that these houses of prayer originated during the Babylonian Captivity as a substitute for Temple worship. Each village had at least one synagogue, and any adult Jew had the right to erect one or even turn his house into one. Sacrifices were never offered in the synagogues, but as we saw in our opening Scripture passage for this chapter, precious scrolls containing the Hebrew Scriptures were kept there. The synagogues would open three times a day for prayer and occasionally for other gatherings, but weekly Sabbath worship was the chief gathering held there. It is hard to overestimate the importance of the synagogue in the life of the believers of Israel. In John's gospel, for example, it is mentioned that those Jews who followed Jesus were threatened with the denial of their synagogue privileges as a severe threat and punishment. After the destruction of the Temple, the synagogue became—and remains to this day—the cen-

The Synagogue

Synagogues were the local centers of Jewish worship, and many were also schools. The drawing is an artist's impression of what such a building would have looked like in Jesus' time, based on the ruins at Capernaum. Many synagogues were not so lavish as this, however.

The courtyard, with a fountain where people could wash their hands and feet

The ark or tabernacle containing the scrolls of Hebrew Scriptures

Women were segregated from the men in Jewish synagogues. Here they have a gallery reserved for them

The pulpit in the middle of the synagogue was made of wood. Here the Scriptures were read and sermons preached

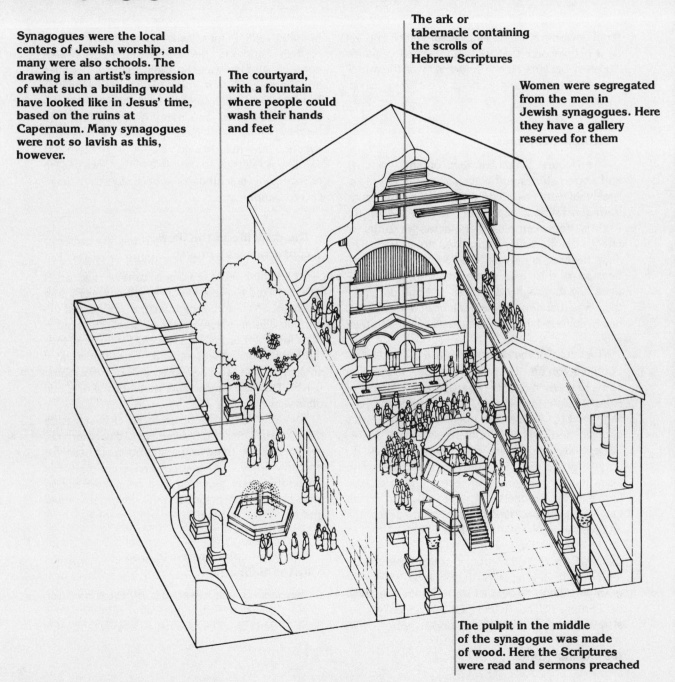

ter of Jewish communal life. It assured their survival as a people over the last two thousand years, as Judaism became strictly a "religion of the word" based on their sacred writings, the Hebrew Scriptures.

Hebrew Scriptures.

The Hebrew Scriptures were originally ancient and sacred stories and teachings of the people of Israel that were passed on orally, by word of mouth, from generation to generation. Some of these—the Psalms, for example—were actually songs or chants before being committed to writing. The Jews became known as "the People of the Book" because of their total commitment to their Scriptures. So thoroughly did these writings dominate their lives that not a single book from ancient Israel has been found that was not directly related to their Bible.

The works of the prophets held a particular importance for the Jews, and we have referred to some of them in our brief overview of the history of Israel—Isaiah, for example, the author of the passage read by Jesus in our opening reading for this chapter, and Jeremiah. Others like Elias, Amos, Osee, and Ezekiel were also cherished. This accounts for the recurring phrase in the gospels and elsewhere about the Jewish commitment to "the Law and the prophets." (The Jewish love for the Law of Moses has already been briefly described, and we will return to it later in this book.)

The Hebrew Bible developed over a very long period. Even individual books of the Bible took a long time to develop, with the Book of Psalms, for example, taking as long as eight hundred years to be compiled! The Hebrew Bible eventually consisted of forty-six different books. About two hundred years before Jesus' time, a Greek edition of their Scriptures developed within the Jewish community. This was the Bible that the Apostles and the early Church would have normally used.

Jesus was deeply and prayerfully aware of the Hebrew Scriptures, and many of his sayings and teachings reflect this fact. Any time we hear him say, "You have heard it said . . ." or "It is written that . . ." he is referring to the Bible of the Jews or, less often, to the teachings of rabbis regarding those sacred Scriptures.

The daily life of the Jews consecrated by prayer.

The faithful Jew (and Jesus certainly was one!) was expected to live a life of personal prayer in the home. At dawn and at nightfall the Jew recited the famous Shema prayer: "Hear, O Israel! The Lord is our God, the Lord alone! Therefore, you shall love the Lord our God with all your heart, with all your soul, and with all your strength" (Deuteronomy 6:4-5). This was the absolute minimum of religious observance.

The truly faithful Jew, however, also set aside three other times for prayer each day: morning, evening, and at three in the afternoon. These were primarily times for prayers of praise and blessing. Therefore Jesus grew up in a religious tradition based heavily on personal and communal prayer and on the sacred Scriptures of his people.

The week consecrated to God by the Sabbath.

The Sabbath is a weekly day of rest and prayer for the Jews based on the creation story from the Book of Genesis when God rested after creating the world. It is also linked historically to the Exodus experience. It is such a significant religious observance that it is mentioned nearly seventy times in the gospels alone. In the early history of the Hebrews, people who violated the Sabbath laws were even put to death, though this severe practice was no longer the case in Jesus' time. Nevertheless, the Sabbath was recognized as a central and sacred sign of Yahweh's presence with his people and of their covenant relationship with him.

Unlike our days which begin at midnight, a day for the Jews began at sunset. Therefore, the Jewish Sabbath actually lasted from what we know as Friday evening and through the daylight hours of Saturday. It was the only day of the week that had a name of its own; all other days were either numbered or identified as "the day before Sabbath," for example. There were strict prohibitions and regulations governing the day: No housework or cooking could be done by the women; no labor of any kind could be performed. It was unlawful to light a fire, so people had "Sabbath lamps" that were fueled and tended by the woman of the house during the Sabbath observance. It was even against the law to use wooden legs on this day! After the Friday evening meal, the people could not eat again until after the Saturday morning synagogue worship service, and special prayers then accompanied each meal during the remainder of the Sabbath.

There were constant arguments among the rabbis and others about how closely these laws were to be followed. Jesus spoke for many of the rabbis when he proclaimed that "the sabbath was made for man, not man for the sabbath." But he added that "the Son of Man [Jesus himself?] is master even of the sabbath," a claim that could not help but offend and greatly anger many of the people (Mark 2:27-28). Once again we see that only a basic background in these realities of Jewish life can make the gospels understandable.

The Jewish year consecrated to God through religious feasts.

A careful reading of the gospels demonstrates the central role played in Jewish religious life by several key religious festivals and feasts. This is true perhaps of all major religions, as in the case of Christianity with its annual observance of Christmas and Easter and the seasonal observances that lead up to these celebrations, Advent and Lent. For the Jews, as for us, these were occasions to glorify, thank, and petition Yahweh, their God. Some of the feasts were celebrated in their homes or in small groups with a master and his disciples. But even these feasts had a strong communal character with individual Jews sensing their unity as one nation turned to its God. Each feast had public ceremonies as well, and many were occasions for great pilgrimages to Jerusalem for those living in distant lands (the Diaspora mentioned earlier).

Initially some of the Jewish feasts were probably nature feasts borrowed from other people—for example, feasts of spring and harvest time—which gradually took on religious dimensions through their long history. Many of the feasts were penitential in nature, reminding Jews of their failures to follow the will of Yahweh, while others were highly festive and had a cheerful, carnival atmosphere.

There were three major feasts that we should be conscious of if we are to understand the gospel accounts of Jesus' life:

1) **Pentecost:** Also called the "Feast of Weeks," this was a celebration of the giving of the Law to Moses. The word *pentecost* is based on a Greek word for "fiftieth," and it reflects the fact that it was fifty days after leaving Egypt before Moses received the Law on Mount Sinai. This feast also celebrated the harvest time for the Jews, a time for experiencing and expressing deep gratitude for the wonderful gifts of Yahweh. It was a great holiday.

2) In autumn there was a series of three feasts which followed in quick succession: the Feast of the Jewish New Year, the Day of Atonement (Yom Kippur), and the Feast of Tabernacles, all happening within twenty-two days of each other. The second of these—**the Day of Atonement**—was the second major feast and one of such central importance to the Jews that if a person simply mentioned "the Day" everyone knew that it referred to this special feast. This was a time for the Jews to solemnly repent of all their sins. There were moving ceremonies, fasting, prayer, and ritual bathings. On this day also the high priest would enter the sacred Holy of Holies in the Temple to purify it with the mingled blood of a goat and a bull.

3) But of all the feasts of the year, the holiest and most celebrated was **Passover,** celebrating the miraculous liberation from Egypt. This marked the beginning of the Jewish religious year. Lasting a week, it included the sacrifice of lambs in the Temple (known as "the paschal lambs" from the word *pasch* meaning "to pass over"), and the ritual of a very special meal recalling one shared by Moses. It was for obvious reasons a very cheerful feast for the Jews and one that plays a central role in the gospel events surrounding the final days of Jesus before his execution.

Concluding comment.

Our point in offering this material is not that you be able to clearly recall the entire history of the Jewish people and know all the details surrounding its religious traditions. Rather, we ask that you view this chapter—and the two chapters that follow—as resources to be returned to periodically as you read the gospels and as we pursue our discussion of Jesus and his message. A careful consideration of all the ideas contained in these chapters will make the reading of the gospels much easier and much more enriching for you. As just a simple indication of this fact, take a moment now to go back to the Scripture reading which introduces this chapter. Read it very slowly, pausing just for a moment to reflect on those terms which have been discussed in this chapter: synagogue, Sabbath, the scroll of the prophet Isaiah, and so on. Does the passage make more sense to you than it did the first time you read it? Can you more clearly sense the wonder and tension that Jesus must have caused during this incident? Can you better understand not only the Jewish response to Jesus at this time, but also his own interior attitudes and feelings as a deeply devoted and faith-filled Jew of his day? This is the intent of this material—not to burden you but, on the contrary, to make the gospels and the Jesus they proclaim come alive for you. The Good News is simply too marvelous to miss because of the lack of this kind of information!

We have begun our discussion of Jesus' roots with his religious heritage as a Jew. We now turn to the family and social life that was so much a part of who he was and of the message he shared.

Review questions and activities:

1) Why must we have a good understanding of Judaism—its history, symbols, and practices—if we hope to understand Jesus?

2) Provide a brief biographical sketch of each of the following persons, including roughly when they lived, what they experienced or did, and why each is so important in Jewish history: Abraham, Jacob, Joseph, Moses, and David.

3) What is a "covenant"? In what major sense did the covenant of Mount Sinai differ from the covenants between Yahweh and persons like Abraham and Jacob?

4) "Yahweh" is actually a *symbolic* name for God. Explain.

5) Write a one-sentence definition or description for each of the following major features of Judaism: Jerusalem, Temple, priestly caste, high priesthood, synagogue, Hebrew Scriptures, Sabbath, Pentecost, Day of Atonement, and Passover.

Terms to identify and remember:

patriarchs	Diaspora
Abram/Abraham	remnant
covenant	Jerusalem
Isaac	Temple
Jacob	priests
Israel	high priest
Joseph	synagogue
Exodus	Hebrew Scriptures
Moses	Sabbath
Sinai	Pentecost
Judah	Day of Atonement
Babylonian Cap-	Passover
tivity or Exile	

Exercise for personal reflection:

Our review of the history of the Jews may seem a bit overwhelming, both because of its complexity and because of the sense that it is all so foreign to our own experience. To "personalize" all of this a bit, try to find in Catholic Christianity parallels to the items listed among the "Terms to identify and remember" above. For instance, is there anything in Catholicism that might be similar to the holy city of Jerusalem? What would be similar to the Jewish Sabbath for Christians? This kind of exercise can make Jesus' sense of his own history more real to us.

4 The World of Jesus and Its Daily Life

Then John's disciples came to him and said, "Why is it that we and the Pharisees fast, but your disciples do not?" Jesus replied, "Surely the bridegroom's attendants would never think of mourning as long as the bridegroom is still with them? But the time will come for the bridegroom to be taken away from them, and then they will fast. No one puts a piece of unshrunken cloth on to an old cloak, because the patch pulls away from the cloak and the tear gets worse. Nor do people put new wine into old wineskins; if they do, the skins burst, the wine runs out, and the skins are lost. No; they put new wine into fresh skins and both are preserved" (Matthew 9:14-17).

1) In Touch with the Land and Its People

One might be inclined to read the passage above quickly and move on, certain either that it is quite familiar and requires little thought or just as certain that it is so confusing that all the thought in the world won't make sense of it! We have chosen this passage to introduce this chapter precisely because of that somewhat mysterious content and its heavy use of the imagery of Jesus' own day. It was noted in the previous chapter that Jesus was a devout Jew whose religious heritage stretched back well over one thousand years to its origins in the story of "the father of the Hebrew people," Abraham. But it is also vital to realize that Jesus was a Jew born into a particular place, with a particular culture, at a particular point in history. A true understanding of him must include a basic sense of his daily world and a certain appreciation for the subtle influences of his culture which are so much a part of who he was and the message he shared.

The gospels are filled—like the passage quoted above—with images and experiences which flow out of the day-to-day lives of the Jewish people: wineskins and old cloaks, festivals and parties, the lilies of the field and the birds of the air, bread baking and storms at sea, planting and harvesting, young children playing and old people dying. In our commitment as Christians to recognize the Jesus of History as the Christ of Faith, there has been a constant but perhaps healthy tension between our acceptance of his divinity and our recognition of his humanity. Without for a moment denying or questioning his existence as God, we must never lose our grasp of a truly wonderful reality: In Jesus God "takes on flesh" to become, as the author of the letter to the Hebrews says, one with us in all things but sin (see Hebrews 4:15). Jesus, as a man, was immersed in the world of his time, steeped in all its religious and social traditions, nourished with the food and drink of his day, brought to laughter by the parties and weddings of his people, and moved as well to tears by the sickness, disease, and death that haunted their daily lives. When he spoke to the people, he used images they would understand and experiences they could identify with:

● **The Pharisees and Sadducees request a sign from heaven to prove he is the Messiah. His response: "In the evening you say, 'It will be fine; there is a red sky,' and in the morning, 'Stormy weather today; the sky is red and overcast.' You know how to read the face of the sky, but you cannot read the signs of the times" (Matthew 16:2-4). His method of forecasting the weather grew out of his culture, but the message he conveyed with that image was of much greater significance to his listeners!**

● **The scribes challenged him because of his dining company: " 'Why does he eat with tax collectors and sinners?' When Jesus heard this he said to them, 'It is not the healthy who need a doctor, but the sick. I did not come to call the virtuous, but sinners' " (Mark 2:15-17). That scene will only strike a chord for those who understand the tremendous importance of meals in the lives of the Jewish people.**

● **His first disciples are called to follow him while working as fishermen by the Lake of Gennesaret. Under Jesus' direction "they netted such a huge number of fish that their nets began to tear," so many in fact that two boats almost sink under their weight. Out of that experience of an almost too successful fishing trip, Jesus draws the point he wants to make: " 'Do not be afraid; from now on it is men you will catch.' Then bringing their boats back to land, they left everything and followed him" (Luke 5:10-11).**

● **He was a carpenter of his day, and the lessons he learned in his shop found their way into his teaching: "Why do you observe the splinter in your brother's eye and never notice the plank in your own? . . . Hypocrite! Take the plank out of your eye first, and then you will see clearly enough to take the splinter out of your brother's eye" (Matthew 7:3-5). The thought of a plank sticking out of one's eye may illustrate Jesus' occasional use of exaggeration to make a point, but there is little doubt that the point is clearly made!**

In this chapter we will provide some very general background into the land and daily life experienced by Jesus. As was true in our discussion of various facets of Jewish religious tradition and history, we will only be able to offer short glimpses into the geography, diet, housing, occupations, and so on, that together provide such a rich human texture to the gospels. It is hoped that this information will allow you to read between the lines of the Scriptures, gaining a deeper appreciation for the profound and often moving message that is so often contained in and expressed through simple and common life experiences.

Palestine: Great Variety in a Small Land

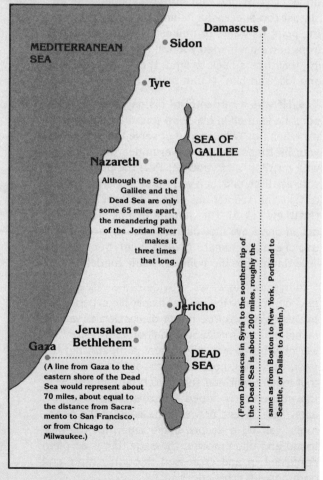

MEDITERRANEAN SEA

Damascus •
• Sidon

• Tyre

SEA OF GALILEE

Nazareth •

Although the Sea of Galilee and the Dead Sea are only some 65 miles apart, the meandering path of the Jordan River makes it three times that long.

(From Damascus in Syria to the southern tip of the Dead Sea is about 200 miles, roughly the same as from Boston to New York, Portland to Seattle, or Dallas to Austin.)

• Jericho

Jerusalem •
Bethlehem •
Gaza •

DEAD SEA

(A line from Gaza to the eastern shore of the Dead Sea would represent about 70 miles, about equal to the distance from Sacramento to San Francisco, or from Chicago to Milwaukee.)

2) The Land: Beauty and Diversity

The land of Jesus—what we today call Palestine—stretched just 145 miles from north to south, and anywhere from 25 to 87 miles from its western coast at the Mediterranean Sea to its eastern borders. This land is often referred to in Scripture as the Land of Israel, and in Jesus' time it was most often called "the Land of Canaan," "the Promised Land," or "the Land of Judah." (It was called Palestine by the Greeks who named it after the Philistines who had inhabited the coastal area at one time.) The significant point to make about the limited size of this region is the fact that this small area is the only world that Jesus ever knew, one that could be traveled from one corner to another by car today in a matter of just a few hours. It was an area roughly the size of Massachusetts, and the distance from its northern to southern extremities about the same as from Philadelphia to Washington, D.C., or from Seattle to Portland. Even though the people of Jesus' time most often had to walk from town to town, it was still relatively easy for them to get around. The Jews were great walkers, thinking nothing of walking distances we might hesitate to drive! An average walker could go from Nazareth to Jerusalem in about two days, for example. This is one reason why there seems to be such continual movement from one place to another in the gospels, and this small size also explains in part the profound love the people had for their land—they simply knew it very well, just as a farmer knows every acre of his land "by heart."

Remarkable variety.

Within this rather restricted area, however, there is tremendous geographical diversity. The gospels speak of lakeshores and hillsides, of deserts and forests. The area surrounding the Dead Sea is desolate and forbidding, while that surrounding the Sea of Galilee to the north is lush and inviting. As one author puts it, "A walk of a single hour will take one from the richest of plains to the bare hills where the sheep graze; and the caravans, toiling under the hot wind of the desert, took hope again from the sight of snow shining on Mount Hermon." The "mountains" of Palestine are really only large hills, but they give a texture and majesty to the land that impress even the traveler of today.

The climate of the area is inviting as well, though not in all areas. The average temperature for the year is 72 degrees Fahrenheit, with an average monthly high of 77 degrees and an average monthly low of 59 degrees. But the variations can be extreme, with frigid nights and hot days. Though rare, snow is known to the people of this region, yet the temperature around the barren Dead Sea can reach 122 degrees Fahrenheit. Rainfall is a problem, with almost all of the annual amount falling in October and in March, often in the form of violent storms like the one mentioned in Matthew 7:24-27, when Jesus reminds his listeners of times when "the rain came down, floods rose, (and) gales blew . . ." The question of water and its sources, therefore, is a very serious one and one often referred to in the Scriptures. The people had to dig many wells, and strict rules governed the use of water. This accounts also for the people's deep love for those bodies of water that *were* available to them, particularly the gorgeous Sea or Lake of Galilee (which is also called the Lake of Gennesaret or the Sea of Tiberias) and the beloved Jordan River, over which the Hebrew people crossed to enter the Promised Land and in whose waters Jesus himself was baptized. In this context, think of the imagery used by Jesus when, in talking to a Samaritan woman by a well, he refers to himself as "living water":

> Whoever drinks this water (from the well) will get thirsty again . . . the water that I shall give will turn into a spring inside him, welling up to eternal life (John 4:14).

Bread and wine—signs of life.

With this great variation in climate and rainfall, it is not surprising that there was also a wide variety of vegetation and foliage in the Palestine that Jesus knew. Trees and fruits were abundant, with juniper and oak the most common trees, and olive and fig trees the most valuable because of the fruit and oil they provided. And of course there was the wonderful "fruit of the vine," the grapes from which the people made their deep, full-bodied red wines, so rich and thick that they had to be mingled with water before being served. Jesus referred to himself as "the vine" (John 15), and the gospels have many references to the vineyards and those who tended them. The common cereals of the time included the most precious—wheat—along with oats and barley. Bread was the essential food of Jesus' day,

so much so that "to eat bread" meant "to have a full meal," a reality we express even today when we speak of "breaking bread together." Bread was to be treated with great respect, and many laws governed its preparation and use. So we can see that when Jesus identified himself with the bread and wine at the Last Supper, it was clear to those gathered with him that he was revealing himself as one who could give them complete sustenance and fulfillment, that he was in fact "the bread of life" who could totally satisfy the deepest hungers of people (see John 6:26-59).

Both wild and domestic animal life was also abundant and varied. Among the common wild animals Jesus would have known were boars, foxes, porcupines, hyenas, wolves, leopards, bears, and lions, many of which find their way into the Scriptures. Fish and birds of many kinds were also plentiful. Domesticated animals included sheep, oxen, donkeys, cows, and, of course, pigs which the Jews considered "unclean" animals not to be eaten. The donkey was the most useful animal because of its strength and endurance, and it was so highly valued that it could never be offered as sacrifice. Perhaps surprising to us, given our modern understanding of the Middle East, camels were quite rare in Jesus' day, and the only people on horseback Jesus would have seen were probably Roman soldiers. Roosters, hens, and geese were common, but there were no family cats in Jesus' time, and most of the dogs were half-wild relatives of the wolves.

3) The People and Their Daily Life

In reading the gospels it seems that nearly every lesson Jesus teaches is expressed through the common experiences of his people and their daily life—their food and meals, their housing and occupations, and the ways in which all these things touched upon their family life. Our awareness of these realities can make the gospels much richer and more meaningful for us, so it is important that we gain a basic sense of the daily life that Jesus experienced.

The food and meals of the Jews.

We have already noted that bread and wine were central to the diet of the Jewish people. It is important to realize as well that the very act of eating, the sharing of meals between people, was considered a sacred act in itself by the Jews. To "break bread" (bread was never cut but always broken) was an outward sign of unity and friendship. Whenever a meal is shared in the Scriptures you can be sure that something very significant is happening. This is why the people reacted so strongly at those times when Jesus ate with obvious sinners. The people were shocked by what they considered a demonstration of outright approval of both the sinners and their sins by Jesus. What Jesus was trying to demonstrate by his actions, however, was that he was offering a continually forgiving love for sinners despite his disapproval of the sins they committed: "I did not come to call the virtuous, but sinners."

The people ate very little meat, which was considered primarily a luxury for the wealthy. When Jesus told the parable of the prodigal son (or, perhaps more accurately, the forgiving father), he knew how to effectively express the profound joy that the father felt when his son returned home: " 'Bring the calf we have been fattening,' the father said, 'and kill it; we are going to have a feast, a celebration, because this son of mine was dead and has come back to life; he was lost and is found.' And they began to celebrate" (Luke 15:23-24). The people listening to Jesus as he told this story knew that one only ate meat on very special occasions or during major celebrations, such as the Passover feast when the paschal lambs were prepared and eaten.

The most common food other than bread was fish, and together these formed perhaps the most common meal of Jesus' day. The fish was often dried and salted to preserve it, and also cooked over a charcoal fire as we see Jesus doing during an appearance after his Resurrection in John's gospel (John 21:9). Fruit was also abundant, as were nuts like walnuts, almonds, and pistachios. The only drink more common than wine was water. The wine was stored either in large jars or in wineskins made of goat hide.

Meals were often eaten in the open air and at flexible times of the day, for the people of Palestine had few of the concerns about schedules and precise times that often frustrate us today. At formal meals the people ate in a reclining rather than sitting position, and they ate with their hands and a flattened metal cup rather than with forks, spoons, and plates. Though most of their meals were simple, the Jews loved their occasional feasts and parties because of the sense of family togetherness

A village in Iraq
with houses built
by traditional methods.
Note the millstone
(See Mark 9:42)

and community provided by them. Many examples from the gospels can be found where feasts and other celebrations form a backdrop for the message of Jesus.

Their homes.

The people's homes were the centers around which their entire lives seemed to revolve, primarily because—as we will see in a moment—Jewish family life was considered very sacred. For the most part their houses were neither large nor impressive. Most of the people were part of what we would call today the lower class, and their houses were usually one-room, whitewashed cubes. They usually had only one door, and the one room was often divided in two, with the people living on one side of the room and their animals living on the other. At times the houses were built into the side of a hill, so that part of the house was actually a cave.

The houses were often made of clay which was sometimes baked into bricks. Only the homes of the rich were made of stone. In the same way, the floors of most houses were simply hard-packed earth, while the wealthy had floors of baked clay tiles. The roof of the common house was made of "wattling," which consisted of poles bound together by reeds and grass which were then covered with earth. These could be lifted off easily as can be seen in the story of the cure of the paralytic in Mark 2 when, in order to get the paralyzed man to Jesus, the people carrying him "stripped the roof over the place where Jesus was; and when they had made an opening, they lowered the stretcher upon which the paralytic lay" (Mark 2:4). The roof usually had just enough slope to carry off rain water. The people often kept tools on the roof, spread linen there to dry after washing, and even slept there in the cool evenings. It was also quite common to sit on the roof during times of prayer and meditation.

Only the houses of the rich contained wood-burning stoves, but every village had at least one communal oven that all could use for baking bread and cooking food. Small lamps were used for light in the homes, which were placed on a lampstand and fueled by rancid olive oil, giving a familiar but not very pleasant odor to all the houses. Furniture was simple, consisting perhaps of just a chest for storage and a bushel or wood container used for measuring grain at the market and then turned over for use as a table in the home. Jesus refers to these things when he says that just as people would not put their lamps under a tub or bushel to be hidden but rather on a lampstand where it can give light, so people must let their good works "shine in the sight of men" (Matthew 5:15-16; Mark 4:21-23; Luke 8:16-18). People slept on mats which they rolled out in the evenings and wrapped themselves in their cloaks at night for warmth. These cloaks were made of camel or goat hair and were very thick, heavy, and waterproof—so heavy, in fact, that they could stand up on their own! The cloak was worn for warmth and protection from the elements over the lighter woolen "tunic" or coat. When Jesus told his followers that "if a man takes you to law and would have your tunic, let him have your cloak as well," he was telling them to turn over some of their most valuable possessions—literally "the shirts off their backs"—to those in need (Matthew 5:40). The people did not use pillows when they slept but rather pieces of wood or even stones for their heads.

Their occupations.

The Jewish people of Jesus' day had a particular love for all kinds of work that had to do with the earth. Many were farmers and shepherds, and images from these occupations fill the gospels: the sower and his seed, fields of wheat, the picking of corn, people tending their sheep or cattle, and laborers in the vineyard. Ploughing, sowing, and harvesting all enter into the teachings of Jesus.

Fishing was naturally another common and respected occupation, given the comments we have already made about the nature of the land and diet of the people. Jesus called his first disciples from this work (Matthew 4:18-22; Luke 5:1-11), and he used imagery from fishing in many of his teachings. Perhaps it was the character and basic qualities that make for successful fishing that attracted Jesus to these men as his first disciples. They were men of courage and patience, and they had hearty spirits. (Jesus called two of them, James and John, "sons of thunder"!) Perhaps most importantly, they had a basic reliance upon and trust in the goodness of God who, after all, supplied the fish they needed for their livelihood.

There were many different kinds of trades practiced in Jesus' day, and the Bible mentions no fewer than twenty-five of them, ranging from carpenters like Jesus and Joseph, to sandalmakers and tentmakers, like St. Paul. Though many necessities were made in the home and often by the women, there was still a need for skilled workers to provide for the other needs of the people. The trade of carpentry which Jesus learned and practiced as a young man was a well-respected one. He built cabinets, carved the yokes which had to be delicately fitted to each ox, constructed small bridges, and so on. No doubt his years in the work gave him a real sensitivity to the needs of the people he lived and worked with. His trade also put him in touch with the glories of God's creation as he roamed the forests in search of good wood and then struggled to create something good and useful out of the varied woods he found there.

4) The Jewish Family: A Community of Faith

Much of Jewish family life, not surprisingly, revolved around religion, including many family traditions and customs, the education of children at the synagogues, and so on. The family was clearly recognized as the essential basis of Jewish society, and the Law was committed to upholding the permanence and authority of the family. In fact for the Jews, the family unit was recognized as a true religious community in and of itself, with the father the chief leader or celebrant of many family religious feasts.

Polygamy, or the practice of allowing a man to have more than one wife, had existed early in the history of the Jews, but by the time of Jesus, monogamy, or the commitment to a single spouse, was more recognized as the ideal. Jesus himself, though never directly condemning polygamy, elevated the role of women in his day dramatically and spoke out strongly on the sanctity of the marriage commitment.

Betrothal and marriage.

People in Jesus' day married very early in life. The men usually married no later than age 20, but women were normally married as soon as they were physically able to bear children, which the law defined as 12½. Mary, the mother of Jesus, was probably no older than 14 when she bore him.

Marriages were most commonly arranged by the parents, chiefly the father of the prospective husband. The actual marriage was preceded by a period of betrothal, usually lasting about a year, during which time the couple got to know each other. The Law recognized many of the rights and obligations during the time of betrothal as being the same as during marriage. For example, a girl found guilty of adultery while betrothed was stoned to death just as if she were married. This is one reason why Joseph wanted to quietly divorce Mary when he found out she was pregnant, for the Law would have demanded she be killed (Matthew 1:18-19). It should also be noted that such punishment generally applied only to the woman. Adultery by a man was only a crime if it involved a married or betrothed woman, because in that case the act would be injuring the stability of the family.

The actual wedding was a great event, sometimes lasting for more than a week! There was much eating and drinking, as illustrated by the wedding at Cana in John's gospel, when Jesus' mother recognizes that the lack of wine might ruin the party and Jesus responds with his first "sign" or miracle (John 2:1-12).

After the marriage, the husband and father was recognized as truly the head of the family. His wife even called him "lord" or "master." Sons and daughters were recognized as his property, and the Law even allowed the father to sell them into slavery if they committed a crime. The commandment to "love thy father and mother" was so strong, in fact, that historically the father had the right to put to death a child who disobeyed! These severe traditions were virtually gone by the time of Jesus, however.

Men and women in Jewish society.

As might be implied by the laws governing adultery, women too were considered the property of men, and it is important to remember that in just about every way imaginable women were considered men's inferiors. For example, women did not eat with the men but rather ate standing while serving them. They kept at a distance from men on the streets and were restricted to certain areas of the Temple. It is only when we recognize this male-dominated society that we can appreciate the tremendous impact of many of Jesus' words and actions with women in the gospels, like the apparently simple yet remarkable scene in the gospel of John when Jesus carries on a discussion with a woman at a public well. His disciples were "surprised to find him speaking to a woman . . ." (John 4:27) simply because the practice was not tolerated. As we will see later in our discussion of Jesus' Resurrection, some of the first witnesses to the event mentioned in the gospels were women, a rather striking fact since the testimony of women was not even recognized or accepted in a court of law.

We should be careful, however, not to overstate the negative side of the lives of Jewish women and children. Despite the obvious inequalities mentioned, they actually had a much better life and were more respected and loved than in many other cultures of the time. Women did have some recognized rights in Jewish society—the right to be housed, clothed, fed, and so on—and Jewish men took this responsibility very seriously. And children were always recognized as a great blessing to Jewish families. (Girls, however, were less desired than boys because they married at such a young age and then became the property of someone else.) But the Jews, to their credit, never resorted to the horrible pagan custom of the day in which unwanted children were simply and cruelly destroyed. In Jewish society, in fact, children were recognized as adults, with adult responsibilities, by age 13.

5) Social Classes in the World of Jesus

Every society it seems gradually develops a series of social classes or groups: the "haves" and the "have nots," the rich and the poor, the politically powerful and the oppressed. Jesus' world was no different, except that the level of inequality and the gaps between the various classes was perhaps far greater than most of us experience in today's world.

Part of what determined social position in Jewish society, predictably enough, was religious tradition. The priestly class, for example, could claim some degree of social importance or nobility on religious grounds, though even they had lost some of their historical power and influence to the scribes by the time of Jesus. We will discuss both these groups a bit more in the next chapter.

A few rich, many poor.

As in most cultures, however, social standing in Jewish society had a lot to do with money and who possessed it. Jesus talked often about the rich and the poor, primarily because the gap between the two was so great and many people of his day were desperately poor. A middle class in our sense of the term simply did not exist. There were very few rich people, only those who had somehow acquired land and the power that goes with it or who had accumulated wealth through trade or political influence. But the vast majority of the people lived in what certainly to us would be described as dire poverty.

Slavery existed at the time of Jesus, and it enters into several of his parables (though the term often used for slaves in the Scriptures is *servants*). But slavery for the Jews was nowhere near as common as it was in Roman and Greek cities where as much as one quarter of the entire population may have been slaves. For one thing, Jews couldn't afford slaves. And the Law of Moses called for much better treatment of slaves than was true in Roman culture, though no doubt that legal principle was not always practiced. Jewish law did demand, however, that all slaves were to be freed after seven years of service, and this fact made a Hebrew slave worth much less money than a pagan slave. Therefore, Hebrew slaves were less popular and fewer in number than pagan slaves, and this may account in part for the fact that Jesus did not seem preoccupied or greatly concerned about the slavery issue directly. Certainly, however, his entire message of love and human freedom contradicted every argument people could develop to try to justify slavery.

In-groups and outcasts.

As we noted earlier, Jewish society included many occupations and trades, and those who worked hard were greatly respected. Some trades and occupations were held in higher esteem than others, however. Sandalmakers and woodworkers were thought to be better, for example, than tanners (who smelled badly!) or perfume salesmen (who were in continual contact with "loose women"). Jewish society did provide the earliest social legislation governing masters and those who worked for them, and there were even the beginnings of trade unions among the Jewish laborers.

Jews felt great contempt for anyone who did not follow the Law of Moses, and this attitude reached outright hatred for the non-Jews who had occupied Palestine during the Babylonian Captivity discussed in the last chapter. The Samaritans were one of these peoples, and the gospels make clear how deeply despised they were. Other social outcasts included those labelled "unclean" (lepers, for example), the extremely poor, the sick, and, as we have seen, women. Judaism excluded all of these people from the center of its religious life which implied, of course, that they were excluded from virtually everything of value in Jewish society.

Think now of the incredible impact of the ministry and message of Jesus in this kind of social setting. **Without exaggerating the point at all, we can say that Jesus challenged and even condemned his own society on virtually every level.** It was a society that rejected the poor and the weak, yet Jesus seemed to make these people the very center of his message and those most to be honored. His people deeply hated the Samaritans, yet in his preaching it is the Samaritan who is seen as "good" while the selfishness of the priest is condemned (Luke 10:29-37). It was a society that at best tolerated women, but Jesus freely associated with them and accepted them as central participants in his ministry. He embraced with love and compassion the sick and "unclean" who were rejected by his people. He attacked those with wealth and power who refused to share with those in need. It is true that Jesus was more than a social revolutionary, more than one committed to changing the social conditions of the people of his time. The message he proclaimed was one of a freedom deeper than freedom from social, economic, or political oppression. But it can never be discounted, ignored, or minimized that Jesus' message included the condemnation of all such social oppression—hunger, racial and sexual discrimination, political domination, and all those things that would keep people from experiencing the fullness of life due them as sons and daughters of a loving God.

One culture among many.

There is a final topic to be discussed before we can move even more directly into a consideration of the person, life, and message of Jesus. We have seen that he was a deeply committed and faith-filled Jew, and we have noted the impact of that reality upon him in chapter 3. In this chapter we have discussed the land and daily life of the Jewish people, catching brief glimpses of the culture that so permeates the gospel story and the marvelous message of Jesus. But the Jewish people and culture during Jesus' time were not free from the profound influences and challenges of other peoples and cultures. They were, in fact, under the near total domination of the Romans, and it is only in the context of understanding that reality and all the personalities and groups involved in it that we can fully comprehend the ministry and message of Jesus. That is the subject of the next chapter.

Review questions and activities:

1) Why is a knowledge of the land and people of Palestine essential for a *balanced* understanding of Jesus?

2) The author writes of the "remarkable variety" of Palestine. Explain.

3) Throughout the Scriptures there are nearly countless references to water. Why is this so?

4) In the context of daily life in Palestine, why does it make sense that Jesus would identify himself with bread and wine at the Last Supper?

5) Why would something as apparently simple as Jesus eating a meal with recognized sinners so deeply anger the people of his day?

6) The Jewish family was recognized as a true religious community in and of itself. Explain.

7) It has been said that Jesus was one of the first "women's liberationists." Explain.

8) The author states that "Jesus challenged and even condemned his own society on virtually every level." Give three examples.

Terms to identify and remember:

Palestine	polygamy	betrothal
Sea of Galilee	monogamy	servants
Jordan River		

Exercise for personal reflection:

Imagine your own family, as you presently experience it, being thrust back through time to the Palestine Jesus knew. Try to construct a typical day in your life under those circumstances: Where would you live? What meals would you eat? How would your parents relate to each other, and what occupation would your father likely be involved in? What trade or occupation do you think you would like to pursue given your own abilities and interests today? You may even find it helpful to do this exercise with your eyes closed and in a relaxed position. Try not only to "see" the situations in your imagination but also to sense the sounds, aromas, and so on that you might experience. Such exercises can help greatly in gaining a rich appreciation for the world Jesus encountered.

5
The Political World of Jesus

1) Making Sense of a Confusing World

A quick reading of the gospels reveals that the world of Jesus was considerably different from our own, with strange names, confusing political and religious groups, rivalries for power between governmental factions, and so on. As just a brief indication of this fact, below are listed some religious and political persons and groups who appear in the gospels and who play at times central roles in the life and ministry of Jesus. How many are familiar to you, and how many do you think you could accurately identify, describe, or discuss?

> Pharisees, Sadducees, the Sanhedrin, Caiaphas, Pontius Pilate, Herod, the high priest, scribes, publicans, tax collectors, Zealots

How did you do? If it's any consolation, the vast majority of adult Catholic Christians would have a difficult time answering this question. And yet it seems clear that we cannot fully understand the gospel accounts about Jesus if we don't have a basic understanding of these groups and individuals. The purpose of this chapter is to offer that understanding in as clear and concise a way as possible.

Our task will not be an easy one. In our earlier treatment of Jewish history, we brought our brief review from Abraham to roughly the year 500 B.C., when the Jewish remnant returned from the Exile to Palestine, the Temple was rebuilt, and the religion

Then the Pharisees went away to work out between them how to trap him (Jesus) in what he said. And they sent their disciples to him, together with the Herodians, to say, "Master, we know that you are an honest man and teach the way of God in an honest way, and that you are not afraid of anyone, because a man's rank means nothing to you. Tell us your opinion, then. Is it permissible to pay taxes to Caesar or not?" But Jesus was aware of their malice and replied, "You hypocrites! Why do you set this trap for me? Let me see the money you pay the tax with." They handed him a denarius, and he said, "Whose head is this? Whose name?" "Caesar's" they replied. He then said to them, "Very well, give back to Caesar what belongs to Caesar—and to God what belongs to God." This reply took them by surprise, and they left him alone and went away (Matthew 22:15-22).

of Judaism formally began. In this chapter we will deal with the historical developments for the Jews from roughly three hundred fifty years before Jesus until about forty years after his death. Though our purpose is to offer a very broad overview of that history, keying in on only those persons, groups, or events which play a direct role in the gospel story, there may still be a tendency for you to feel overwhelmed by the strange names and complex history you encounter here. Our first suggestion is an important one: relax! Though you may be expected to be able to identify and describe the key groups and persons mentioned at the end of this chapter, you will likely not be tested on all the dates and details of the history which led to their development. The next few pages, in other words, are intended to help make sense of the review of key concepts made later. Read this material carefully and try to gain a broad sense of this historical development, but don't be threatened by it.

Some helpful hints.

We would also like to offer a few suggestions that may help to make this material more easily understood:

1) Naturally our discussion will include some names of places or regions of Palestine. The map included on page 92 of this text is designed to show these areas in the clearest and simplest fashion with few names of towns and cities. Refer often to the map as you read.

2) For names of persons or regions that may be difficult to pronounce, a phonetical spelling is provided to help you. We suggest that you say these words out loud as you read. The combination of both seeing and hearing the names will make it easier for you to remember them.

3) Work your way through the material quickly the first time to gain a general sense of the progression of ideas. Then reread the material very slowly and carefully, moving from one point to the next only when you feel fully confident that you understand the material presented. If a particular point seems somewhat confusing to you, don't skip over it assuming that it isn't very important. It is quite possible that much of the material following that point won't make sense without understanding it.

4) Finally, a simplified summary of this historical development is presented on page 98. The chart indicates the basic material with which you should be fully familiar. Use the chart as a kind of checklist for yourself. If there is a point on it that you can't understand or remember, return to the detailed explanation in the chapter for more information. When the material on the chart seems clear to you, you have gained an adequate understanding of the information in this chapter.

Providing these aids for understanding this material may make it seem even more threatening and difficult than it is. That is, of course, not our intent. The fact is that this history is downright fascinating and enjoyable to study, making the work of Jesus and so much of what we have heard about it through our Christian education come alive for us. Again, relax . . . and enjoy!

2) The Greeks Dominate Palestine: 323-142 B.C.

Alexander the Great was unquestionably one of the most remarkable figures in all of history. He lived only thirty-three short years (356-323 B.C.), but in that time he literally dominated his world. He was a Macedonian, born in a country north of Greece, but he was a Greek in spirit, educated by the great philosopher Aristotle, and convinced that the Greek vision of life offered civilization its greatest hope of fulfillment and excellence. He was just twenty when he became king of Macedon, but he won the hearts and minds of the Greeks in six short years as he led his armies in victories over all the enemies of Greece. By the time he died in 323 B.C. he had conquered much of the Mediterranean world and lands as far east as India.

The empire divided.

After his death the land that Alexander had conquered was divided among the leading generals of his army. Our concern, of course, is what happened to one part of the empire, namely the Middle East which included Palestine, the land in which Jesus would be born some three hundred years later. This region was divided between two of Alexander's generals: Seleucid (sell-oo'-sid) and Ptolemy (toll'-eh-mee). These two men and their successors would dominate Palestine for 150 years.

The Seleucid dynasty was based in the city of Antioch in Syria, the region just north of Israel. The Ptolemean dynasty was based in Alexandria, a major city in Egypt to the southwest of Palestine.

Looking at the map you can see that Israel was located directly between these two centers of power, and it was inevitably caught in the struggle for control between them. It was out of that struggle that many of the factions and groups we find in the gospels would later develop.

"Galilee of the Gentiles."

For about the first one hundred years of Greek domination, Israel was ruled by the Ptolemies in Egypt. Because of the distances which separated them, there was little interference in the internal affairs of the Jews. Nevertheless there was a subtle impact of Greek culture upon the people of Palestine. For example, there was an increasing use of the Greek language throughout Israel. In fact in the northern region of Israel named Galilee, where the Seleucids ruled, the Greek influence on all levels of their culture was profound—so much so that the region is often referred to as "Galilee of the Gentiles" in the Bible. Gentiles, as you know, are non-Jews, and we will see that by Jesus' time to be born a Jew in Galilee was similar to our notion of being "born on the wrong side of the tracks."

As an aside here, it will prove helpful to keep in mind that by the time of Jesus Israel was divided into several regions, the key ones for our discussion being Galilee to the north, Samaria in the north central, Judea in the south central, and Idumea to the south. Judea was considered the center of the state for, among other reasons, it was there that Jerusalem was located. All of these names come into play often throughout our study of Jesus.

The tolerant kind of Greek occupation practiced by the Ptolemies ended in the year 198 B.C. when all of Israel came under control of the Seleucids. At first Israel was allowed to maintain local control of its affairs, but that situation changed gradually as the Seleucids developed a need for increased finances. The Romans from the west had defeated the Seleucids in a naval battle and then demanded an enormous amount of money as a price of defeat. To pay off the Romans—as well as to support all their other war efforts—the Seleucids began a heavy taxation of Israel. Any peace and good will that had existed between the Greeks and the Jews were shattered by this.

Reactions to Greek rule.

There were two different reactions to these foreign influences by the people of Israel, particularly by those living in the region of Judea:

1) The wealthy landowners and priestly class tried to get along with the foreigners, simply because they had the most to lose in any conflicts with them.

2) Another group, called the "Hasidim" meaning "the pious ones," resented the Seleucids and thought that any compromise with them amounted to a rejection of their Jewish faith.

It was out of this basic philosophical and religious tension that many of the factions which appear in the gospels would eventually develop, particularly the Sadducees and the Pharisees.

An incredible victory.

Seleucid domination led to one of the greatest events in the entire history of the Jews, one that eventually resulted in a religious festival that is celebrated by the Jews even today. (This is a bit complex, so think through this development carefully.) The ruler of the Seleucids, in an effort to extend his control over the land, tried to take possession of the land held by the Ptolemeans in Egypt. The Romans

An ancient Roman mosaic depicting Alexander in battle

stepped into the conflict, however, and stopped the Seleucids. Some rebels within the Jewish community were so heartened by the defeat of the Seleucids by the Romans that they thought they too could overthrow them and regain their freedom. They guessed wrong. The Seleucid ruler, who was already deeply angered about his defeat at the hands of the Romans, took out his rage on the rebelling Jews. He not only crushed the rebellion but sacked Jerusalem, desecrated the beloved Temple, and even went so far as to build an altar to the Greek God Zeus in the Holy of Holies, that most sacred part of the Temple where even devout Jews could not enter.

The Seleucid ruler had clearly gone too far and had underestimated the power of a people whose religious convictions ran as deeply as did those of the Jews. All of Judea erupted in outrage at what the Seleucids had done. Though the odds were strongly stacked against them, the rebelling Jews— under the leadership of a family named the Hasmoneans (haz-mo′-nee-ans)—won a decisive victory over their oppressors! One of the Hasmoneans was nicknamed Maccabeus, meaning "the hammer," because of his ferocious fighting. The revolt came to be known as the Maccabean War or Revolt, and its story is told in two books of the Hebrew Scriptures. In the year 164 B.C., the hated altar of Zeus was removed and the sacred Temple was rededicated, an event remembered and celebrated even today by the Jews with the Feast of Dedication or Hanukkah. By the year 142 B.C., the Seleucids had granted complete freedom to Israel, and about a century of national freedom followed, a period of independence not to be experienced again by the Jews until, incredibly, the founding of the modern state of Israel in our own era.

3) Jewish Independence: 142-63 B.C.

The Hasmonean family assumed leadership of the Jewish state after the Jews had gained independence, but they failed as political leaders almost as totally as they had succeeded as fighters. Even before achieving complete independence, one of the Hasmonean family members accepted the "gift" of the high priesthood from the Seleucids. As we discussed in an earlier chapter, the priesthood had traditionally been restricted to members of certain families coming from one of the original twelve tribes of Israel. The Hasmoneans were not members of any of the accepted priestly families, and by accepting that role they publicly violated the traditions of the Jewish people. This act greatly lessened the prestige and respect accorded the priesthood, a fact we will see represented in the tensions of the gospel story.

Factions within Judaism.

Just as "the pious ones" were moved to react to their Greek rulers earlier, so now they had to deal with their own Jewish leaders. There was no uniform reaction, however, and many factions began to take shape, most of which we find in the gospels:

1) The priestly class again worked out accommodations with the Hasmoneans just as they had with the Seleucids earlier. These people became known as the **Sadducees** (sad'-yoo-seez).

2) Some people reacted so strongly to the weaknesses of the Hasmoneans that they withdrew from Jewish society altogether in order to observe strict religious traditions. These people were known as the **Essenes,** and though never mentioned in the Bible, it is likely that Jesus knew of them and may even have been influenced by their deep religious convictions and practices.

3) Another group tried to find some kind of middle ground or compromise between the political accommodation of the Sadducees and the withdrawal of the Essenes. These were the **Pharisees** (fare'-eh-seez), an extremely important Jewish party and one mentioned often in the Christian Scriptures. The Pharisees refused to compromise their religious beliefs and therefore lost some influence in the higher levels of religious and political power. But they gained a strong reputation for strict faithfulness to the covenant among the common people, and they were very much respected and therefore influential among them.

Eventually the Hasmoneans further abused their position of power by trying to expand their central power base in Judea. Much of the prejudice and bitterness between various sections of the country in Jesus' time originated during this period:

1) On the map you will see that just south of Judea was the territory of **Idumea** (id-oo-mee'-ah). Under the Hasmoneans this region was quickly absorbed by Israel and *forced* to accept Judaism. The fact that their "acceptance" of the Jewish faith was brought about by force would always make the Idumean Jews suspect to the "mainline" Jews of Judea. There is a real irony here that we will discuss more thoroughly in a moment. A man named Herod—an Idumean Jew—would eventually be appointed king of the Jews by the Romans who would soon overthrow the Hasmoneans, the same Hasmoneans who had forced the Jewish faith upon the Idumeans in the first place!

2) **Samaria,** the territory just north of Judea, was also suspect. The Samaritans, as we mentioned earlier, were among the remnants of the old northern tribes of Israel who had *not* been sent into Babylon during the Exile. As a result, many of their religious practices and traditions—including their Scriptures—were different from those of mainline Judaism. When the Judeans returned from the Exile, they completely rejected the Samaritans and would not allow them any participation in Jewish religious or national life. The Hasmoneans, in their effort to expand their power, went so far as to destroy the temple that the Samaritans had built in their own territory and then tried to force them to accept orthodox Judaism. The intense hatred between the two deepened dramatically, and by the time of Jesus there was great bitterness between them. Imagine now the impact of Jesus' story about the "Good Samaritan" who comes off as a hero when compared to the priest in the story

The Roman Empire in A.D. 14

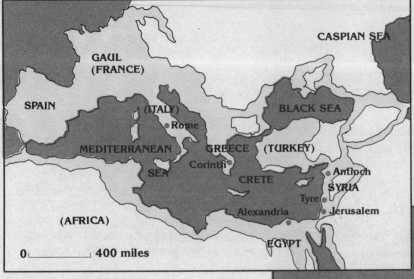

GAUL
(FRANCE)

SPAIN

CASPIAN SEA

(ITALY)

• Rome

BLACK SEA

MEDITERRANEAN

GREECE

(TURKEY)

Corinth

CRETE

SEA

Antioch

SYRIA

Tyre

Alexandria

Jerusalem

(AFRICA)

EGYPT

0 ⌐————⌐ 400 miles

Palestine at the Time of Jesus

Place names in parentheses
are modern names.

The dashed line indicates
the political boundaries
in A.D. 6-34.

NOTE: This map
contains only those
towns and geographic
regions which are
mentioned in the
synoptic gospels.

NOTE ALSO: The area
near Capernaum is at
times referred to as
Gennesaret.

*The Decapolis was a
loose federation of
ten towns and their
surrounding areas.

**Perea is also referred to
as Transjordan or
"across the Jordan" in
the gospels.

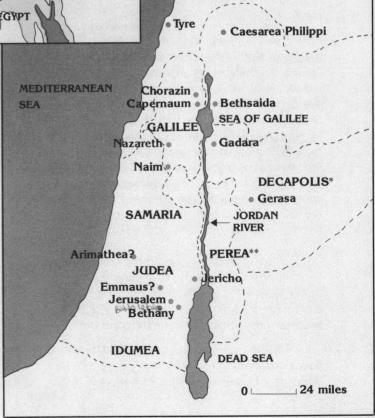

• Tyre

• Caesarea Philippi

MEDITERRANEAN
SEA

Chorazin
Capernaum •

• Bethsaida

SEA OF GALILEE

GALILEE

Nazareth •

• Gadara

Naim •

DECAPOLIS*

• Gerasa

SAMARIA

JORDAN
RIVER

PEREA**

Arimathea? •

JUDEA

• Jericho

Emmaus? •
Jerusalem •
Bethany •

IDUMEA

DEAD SEA

0 ⌐————⌐ 24 miles

4) Israel Under Roman Domination

(Luke 10:29-37), or his public conversation with not just a woman (which would have been scandalous enough) but with a *Samaritan* woman, no less (John 4:1-30)! No wonder he seemed to cause problems wherever he went!

3) Galilee, too, was annexed by the Hasmoneans, and the non-Jews there were also forced to either accept Judaism or leave the region. Many accepted, and by Jesus' time most of Galilee was Jewish. This, as indicated earlier, led to a negative attitude about Galileans among mainline Jews. Their late acceptance of the Jewish faith gave the Galileans a reputation as "second-class citizens." As you can see on the map, **Nazareth**—where Jesus was raised—was located in Galilee. This explains the comment made about him in the gospels by mainline Jews: "Can anything good come out of Nazareth?" (John 1:46)

Thus the century of independence under the Hasmonean family quickly deteriorated into bitter factions, nearly to the point of civil war. Finally, both the Pharisees and the Sadducees appealed to Rome for help in settling their conflicts. The Romans had just been waiting patiently for such an invitation, and when it came they were ready to offer more "help" than the people had bargained for. In 63 B.C., some sixty years before the birth of Jesus, the Romans occupied the country and took over complete control.

One of the reasons the Romans built such a powerful empire in their day was the wise way in which they governed the people they conquered. For example, when they defeated a country and took control of it, the Romans would carefully select leaders from among the conquered people themselves. This practice gave stability to the entire empire. By 37 B.C. the Romans had selected the shrewd Idumean Jew, Herod, to rule Israel. Herod would rule until his death in 4 B.C., and it was during the end of his reign that Jesus would be born. The sons of Herod would continue his dynasty until almost the end of the first century after Jesus.

Herod "the Great."

If one were to judge Herod on purely political grounds, with no regard to his morality, he would have to be judged a success as a ruler. He combined the qualities of political cunning with absolute terror. He was a master builder and, as was mentioned in an earlier chapter, he began the restoration of the Temple to its original splendor during Jesus' time. But he was an incredibly cruel man. The story is told, for example, that Herod ordered that all the prominent men of the town in which he lay dying were to be executed right at the moment of his own death, so that the grief of the town's people would be "real"! In Matthew 2:13-18, we find the story of Herod's execution of all male children under the age of two in the hope of destroying "the Christ" who might assume his role as "king of the Jews." This event, called "the Slaughter of the Innocents," has not been historically verified, but Herod's reputation for brutality certainly makes it seem possible.

It was Herod's political ability that managed to hold the country together during his reign. But when he died, the Romans allowed his power to be passed on to his sons who seemed to have all of his cruelty but none of his political intelligence. They were such poor leaders, in fact, that by the year A.D. 67 (about forty years after the death of Jesus) there would be a massive revolt against the Roman occupation by Jewish rebels, a revolt that would quickly lead to the total and final destruction of the city of Jerusalem, the Temple, and Judaism itself as it had been known to this time. This political division and the names of the three sons of Herod the Great who ruled Palestine became the backdrop for the gospel story of Jesus:

1) **Philip** was the most capable of the three sons of Herod. He took over control of the land to the extreme northeast of Palestine proper, and he built the town of Caesarea Philippi there. Of all the sons of Herod, Philip was the only one who proved to be a balanced and humane leader.

2) **Herod Antipas** (often called simply Antipas to avoid confusion with his father) was given control of Galilee and Perea, a region just east of the Jordan River. His marriage to the wife of his half-brother brought about the rage of John the Baptist against him which in turn led him to have John beheaded (Matthew 14:1-12). Jesus referred to him as "that fox" in a discussion with the Pharisees (Luke 13:31-33). It was this man whom the gospels refer to as simply Herod or occasionally as Herod "the tetrarch," a title based on the Greek word for "four" and referring to a person who governs one-fourth of a province.

3) **Archelaus,** the third son of Herod the Great, was by far the worst leader of the three, but he was given the most important area to rule: Judea, Samaria, and Idumea. He was so inept as a ruler that he was eventually removed and sent into exile by the Romans, who in turn replaced him with a Roman official variously called a "prefect," a "procurator," or, less often, a "governor." The first of these was installed by the Romans in A.D. 6, and by the time of Jesus' public ministry five different men had held the position. The fifth procurator began his rule in the year A.D. 26, just a year or so before Jesus began his public life. The man was named Pontius Pilate, and he was to play a key role in the trial and execution of Jesus.

So the two key ruling figures we encounter in the gospels are Herod Antipas, the tetrarch of Galilee, and the Roman official, Pontius Pilate. If, in reading the gospels, you have felt at times baffled by all the political intrigue, at least this brief review may make it more clear what all the confusion is about!

This confusion and division would last throughout Jesus' lifetime and beyond. Eventually the strong anti-Roman feelings among the Jews would build to the point of exploding, fueled by the memory of the Hasmoneans' successful rebellion against the Seleucids years earlier. Under the leadership of the Zealot party (see page 96) in the year A.D. 67, an open rebellion against the Romans would begin. But this time the Jews would take on a power far too great in strength. The Romans totally crushed the rebels and destroyed Jerusalem and its Temple by the year A.D. 70. Jewish hopes for freedom were destroyed, and as we shall see in a moment, it was only because of the strength of the Pharasaic Party that Judaism was able to survive until today.

5) A Review of Key Religious and Political Groups Mentioned in the Gospels

Our review of the history of the Jews through the time of Jesus has now given us some sense of the turmoil and confusion of the world into which he was born and the one to which he proclaimed his message. As a kind of summary here, we will attempt to flesh out a few of the more important and prominent persons, groups, and movements in the religious and social life of the times. All of these are mentioned in the gospels, and our understanding of these will greatly enhance our understanding of the Good News of Jesus.

Sadducees: The Sadducees were the priestly aristocracy based in Jerusalem. **They were liberal in politics (in that they were willing to compromise with the people in power) but they were very conservative in religion.** For example, they accepted only the first five books of the Hebrew Scriptures (called the "Pentateuch" [pent'-ah-took] or "Torah"), and they rejected all later attempts to add to or interpret the basic Law contained there. They rejected any belief in a resurrection after death for people, which was a rather recent religious belief among some Jews. An example of their conflicts with Jesus on this point can be found in Mark 12:18-27, in which they pose a problem for him about a woman who had seven husbands. As noted, the Sadducees were the priestly class, and with the destruction of the Temple by the Romans in A.D. 70, they eventually lost power and died out.

Pharisees: Perhaps no single group receives a more negative treatment in the gospels than the Pharisees. A reading of Jesus' comments about this group (along with the scribes discussed below) in Matthew 23:13-36 can make the reader wince, nearly embarrassed by the rage of Jesus against these people. We have to be very careful, however, about stereotyping the Pharisees according to this limited impression of them. **The strongly negative image of them presented in the gospels may well reflect some of the early Church's conflicts with this group.** And this exaggerated understanding of them, when used as a description of the Jewish people generally, has led at least in part to the bitter anti-Semitism and social rejection of the Jews throughout their long history. Christians have an obligation to change this false perception, and nothing will help to accomplish that more than a clear understanding of the facts.

The Pharisees of Jesus' day, as we saw earlier, originated in the Hasidim group mentioned earlier—the group known as "the pious ones." They were called this because of their strict adherence to the Law, but in fact they were far more liberal in religious matters than were the Sadducees. In fact, the Pharisees and the Sadducees often held opposite opinions on matters of politics and religion, and

Like the Zealots of Jesus' time,
contemporary rebels in Afghanistan
seek national liberation
through guerrilla warfare

there was often great tension between the two groups. **Unlike the Sadducees, the Pharisees were very conservative in politics and rejected any attempt to compromise with their political rulers.** Because of this attitude they were greatly respected by the common people. **But in religious matters they were liberal in that they were open to new developments in Jewish thought.** In fact they created an extensive oral commentary on the Law in an attempt to help the people live it more fully. Their commitment to the Law rather than to the Temple worship as in the case of the Sadducees allowed the Pharisaic Party to survive the destruction of the Temple in A.D. 70. The Judaism of today is derived from Pharisaism.

There can be no doubt that Jesus did have serious conflicts with the Pharisees over their interpretation of the Law and their tendency to become overly legalistic. But, as mentioned, the early Church likely exaggerated this division because of its own conflicts with the Pharisees after the death and Resurrection of Jesus. It should be noted as well that the Pharisees had no official part in the trial and execution of Jesus.

Zealots: (zell'-otts) The beginnings of this group—at least in the attitudes which they represented—may go back to the time of the Hasmoneans and their revolt against the Seleucids. But the Zealots were not a clearly defined party or movement until the time of the revolt in A.D. 67. **They maintained that Jewish independence could be attained only through a military overthrow of the Romans.** It is possible that some of them may have been attracted to Jesus at first because of his strong leadership, but his obvious commitment to nonviolence would likely have led them to reject him eventually.

Tax collectors or **publicans:** We mentioned in an earlier discussion that a taxation of the Jews was begun by the Seleucids to help pay off their debts to the Romans. The Jews were also expected to pay a Temple tax to their own leaders, and this double taxation became nearly unbearable, amounting to some 40 percent of their total income. In order to collect the taxes from the Jews, the Romans would hire Jewish agents who were expected to attain a certain quota of taxes, after which they could keep whatever "extra" money they managed to collect. These were the notorious tax collectors in the gospels, and they were a clearly despised group of men. They were also called "publicans."

Scribes: The scribes were a class that had its origins during the Exile in Babylon. They were both writers (as the term *scribe* indicates) and jurists, or interpreters of the Law. They had the task of carefully studying the Law and passing judgment on those who broke it. It was this group that organized the Hebrew Scriptures much as we know them today. **The most respected of the scribes were given the title "doctors of the Law" and, when they were in a position of teaching, they were given the title *rabbi*, meaning "master" or "teacher."** They taught in the synagogues and were consulted in matters of justice. The scribes, as noted above, are often mentioned in the gospels along with the Pharisees, but the two groups were not identical. Though many of the scribes no doubt belonged to the Pharasaic Party, not all of them did.

The Sanhedrin: The word *sanhedrin* means literally "assembly" or "senate." The Great Sanhedrin (some local governing bodies were also known as sanhedrins) was the official governing body of the Jews, and it was recognized as such by the Romans. It consisted of seventy members plus a president. The members of the Sanhedrin were representatives of the priestly families, the scribes and doctors of the Law, and the elders—the name given to outstanding Jewish laymen. Both the Pharisees and the Sadducees were represented, but the Sadducees had much greater influence because of their strong relationship with the political powers. **This body voted the laws, had its own police force, and controlled everything to do with religion which, as we have noted repeatedly, meant virtually all of Jewish life.** In the trial of Jesus, the Great Sanhedrin acts like a kind of supreme court.

The high priest: The high priest was the head of the priestly class and recognized as the president of the Sanhedrin as well. As we noted earlier, the right to appoint the high priest was assumed by the political powers during the Maccabean period, so there was a great deal of political power that went with the position even though the high priesthood was presumably a religious position. He was recognized by the people as a kind of symbol or embodiment of the Law itself. He lived in a grand palace close to the center of political power. During the trial of Jesus, the high priest was a man named Caiaphas (ky'-ah-fas) whom Pontius Pilate treats with real caution and consideration because of his position of importance and influence among the Jewish people.

Summary of Jewish History: 350 B.C. to A.D. 100

Key persons and events indicated by capitalization

350 B.C.	ALEXANDER dies in 323 B.C. and the Greek empire is divided. In Palestine the SELEUCIDS (in Syria) and the PTOLEMIES (in Egypt) are given control.		withdrawn); PHARISEES (politically conservative, religiously liberal). TENSION GROWS between mainline Jews and Galileans, Samaritans. Romans occupy Israel in 63 B.C.

350 B.C.

ALEXANDER dies in 323 B.C. and the Greek empire is divided. In Palestine the SELEUCIDS (in Syria) and the PTOLEMIES (in Egypt) are given control.

300 B.C.

Israel is ruled by the Ptolemies in Egypt for about one hundred years. Though Greek influence is experienced throughout Israel (especially in Galilee), generally the Jews are allowed to conduct their internal affairs without interference.

250 B.C.

200 B.C.

From 198 to 142 B.C. the Syrians, under the Seleucid leadership, control Israel. Heavy taxation begins, and political and religious factions begin to develop among the Jews. After the SELEUCIDS DESECRATE THE TEMPLE, the outraged Jews successfully rebel under HASMONEAN leadership. The Temple is rededicated in 164 (HANUKKAH) and Jewish independence is gained by 142 B.C.

150 B.C.

Jews are independent from 142-63 B.C. Hasmoneans are poor leaders, and their acceptance of the priesthood causes tension. Factions within Judaism become defined: SADDUCEES (political liberals, religious conservatives); ESSENES (religiously strict and

100 B.C.

withdrawn); PHARISEES (politically conservative, religiously liberal). TENSION GROWS between mainline Jews and Galileans, Samaritans. Romans occupy Israel in 63 B.C.

50 B.C.

From 63 B.C. until well after the time of Jesus, the ROMANS RULE PALESTINE. In 37 B.C. HEROD "THE GREAT" is appointed king. He's a political "success" but extremely cruel. He rules until 4 B.C., and JESUS IS BORN very near the end of his reign (about 6 or 5 B.C.). After Herod's death, PALESTINE IS DIVIDED among his three sons: PHILIP (ruler of area northeast of Palestine); HEROD ANTIPAS (ruler of Galilee and Perea); ARCHELAUS (ruler of Judea, Samaria, Idumea). Archelaus is such a poor leader that he is replaced by a Roman "PROCURATOR." From A.D. 26-36 the procurator of Judea is PONTIUS PILATE, and it is during his term that JESUS IS CRUCIFIED (about A.D. 30). In A.D. 67 the ZEALOTS lead a revolt against the Romans but are totally crushed. JERUSALEM AND THE TEMPLE ARE DESTROYED by the year 70, and it is only on the strength of the Pharisaic Party that Judaism is able to survive.

0

A.D. 50

A.D. 100

6) An Oppressed People Dreams of a Liberator

Throughout this book we have only briefly mentioned or occasionally alluded to a central figure in Jewish history, one spoken of and described in different ways by different people from the time of King David—about one thousand years before Jesus. That figure is the "Messiah," "the anointed one," "the one who is to come," the person whose title in the Greek language is "the Christ." By the time of Jesus, the yearning among the Jews for the one who was to set them free from all oppression had grown to great intensity, and it is important now that we pause for a moment to reflect more on just who the Messiah was expected to be.

The hope and expectation of "God's promised deliverer" was strongly associated with the experience of the kingship of David, the greatest of the Israelite kings. As we saw in an earlier discussion of Hebrew history, the Israelites had turned to a king to unify them and lead them at a time when they were in chaos as a people and their very existence was threatened by their enemies. It was under David's kingship that all the tribes of Israel were finally united, and it was then David who led the armies of Israel in defeating all its enemies. **For generations to come the Jews would yearn for a "son of David," one from the line of that beloved king who would restore them to their place of prominence in the world, who would lead them to victory over new enemies, one who would bring them into an age of peace and prosperity.**

Two important observations.

The development of the Jewish understanding of the Messiah, his nature, and characteristics is a complex one. It is sufficient for our purposes to note two major factors involved in it:

1) By the time of Jesus, as the Jews lived under the complete domination of the Romans, the Messiah had taken on the image of a mighty warrior-king, a great military leader, one who would overthrow the Romans and make of the Jews a mighty and free nation once again. **This militaristic image of the Messiah would clash dramatically with the life and message of Jesus and have major implications in the gospel story.**

2) Though there were no doubt various understandings about the nature and role of the Messiah throughout the history of the Jews, **it is certain that the Jews would *never* have considered the Messiah to be the *divine* Son of God, as we understand that term.** This is an important point to make because of our common tendency today to somehow lump all of the titles associated with Jesus together as if they were interchangeable. To do so is virtually to guarantee ourselves confusion in our attempts to understand how the Jewish people

understood—or failed to understand—Jesus and, indeed, how he understood himself. Remember that the Jewish understanding of Yahweh was such that they could not bring themselves even to utter his holy name. The idea of a man, a human being, in some way embodying God himself would have been nothing short of unthinkable, even blasphemous, for the devout Jew. This understanding of Yahweh, too, would have great implications for the Jewish response to Jesus and his message.

Conclusion.

We have spent the last three chapters providing critical background for the gospel story. We have discussed the world of Jesus—the one he would enter, preach to, and be largely rejected by. It was a complex world of deep religious convictions and great political tension. The oppression and near despair of the people of God was profoundly real, and their hunger for salvation and a savior was intense.

We are now ready to begin a more direct discussion of Jesus of Nazareth. To fully comprehend his story, you may have to return often to these chapters for a review of some of these key ideas. We encourage you to do so, not as a burden to you in this study but as a very helpful resource in making the Good News of Jesus speak not only *of* him but *to* you.

Review questions and activities:

1) Three hundred years before Jesus, Israel was located between two centers of power and deeply affected by both. Name the two powers and explain Israel's difficult position between them.

2) How did the region where Jesus lived come to be called "Galilee of the Gentiles"?

3) What were the two basic reactions of the Jews to Greek rule within Israel?

4) Explain the origins of the major Jewish feast of Hanukkah, or the Feast of Dedication.

5) The factions begun within Judaism during Greek rule were deepened during the period of Jewish independence. Define and explain the origins and basic stance of these groups: Sadducees, Essenes, and Pharisees.

6) Identify and describe the basic characteristics of these Palestinian regions: Idumea, Judea, Samaria, and Galilee.

7) According to the author, Herod the Great and his three sons—along with the political events surrounding them—became "the backdrop for the gospel story of Jesus." Explain.

8) A central figure gradually emerged out of the long history of the Jews—"God's promised deliverer," the Messiah. Explain the origins of this Jewish belief and the major characteristics which were expected of the Messiah by the Jewish people of Jesus' day.

Alexander	Hasmoneans	Pontius Pilate
the Great	Sadducees	Zealots
Seleucids	Essenes	tax collectors
Ptolemies	Pharisees	publicans
Galilee	Herod the Great	scribes
Samaria	Philip	Sanhedrin
Judea	Antipas	high priest
Idumea	Archelaus	Messiah

Exercise for personal reflection:

The complex world described in this chapter is the one in which Jesus was born and to which he would bring his message. Try to imagine yourself as a person living at that time, oppressed by all the social and political realities, and yearning for freedom from it all. Then read Matthew 5:20-48. Would you be moved to follow Jesus, as did the first disciples mentioned in Matthew 4:18-22? Or do you think you might react like the Zealots, who preferred to fight their oppressors physically rather than by "turning the other cheek"? How would you react if you were a Sadducee? a Pharisee? a tax collector?

6
The Mission Begins

The beginning of the Good News about Jesus Christ, the Son of God. It is written in the book of the prophet Isaiah:

Look, I am going to send a messenger before you;

he will prepare your way. . . .

and so it was that John the Baptist appeared in the wilderness, proclaiming a baptism of repentance for the forgiveness of sins. All Judaea and all the people of Jerusalem made their way to him, and as they were baptised by him in the river Jordan they confessed their sins. . . . In the course of his preaching he (John) said, "Someone is following me, someone who is more powerful than I am, and I am not fit to kneel down and undo the strap of his sandals. I have baptised you with water, but he will baptise you with the Holy Spirit."

It was at this time that Jesus came from Nazareth in Galilee and was baptised in the Jordan by John. No sooner had he come up out of the water than he saw the heavens torn apart and the Spirit, like a dove, descending on him. And a voice came from heaven, "You are my Son, the Beloved; my favour rests on you."

Immediately afterwards the Spirit drove him out into the wilderness and he remained there for forty days, and was tempted by Satan. (Mark 1:1-13).

And so the mission of Jesus begins—at least as it is described by the evangelist Mark. After this brief introduction to his gospel, Mark begins a discussion of the public ministry of Jesus.

But pause for a moment and ask yourself: Isn't there something missing here? Is this where the story of Jesus begins—with John the Baptist and the baptism of Jesus? What about the birth of Jesus, the event celebrated to this day with elaborate and joyous traditions by Christians throughout the world? Well, that was precisely the question raised by the early Christians as the gospels began to take shape. Many people could recall from personal experience the early days of Jesus' public ministry. Many had heard his words and seen his works. But where did he come from, what was his childhood like, what did he do *before* he came among them as about a 30-year-old man?

1) The "Infancy Narratives"

In an effort to provide a faith-filled response to these natural questions of the early faith community, Matthew and Luke began their gospels with writings that have come to be known as "infancy narratives"—stories about the "hidden life" of Jesus. In Matthew, for example, we do not hear of the public preaching of John the Baptist or of the baptism of Jesus until the third chapter. That material is preceded by an introduction that includes the following information, much of it familiar to us:

- The gospel begins with a genealogy or family tree of Jesus, tracing his roots back to Abraham (Matthew 1:1-17).

- This is followed by the story of Mary and Joseph, including the statement that Mary became pregnant with Jesus "by the Holy Spirit," and then a simple description of his birth and the giving of his name (1:18-25).

- We then learn of the visit of the Magi, the "wise men" sent by Herod to find Jesus. They follow a star to the place of Jesus' birth where they present gifts of gold, frankincense, and myrrh (2:1-12).

- The story of the Magi is followed by that of the flight into Egypt by Joseph, Mary, and Jesus as Herod begins to slaughter innocent children in the hope of eliminating a possible rival to his throne (2:13-18).

- And, finally, we read of the return by Jesus' family to Israel and the town of Nazareth in Galilee where he is to be raised (2:19-23).

These are of course very familiar scenes to most of us, touching images that are recalled by families and parish communities each Christmas season. But there is still more. If we look now at Luke's treatment of the hidden life of Jesus, we discover other stories, information not contained in Matthew's account:

- In Luke we find a rather detailed description of John the Baptist's conception by a priest named Zechariah and his elderly wife, Elizabeth (Luke 1:5-25).

- This is followed by the announcement made to Mary by the angel Gabriel that she is to bear a son named Jesus who will be called "the Son of the Most High." (We celebrate this event even today with the Feast of the Annunciation on March 25.) Mary then visits Elizabeth who, upon discovering Mary pregnant, exclaims "blessed is the fruit of your womb." We therefore find in this section of Luke's gospel the origin of part of the prayer we now know as the Hail Mary (1:26-45).

- We then find Mary's beautiful response to the realization that she is to bear a very special son in a prayer now called the Magnificat. This is actually a collection of many verses from the Hebrew Scriptures (1:46-56).

- And next we find several scenes centering on John the Baptist: his birth, his circumcision and naming, and a beautiful prayer by his father, Zechariah (1:56-79).

It is only after all this information has been shared that Luke even begins to describe the birth of Jesus and the events that follow it. There is much in Luke's version of these events that has found its way into our Christmas season traditions and therefore into the minds and hearts of most Catholic Christians. It is interesting—and important—to note that some of these ideas are found only in Luke:

In Luke we find the familiar description of Jesus' birth: "(Mary) wrapped him in swaddling clothes, and laid him in a manger because there was no room for them in the inn" (2:7).

As we noted, in Matthew the Magi are led by a star to a house where they find Jesus (Matthew 2:11). But in Luke's gospel we find poor shepherds hearing of the marvelous birth from an angel who announces, "Today in the town of David a saviour has been born to you; he is Christ the Lord" (2:11). Luke doesn't mention the wise men, nor does Matthew ever mention the shepherds.

Luke then describes the circumcision of Jesus, his presentation in the Temple, and prophecies by a man named Simeon and a woman named Anna (2:21-38).

And, finally, Luke is the only evangelist to offer the familiar story of Jesus at age 12 when his parents lose track of him during a trip to Jerusalem and then eventually find him in the Temple, "sitting among the doctors, listening to them, and asking them questions; and all those who heard him were astounded at his intelligence and his replies" (2:46-50).

Luke then closes his discussion of the hidden life of Jesus with this important statement: "(Jesus) then went down with them and came to Nazareth and lived under their authority. His mother stored up all these things in her heart. And Jesus increased in wisdom, in stature, and in favour with God and men" (2:51-52).

What's going on here?

Most Catholic Christians have arrived at a pretty clear and firm understanding of the birth of Jesus and the events that surrounded it through a life-long experience with Christmas traditions—with manger scenes, for example, and with Christmas carols and other religious practices that have developed through our history as a Church. It can be a bit confusing and even disturbing for some to discover the difficulties involved in sorting all these events out in terms of the gospels, those documents which we have said must ultimately be the foundation and source of our understanding of Jesus. But, as we said early in this book, our intention in this course is not to provide simple answers but rather sound ones, not just to affirm the understanding of our faith gained as children but to help us move toward a more mature, adult, and therefore more fulfilling and meaningful understanding of our faith.

How can we explain the stories of Jesus' birth and early years as they are presented in the gospels of Matthew and Luke? (As we saw in our opening reading for this chapter, Mark does not discuss these events at all. The gospel of John doesn't either, but offers instead a very profound and poetic statement of what it meant for the "Word of God" to become a man in the person of Jesus. See John 1:1-18.) How are we to make sense of the differences between all these accounts? You may be surprised to learn that you already know the answers to these questions—at least if you have carefully read and studied the material already presented in this book! The clues for solving our puzzle were all provided in chapter 2 when we discussed the nature, purpose, and development of the gospels. A brief refresher on the major points

Adoration of the Shepherds, a woodcut by Jules Chadel (1870-1942), from the Mr. and Mrs. Ross W. Sloniker Collection at the Cincinnati Art Museum

raised there will provide the framework we need for understanding the stories of Jesus' early life as well as much of what we will discuss later about his life and works as an adult. Recall these important points about the gospels:

1) The gospels are *not* biographies or life stories about Jesus, but rather testimonies of faith and proclamations of the Good News written by people *after* they had experienced Jesus as the Risen Lord.

2) Each gospel was written by different persons, at different times, to different groups of people, and for different purposes. Briefly:
  a) Mark was the first gospel written. It was directed to non-Jewish Christians, and it stressed the humanity and suffering of Jesus.
  b) Matthew was written ten to fifteen years later than Mark and was directed toward devout Jews. It stressed the conviction that Jesus fulfills the Law of Moses and is the Messiah the Jews had been awaiting.
  c) Luke was written roughly the same time as

Matthew, but it was directed to Gentiles and emphasizes the fact that the Good News of Jesus is offered to all people—rich and poor, men and women, Jews and Gentiles.
As we noted earlier, we will rely primarily on the three synoptic gospels in our discussion because of the unique nature and purposes of John's gospel.

3) Very importantly, the gospels as testimonies of faith written by believing Christians intend not simply to provide historical facts about Jesus but also to provide the *meaning, significance, and impact* of his life and teaching upon the people and events of his time.

Special stories about a special event.

So what we find in the infancy stories and throughout the gospels are *statements of faith* about the meaning of Jesus and the events of his life. There is little doubt or argument among Scripture scholars, for example, that there is a great deal of symbolism involved in the stories of Jesus' and the occult, the mysterious dimension of life. (Our words *magic* and *magician* come from the same root word.) Matthew is showing his Jewish readers that Gentiles will often accept Jesus as the Messiah even though many of the Jews will often reject him, a theme that is repeated throughout his gospel. Finally, Matthew fills his entire account with quotes and images from the Hebrew Scriptures, all of which would have had a profound significance and impact on his Jewish readers. For example, Matthew has the Holy Family flee into Egypt, and then the angel calls them out of Egypt to Israel after the death of Herod. Who else was "called out of Egypt" by God? The Israelites, of course, who were led out of their bondage in Egypt by Moses. So, in Matthew, Jesus is recognized as "the new Moses," one who totally fulfills the Law, "the one sent" who will lead the people to salvation as their Messiah.

2) Luke, on the other hand, has a different audience and different messages in mind as he writes his story of the birth and early years of Jesus. Though Luke makes it clear that Jesus is the Messiah who fulfills Jewish hopes and expectations, he doesn't use a lot of quotes from the Hebrew Scriptures simply because his readers, as non-Jews, would not be as concerned about this as Matthew's Jewish readers. As we mentioned before, **Luke's gospel stresses that the Good News is for everyone and, in a special way, for the poor and downtrodden.** That is his reason for including the shepherds in his story, indicating that the poor will be the first to recognize and respond to Jesus. Luke's emphasis on the fact that Jesus offers the Good News to everyone is also illustrated later in a genealogy he offers for Jesus that differs dramatically from that of Matthew (see Luke 3:23-38). Matthew, we noted above, starts with Abraham and

birth and early years. There were, after all, very few eyewitnesses to the events themselves. Other than his parents, few people knew anything about Jesus' early years. But just as importantly, even *if* the evangelists had known that kind of information, they probably would not have used it, simply because that was not their purpose. In a moment we will try to offer some ideas on what we can know with some certainty about Jesus' early historical life based on our knowledge of the Jewish people and the times. But first, what are the gospels of Matthew and Luke trying to tell us about the Christ of Faith through the infancy stories? These major points are at the core of these stories:

1) **Matthew wants to show his Jewish readers as clearly as possible that Jesus is the Messiah they have been waiting for.** In providing a genealogy or family tree for Jesus at the beginning of his gospel, for example, Matthew refers to Jesus as a "son of David, son of Abraham," and then charts Jesus' roots directly back to Abraham (Matthew 1:1-2). He carefully notes that Joseph was born in Bethlehem from the line of David. As we saw earlier in our discussion of Jewish history, the Jews expected the Messiah to descend from David, whose hometown was Bethlehem. Matthew also includes the story of the *Magi,* non-Jewish men who were known for their understanding of astrology

2) The Early "Hidden Years" of Jesus

works his way up to Jesus. Luke, on the other hand, begins with Jesus and works all the way back to *Adam*. As the "first man," Adam is the father of *all* people, not just of the Jews, and with this clever bit of writing Luke again affirms the universality of the message of Jesus.

There is no way to explain these differences other than to repeat our major point here: The gospels are trying not only to provide historical facts but also to provide the meaning and significance of historical events for believing Christians.

We do not want to overdo our discussion here. The intent of this course is not to explain every line of the gospels. But we do want to establish as clearly as possible the way in which we understand the meaning of Jesus and his message as revealed in the gospels. From this point on, whether in discussing specific events in the life of Jesus, or his miracles, or the parables he shared, our constant emphasis will be on this question: *What do these things mean?* What is the point that the gospel writers are trying to make? What are we to understand about Jesus from this? These were the questions the evangelists were trying to answer, and if we lose touch with that fact we will become very confused if not hopelessly lost in our attempt to understand the Jesus of History whom the gospels proclaim as the Christ of Faith.

In chapters 3, 4, and 5 of this book, we offered quite a lot of information about the history of the Jewish people, their beliefs, their religious practices, their family and social life, and so on. In answering the question "What can we know about the childhood of Jesus as he actually experienced it in Palestine some two thousand years ago?", we can with some reservation say this: the historical Jesus experienced life as a typical Jew of his day. Note that we claim this "with some reservation." Jesus was clearly a very special person even as a young boy. He must have been particularly gifted, intelligent, and sensitive. We can surmise as much just by studying him as an adult.

An important caution.

Yet we must be very careful not to think of Jesus as strange, weird, or so different from us as to seem almost inhuman. In the early Church, for example, there were writings and stories about Jesus that did not find their way into our gospels. One of the stories described Jesus as a young boy who, in order to entertain and impress his young friends, would take clay models of birds and magically make them come alive and fly away!

Many of us might have impressions of Jesus that are not all that far removed from this kind of fanciful image. For instance, we might think of the baby Jesus lying in the manger with the power to know all things, to read people's minds, or to be able to go without food and drink. Such images can make Jesus seem like a freak of sorts, rather than what the Church has continually claimed him to be—the Son of God, certainly, but also a man who was one with us in all things but sin. In the introduction to this book we quoted St. Paul: "His state was divine, yet he did not cling to his equality with God but emptied himself to assume the condition of a slave, and became as men are . . ." (Philippians 2:6). Jesus "became as men are," with all the physical, emotional, intellectual, and spiritual needs each of us experiences. So what can we say about his early hidden life based on our understanding of the Jewish people and their history?

An unknown birthday.

We mentioned earlier in this book—perhaps to your surprise—that Jesus was born around 6-5 B.C. If B.C. means "before Christ," this can obviously be a bit confusing! The solution to this problem is too complex to discuss in full here. Basically what happened is this: In the development of our own calendar during the sixth century, there was a miscalculation made in determining the year in which Jesus was born, and that mistake was never corrected. We know from the Scriptures, however, that Jesus was born during the reign of Herod the Great, and we know with certainty from other sources that Herod died in the year 4 B.C. So Jesus was certainly born before that time. Scholars differ on the precise year of his birth, most claiming anywhere from 8 B.C. to the year 5 B.C. **What is obvious from this is the fact that the people of Jesus' day, and the evangelists, did not share our concern for such precise information about these events.** In a typical biography today, one of the first bits of information we would gain about the subject would be his or her date of birth. That didn't concern the authors of the gospels at all!

Eight days after his birth in Bethlehem, Jesus was circumcised according to the Law of Moses. **The circumcision was a religious practice which involved removing the foreskin of the male child's penis as a permanent sign of the child's membership in the covenant community of the Jews.** It can be traced back to Yahweh's first covenant with Abraham as described in Genesis in which it is stated that God said, "You shall circumcise your foreskin, and this shall be a sign of the Covenant between myself and you. When they are eight days old all your male children must be circumcised" (see 17:10-14.). At that time he was given the name Jesus, a popular Jewish name of the day and one meaning "Yahweh saves" or "Yahweh is salvation." Then Jesus' parents took him to the Temple in Jerusalem, where they consecrated him to Yahweh with the offering of a pair of turtledoves or pigeons, the common sacrifice of the poor.

Childhood in Nazareth.

Jesus was raised in the Galilean village of Nazareth, a community of just a few thousand people. He probably lived in the kind of one-room house described earlier. His stepfather, Joseph, was a carpenter by trade, and as was the common practice of the day, Jesus worked along with him and eventually became a carpenter himself. The carpenter of Jesus' day was a relatively skilled craftsman, and the occupation was a respected one.

Jesus seems to have had a good education. He could read Hebrew, which was fairly rare at the time. Because of the historical setting in which he was raised and also because of the location of Nazareth geographically, he probably spoke three languages: Hebrew, Greek, and Aramaic, the common language of Palestine. He likely attended school in a room attached to the synagogue where, of course, his study would revolve entirely around the Hebrew Scriptures and the faith and history of his people, the Jews. Jesus' education was also enhanced by life in Nazareth itself. Though we noted earlier that Galilee was held in low esteem by many Jews, it was an area in which Jesus would have encountered many of the new ideas of the Greeks and Romans as he grew and matured.

A faith-filled family.

Ultimately Jesus' strong Jewish faith had its source and solid foundation in the faith of his parents. Both Joseph and Mary were devout Jews, and as we described it earlier, the Jewish family was recognized as a religious community in itself. No doubt they were a deeply prayerful family and one committed to faithfully following not only the Law but the spirit of their religion.

From that early foundation of a strong, loving, and truly religious family, Jesus grew. He was unquestionably a person of deep prayer, a reality constantly reflected in the gospels. He was a man who developed a profound love and understanding of the Hebrew Scriptures, and one fully committed to the family and communal worship of his people. For thirty years "he grew in wisdom, in stature, and in favour with God and men" (Luke 2:52). Out of that long development, Jesus grew to an intense religious awareness, an understanding of God and his relationship with people that would one day put Jesus in direct conflict with his people, his friends, and even his family. It was a vision that would eventually lead him to death on the cross, a death that would offer for all people the possibility of fullness of life.

3) The Public Life of Jesus

John the Baptist was one of many wandering prophets at the time of Jesus, but he was unique in that he did not try to proclaim himself as a messiah or savior. Rather his purpose was to point to another, "someone who is more powerful than I am." His task was to "prepare the way" for Jesus' ministry by calling people to an awareness of their sin and to repentance. He announced that a whole new "kingdom," a new society, was about to begin and that the people were to get ready for it. The sign or symbol he used to express this change of heart, this openness of mind and spirit to what was to come, was a ritual bathing called **baptism. The act of bathing in water as a sign of spiritual purification was a common religious symbol for many religions, including Judaism.** By accepting the baptism of John in the Jordan River, people acknowledged both their own sinfulness and their desire to join the new kingdom he was announcing by changing the way they were living. Later Jesus would praise John, saying that "of all the children born of women, there is no one greater than John" (Luke 7:28).

The baptism of Jesus.

All of the synoptic gospels record the baptism of Jesus, and John's gospel alludes to it, but there are some significant differences between the accounts. In Mark's version (1:9-11) Jesus is quickly baptized, and then he "saw the heavens torn apart and the Spirit, like a dove, descending on him. And a voice came from heaven, 'You are my Son, the Beloved;

my favour rests on you.' " In Matthew's account (3:13-17) Jesus is baptized only after some disagreement with John about whether he should be. After the baptism Jesus sees "the Spirit of God descending like a dove," and a voice from heaven proclaims, "This is my Son, the Beloved; my favour rests on him." And in Luke, Jesus is seen at prayer *after* the baptism has taken place, and it is then that the Spirit descends "in bodily shape, like a dove," and the voice proclaims again, "You are my Son, the Beloved; my favour rests on you" (3:21-22).

Certainly there is some symbolism here: The dove was likely a Jewish symbol for Israel as a whole and, less often, for "the Spirit of God" which, for the Jews, meant the saving power of Yahweh active among his people. And in the Hebrew Scriptures there were a number of occasions when Yahweh was depicted as speaking to the people "as a voice from the heavens," often concealed by a cloud. **It appears that these were manifestations of God experienced by Jesus in an interior way during his baptism, rather than events that could be readily seen by those gathered about him.** Note, for instance, that it is Jesus who "sees" the Spirit of God descending, and that, in two of the accounts, the voice speaks directly to him: "*You* are my Son . . ." rather than "This is my son . . ."

A good question.

What is particularly interesting is the development of the accounts of Jesus' baptism from the earliest version of Mark to the later ones of Matthew and Luke. The scene in Mark is straightforward and direct, while Matthew introduces the disagreement with John over whether Jesus should be baptized at all, and then Luke almost skips over the actual baptism and shows Jesus in prayer *after* the event.

An artists' interpretation of the baptism of Jesus

Scholars claim this reflects the evangelists'—and in them, the early Church's—discomfort with the whole notion of Jesus accepting baptism at all. **It *is* a good question: Why should Jesus, as the Messiah and sinless Son of God, accept a baptism which John himself proclaimed was one of "repentance for the forgiveness of sin?"** Matthew's statement about John's reluctance to baptize Jesus is an attempt to offer an explanation. Jesus accepts baptism because it "is fitting that we should, in this way, do all that righteousness demands" (Matthew 3:15). Jesus sees the act as part of God's design or plan, and he accepts it on that basis. His acceptance is not an admission of sin on his part but, rather, indicates his willingness to completely immerse himself in the life and concerns of his people, to live life as they had to live it. His water baptism was the first step on the road to the cross, which he would later refer to as "the baptism with which I am to be baptised" (Mark 10:38; Luke 12:50).

Jesus learned two chief lessons from his baptism, both symbolized by the writers of the gospels with vivid, biblical imagery:

1) He recognized that he was chosen in a special way to proclaim and begin a new kingdom. The words spoken from heaven echo those of Isaiah 42:1 in which we hear of the "Suffering Servant of Yahweh" who will one day save his people.

2) And in his baptism Jesus learned that he would be given the power to fulfill his role through the Spirit of God, represented by the descending dove.

It was that same Spirit of God which immediately "drove him into the wilderness" following his baptism and the same Spirit which would continue to lead him throughout his ministry.

Jesus decides his priorities.

In our opening reading for this chapter, Mark simply states that immediately after Jesus' baptism, "the Spirit drove him into the wilderness and he remained there for forty days, and was tempted by Satan." Matthew and Luke expand this scene and describe a threefold temptation that Jesus experiences while in the desert (Matthew 4:1-11; Luke 4:1-13). In Matthew "the tempter" or "devil" asks Jesus first to turn stones into bread, then to throw himself down from a high point of the Temple in order to prove his special relationship with God, and finally to fall at the feet of the devil and worship him, for which Jesus would receive "all the kingdoms of the world." In Luke's gospel, the order of the second and third temptations is reversed, but the content is essentially the same. Jesus' response to all three temptations is a direct quote from the book of Deuteronomy of the Hebrew Scriptures. In response to the first temptation he says, "Man does not live on bread alone, but on every word that comes from the mouth of God" (8:3). For the second one in Matthew: "You must not put the Lord your God to the test" (6:16). And for the third temptation, again in Matthew: "You must worship the Lord your God, and serve him alone" (6:13). Again we must ask, what does this mean? What are the

The Mission Begins 111

gospel writers trying to tell us here about Jesus and his mission?

First of all, each of the gospels refers to the forty days that Jesus spends in the desert, and every Jew would immediately be reminded of the forty years that the people of Israel wandered in the desert, a time when they were severely tempted and when they ultimately failed. Jesus, as "the new Israel," is tempted as well, but he does not fail. **The three temptations deal with the kind of power Jesus is going to exercise in his ministry, and his rejection of the kind of political and militaristic messiahship the people had come to expect and hope for.** His was not to be an economic kingdom based on his ability to provide for the material wants and needs of the people (symbolized by turning stones into bread). Rather, he came to provide for the spiritual hunger of the people by proclaiming the "word of God" which offers true life. Nor would his kingdom be based on magic and works of wonder which might somehow capture the imagination of the people and almost force them to believe in him (symbolized by throwing himself off the top of the Temple and surviving). Jesus responds that "the Lord, your God" (meaning Yahweh here, not Jesus) does not reveal himself through trickery and magic. Such wonder-working would be a constant temptation for Jesus throughout his ministry as we will see in our later discussion of his miracles. Finally, the kingdom Jesus is proclaiming would not be based on political power (symbolized by the temptation to control all the kingdoms of the world). Jesus says that God alone is to be worshipped and that the reign of God in the world would take place in the hearts of the people, not in political domination of them.

Therefore, the three temptations we see Jesus confronting—and defeating—represent the kind of temptations he would have to deal with throughout his ministry. We must remember as well that the gospels were written for the Church and its members, and that we too are being warned here to resist the temptations to find our own meaning and purpose in life in economic security or in personal or political power over others.

Wandering preacher, unique teacher.

After his baptism, Jesus became a wandering preacher and religious teacher. It was common for the Jewish rabbis or teachers of the Law to roam from place to place teaching, often accompanied by a band of disciples or young men who would freely choose to follow and study under a rabbi they particularly liked. And it was common for the rabbis to teach in the synagogues and, less often, wherever people would be willing to gather to listen to them—mountainsides, fields, or along the roadsides. Therefore, though Jesus was probably not a rabbi in an official or legal sense, his ministry appears similar to theirs in many ways.

There were, however, several unique factors in the content of the message Jesus proclaimed, in the way he shared it, and in his relationship to his disciples—factors that clearly set him apart from the other teachers of his day:

1) **First, Jesus proclaimed in both his words and his actions the coming of a new "Kingdom of God."** The notion of such a kingdom was a central one for the Jewish people of his day, so it was not surprising in itself that Jesus would speak of it. But his sense of the kingdom was truly unique, so much so that we will devote the entire next chapter to a discussion of it.

2) **In his teaching, Jesus not only proclaimed the coming of a new kingdom but also claimed a very special role for himself as the one who would personally establish and manifest it, not simply announce it.** Again, this will be clarified later.

3) Jesus amazed the crowds not only with the content of his message but with the attitude he possessed while sharing it. As we find it in Matthew, "his teaching made a deep impression on the people because he taught them with authority, and not like their own scribes" (Matthew 7:28-29). The rabbis at the time of Jesus were called to study the Hebrew Scriptures and the teaching of other rabbis thoroughly. Whenever they taught they were expected to back up what they were saying with direct quotes from Scripture or with statements from other respected rabbis which supported what they were teaching. **Jesus, on the other hand, claimed himself as the sole judge of the truth of what he taught.** At times he would even say, for example, "You have heard it said by others that . . . but this is what *I* say to you" (see Matthew 5:20-48). This was a clear break from the common practice and one that both impressed and alienated many people who would listen to him preach.

4) Finally, Jesus differed dramatically from other teachers of his time in his use of parables (which we will discuss in chapter 8) and, of course, in the miracles or "signs and wonders" he performed (which we will discuss in chapter 9).

Sermon on the Mount, an engraving by Gustave Dore, dated about 1875

4) Jesus and His Disciples

It is important to note the unique relationship which Jesus chose to establish with his disciples. As we have mentioned, it was typical for a rabbi to attract disciples who would then study under him. The disciples would learn from the rabbi through a process of lengthy discussion, memorization through word games, and so on. The goal was for the disciples to learn perfectly what the rabbi taught to the point of being able to repeat his teachings word for word. Once they had perfected the teaching, the disciples would then leave the rabbi and become independent rabbis themselves.

With Jesus and his disciples, however, the relationship is different:

- First of all, they do not choose him but rather he calls them, and he expects and receives an immediate and complete response from them (Mark 1:16-20; Luke 5:1-11).

- Unlike other rabbis, Jesus does not simply share a body of teachings with his disciples which they are expected to memorize word for word. Rather he calls them into a lasting, never-ending personal relationship with himself (Matthew 23:8-10).

- And, finally, the disciples of Jesus are not simply expected to watch and learn from Jesus, but also are actually called to share in his mission of proclaiming the Kingdom (Luke 9:1-6).

It is important that we recognize this unique role of the disciples of Jesus because it is also a model of what it means to be his disciple *today*. Jesus calls each of us as well to a personal lasting relationship of love with the Father and also sends us out to share in his mission of proclaiming the Good News of the Kingdom.

The Twelve Apostles.

There were many people who responded to Jesus, all of whom might—depending on our precise definition of the term—qualify as his *disciples.* But the gospels are clear that there were also twelve special men carefully selected by Jesus who were to play a very central and significant role during his ministry and in the future. These were the "Apostles," most frequently referred to in the gospels as "the Twelve." (Their names are given in Matthew 10:2-4; Mark 3:16-19; Luke 6:13-16; and in the Acts of the Apostles 1:13.) **It is significant that Jesus would choose exactly twelve such men and that the early community of faith would work to maintain that number after the death of one of them.** (See Acts 1:12-26.) Think back to our discussion of the history of the Jews. When have you heard that number twelve mentioned before? You will recall that the Israelites at one time consisted of twelve tribes, each descending from one of the twelve sons of Jacob. It seems certain that Jesus and the early Christian community recognized that the Twelve Apostles would be the foundation of a new community of faith, a "new Israel," what we today recognize as the Church. But what was so special about the Apostles as they walked with Jesus nearly two thousand years ago?

The Twelve were, of course, disciples of Jesus, but they were selected by him to be his constant companions, traveling with him from place to place and becoming thoroughly instructed in the truths he shared. The word *apostle* comes from a Greek word meaning "to send forth," and in a very special way these men would be sent forth or commissioned to carry on the Good News of Jesus after his death and Resurrection. They were men who shared in his power and who, in his name, would continue to preach his word, to heal, and to make disciples through baptism (Matthew 28:16-20).

Ordinary people with an extraordinary calling.

What sort of people did Jesus seek for this mission as Apostles? Some were simple fishermen. One was a hated tax collector. Two were such hotheads that Jesus referred to them as "sons of thunder." One would eventually betray him. One was a leader who could show signs of great insight but also demonstrate outright cowardice. The gospels often portray these men as dull, baffled, unable to understand what Jesus is telling them. At times they seem to hunger for great power, and yet they were people who, in the end, would desert Jesus out of fear. But eventually all of them would be reconciled with Jesus after his Resurrection and go on to die as heroes in the early Church. **In short, the Apostles chosen by Jesus were ordinary people who, because of their association with him, were capable of extraordinary things.**

The proclamation of the Kingdom.

Central to Jesus' identity, his life, his mission and message, and all of his words and actions is the notion of the Kingdom of God. His history as a Jew inspired the notion of the Kingdom. His prayer and life experiences led him to identify himself as the proclaimer and possessor of it. His parables were stories that pointed to and described the Kingdom, and his miracles were signs of its presence in their midst. The obvious question for us, then, is what is this Kingdom? Clearly we have to understand it if we are to understand Jesus. That is the goal of the next chapter.

1) Which two gospels contain introductions called "infancy narratives"? Why did the authors of these gospels include these stories? Finally, what are the major differences between the two accounts of "the hidden years of Jesus"?

2) Try to respond to this statement from the point of view of a mature Christian: "The stories of Jesus' birth are just a bunch of fairy tales, and only children will accept them as anything more than that."

3) Contrary to the understanding of some, we know neither the day nor even the year of Jesus' birth. This was simply not important to the people of his day or to the evangelists. Explain why this was so.

4) John the Baptist and his ministry are often viewed as a kind of transitional stage between the Hebrew and Christian Scriptures, between the "old" Judaism and the new vision proclaimed by Jesus. In what way was John related to the Judaism of his day? What role did he play in the ministry of Jesus?

5) Why did Jesus, though sinless, accept the baptism of John? What two major realities are symbolized by the accounts of his baptism?

6) In the accounts of Jesus' temptations in the desert, the evangelists illustrate the kind of power Jesus chose to exercise in his ministry. Explain the three temptations in terms of the choices Jesus had to make about his ministry.

7) What factors made the teaching ministry of Jesus different from that of the Jewish rabbis of his day?

8) What does Jesus' unique relationship with his disciples imply about the role to be played by all Christians?

9) Why is it significant that Jesus would select *twelve* Apostles?

Terms to identify and remember:

Infancy narratives	John the Baptist
Magi	baptism
Annunciation	disciples
Magnificat	Apostles
circumcision	

Exercise for personal reflection:

Read the account of the desert temptations of Jesus in Luke 4:1-13. Then imagine yourself facing similar temptations in your life today. In what ways are you challenged in your life regarding economic values? In what ways does society offer you "magic solutions" or escapes from problems? What pressures do you experience that lead you to want to have power over others? And, finally, who—or what—are the "tempters" in your life in these areas?

7
The Kingdom of God Proclaimed

One of the scribes . . . put a question to him, "Which is the first of all the commandments?" Jesus replied, "This is the first: 'Listen, Israel, the Lord our God is the one Lord, and you must love the Lord your God with all your heart, with all your soul, with all your mind and with all your strength.' The second is this: 'You must love your neighbour as yourself.' There is no commandment greater than these." The scribe said to him, "Well spoken, Master; what you have said is true: that he is one and there is no other. To love him with all your heart, with all your understanding and strength, and to love your neighbour as yourself, this is far more important than any holocaust or sacrifice." Jesus, seeing how wisely he had spoken, said, "You are not far from the kingdom of God" (Mark 12:28-34).

1) New Insights into Old Ideas

One of our common mistakes as Christians in attempting to understand Jesus is to somehow separate him from his Jewish roots, to isolate him from his own heritage as a faith-filled man of Israel. We have discussed this problem in earlier chapters and have tried to correct it by reviewing Jesus' religious, social, and family background as a Jew. In this chapter it is important to again raise this concern, for we will be dealing here with the central issues of the nature of God and of people's relationship to him as understood both by the Jewish people and by Jesus. Many Christians have simple stereotypes of the Jewish position on such matters, stereotypes that do an injustice both to the Jews and to Jesus.

One example of our common misunderstanding is the sense many have that every teaching of Jesus was an idea that originated with him and that—according to the stereotype again—was directly contrary to popular Jewish teaching. Our opening reading for this chapter clearly contradicts this common misunderstanding. Notice that Jesus responds to the scribe's question about the commandments, not with an original statement of his own creation but, rather, with verses taken directly from the Hebrew Scriptures, the sacred writings

117

King David, a lithograph
by Marc Chagall, dated 1956

revered by both Jesus and the scribe. Jesus' response concerning the "first commandment" is the famous "Shema" prayer which, as we briefly mentioned in chapter 3, the faithful Jew said twice each day: "Listen, Israel, the Lord our God is the one Lord . . ." (Deuteronomy 6:4-5). And Jesus' second response—about the need to "love your neighbor as yourself"—is taken directly from the book of Leviticus 19:18. So Jesus was responding to the scribe as *all* loyal Jews would—so much so that, interestingly, it is the scribe who judges Jesus' response, not the other way around.

Most central to our purposes in this chapter, however, is the closing statement by Jesus in our opening passage: "Jesus, seeing how wisely he had spoken, said, 'You are not far from the kingdom of God.' "

Just what is this Kingdom of God? Scripture scholars recognize that Jesus' preaching about the Kingdom is at the very core of his entire message, the subject of many of his parables and both the motivation and the goal of many of his miracles. As we will see, the notion of the Kingdom is a complex one, but our opening reading indicates that it is closely bound up with an understanding of the relationship between God and people and with the two challenges to love God and one another. Let's try to make some sense of this.

Roots of the Kingdom in Jewish history.

The basic notion of the Kingdom was not introduced by Jesus. It was commonly accepted by the Jews, for example, that Yahweh was the king over all creation. Many of the Hebrew religious hymns which we call Psalms celebrate the kingship of God:

> Yahweh is king, robed in majesty,
> Yahweh is robed in power,
> he wears it like a belt.
> You have made the world firm, unshakeable;
> your throne has stood firm since then,
> you existed from the first, Yahweh
> (Psalm 93:1-2; see also Psalm 96).

So God's kingship was recognized first in the wonders of creation. Some rabbis taught as well that the Kingdom of God was present in the Law, in the Torah. They felt that the Law was God's instrument for ruling his people.

It was also clear to the Jews that the Kingdom of God had not yet been fully established, because there was still obviously so much evil in the world. They recognized as well that this was in large part due to their own failure to cooperate with Yahweh, their failure to follow his will completely.

Gradually the Jews evolved a belief that the Kingdom of God would be fully established through a great prophet. With the experience of the monarchy during David's time, this belief became bound up with the notion of the establishment of a national, political kingship. And by the time of Jesus' life, after nearly a hundred years of Roman domination, many Jews expected the Kingdom to begin with a military takeover of the country and the expulsion of the Romans. This overthrow was to be led by the Messiah who now expected by some to be a military leader, a warrior. Jesus would contradict all such expectations, and his understanding of the Kingdom would prove far different from the common understanding of his people.

What the Kingdom *was not* for Jesus.

It is clear from all his teaching and actions that Jesus was not trying to begin a new political reign over his people nor, certainly, a military one. There are times in the gospel story when people try to make Jesus a king or political ruler and he firmly rejects the idea, and his stand on nonviolence eliminated the possibility of a military takeover of any kind. It is also clear that he did not have in mind a geographical state or nation when he spoke of the Kingdom. His Kingdom would have no boundaries, no borders separating one nation from another. Nor was Jesus' concept of the Kingdom of God simply a new philosophy of some kind or a new plan of social reform. But if the Kingdom was none of these things, what was it?

2) Jesus and the Kingdom of God

Perhaps we become a bit confused by the very word *kingdom* itself. The word for us automatically implies a place or region. A better term would be "the reign of God" or "the kingship of God." But what did God's kingship over the world mean?

Jesus was thoroughly Jewish, so his understanding of the kingship of God necessarily flowed out of Jewish history, Scriptures, worship, and, of course, out of his own personal prayer and reflection on all of these. That personal reflection and prayer led him to a unique and remarkable vision or recognition of God as his "Father." The notion of the fatherhood of God was not entirely new to Jesus. The Hebrew Scriptures occasionally used this term for Yahweh. But we have seen that the Jewish understanding of Yahweh was one of such awe and reverence that they would not even consider using his name in prayer and worship, always replacing it with words like "the Lord," "the Most High," or "the Holy One." **Jesus, however, shatters this belief and practice and takes the incredible position of referring to God as "Abba, Father"** (Mark 14:36). *Abba* was an Aramaic word which means something far more intimate than simply "father." It was the word used by little Jewish children for their fathers, one having the sense of the word *dada* uttered so easily by infants. In other words, Jesus was saying we not only could call God by his name but also could even refer to him with an equivalent of our word *Daddy!* No Jew would ever dare such intimacy, and it must have shocked many to hear Jesus speak of God with such a sense of childlike affection. Jesus was claiming by this that God had unleashed his unconditional love upon the world and upon all people. The Kingdom which Jesus announced, therefore, was in fact a new relationship between God and people or, perhaps more accurately, a new understanding of a relationship that God had always offered. **Jesus was sharing a new insight into nothing less than the very nature of God himself.**

A problem with language.

We must pause briefly here and admit to a problem with our own language in discussing these things. Jesus found the need to speak of God with a new vocabulary, a new set of words and terms. Many today sense a similar need because of the common difficulty of our use of sexist language in talking about God. If we are to avoid terribly clumsy language and poor grammar, it seems impossible to avoid the occasional use of masculine pronouns in referring to God—words like *him, himself, he,* and so on. The problem is based on our past practices (many of which, admittedly, are deeply affected by sexism), Jesus' own use of the notion of God's fatherhood, and the constant gospel use of masculine images. The fact is that God is neither masculine nor feminine in our common sense of those terms. God does not have a sexual identity in the same sense that we do. It may be more accurate, for example, to speak of God as "parent" rather than as "father" or "mother." Somehow we have to arrive at some acceptable way to deal with this problem in both religious and secular language, but it does not seem appropriate for us to attempt that in a text of this kind. We must simply acknowledge the problem as a real one and apologize for our own limitations in dealing with it.

Time to turn it around.

For Jesus, the ability to recognize and fully participate in the kingship of God required a conversion, a change of heart, a turning from selfishness to openness to God and his call to love. When this happens, the Kingdom takes root in the heart of the believer. Jesus' initial call, therefore, is to repentance, to a change in the way we live. "The time has come," he said, "and the kingdom of God is close at hand. Repent, and believe the Good News" (Mark 1:15).

The Kingdom—the reign of God—was not to be only a one-to-one relationship between God and individual persons, not simply a "me and God" kind of reality. Rather, Jesus clearly understood the Kingdom as also being communal in nature, implying a new relationship not only between God and individuals but between individuals and others. **Therefore, Jesus saw the Kingdom as the rule or reign of God's love over the very hearts of people and, as a consequence of that, a new social order based on unconditional love for one another.** Together this meant that an entirely "new age" (another possible meaning of "Kingdom") had begun, that history had been in a sense "turned around" by Jesus, and that a new era of peace, joy, freedom, and love was beginning.

We began this chapter by stating that Christians often misunderstand the nature of the Jewish notions of God and of people's relationship to him and to one another. For example, it has been a common practice to claim that the Jews believed in an angry God while Jesus proclaimed a loving one, or that the Jews practiced a morality based on revenge while Christians practiced one based on forgiveness and acceptance of others. There is no question that Jesus proclaimed a different under-

A Jewish father in traditional prayer garments

standing of these realities than those commonly accepted by the Jewish people, but it was more a matter of expanding and deepening their ideas than it was of directly contradicting them.

Jesus' understanding of God.

It is unfair to stereotype the Jewish sense of God as "a God of fear and justice" and Jesus' understanding of him as a "God of love." The Jewish notion of a loving God was and is very strong. But, as we have seen, Jewish reverence for God was *so* strong that they could not even utter his name, and they experienced God as distant and removed. One way they expressed this sense was by referring to God as "the heavens." This explains an interesting expression that Matthew uses in his discussion of the Kingdom of God in his gospel. Remember, Matthew was writing to a Jewish audience, and he was very sensitive to their feelings and religious practices and convictions. Therefore, instead of using the term "Kingdom of God," Matthew says "Kingdom of heaven." The God of the Jews was full of mystery, demonstrated by the Holy of Holies in their Temple, that sacred place reserved for Yahweh alone.

For Jesus, however, God's intimate union with him and with people is profound. Jesus experienced the nourishing love of God in a deeply personal sense, and he then shared that vision and relationship with us. He refers often to "my Father" in the gospels, indicating a very special relationship that he alone had with God. But he also teaches us to pray to "our Father." **Jesus sees the Father as one whose love is tireless, healing, unlimited, and unreserved. God offers his love to sinners as well as to the just, to rich and poor alike, to men and women, to both slaves and free people.** This is a radically new vision, a vision of a God in whom we can put our complete trust. This is beautifully expressed in a passage from Matthew that has been greatly treasured by Christians throughout the ages:

Look at the birds in the sky. They do not sow or reap or gather into barns; yet your heavenly Father feeds them. Are you not worth much more than they are? Can any of you, for all his worrying, add one single cubit to his span of life? And why worry about clothing? Think of the flowers growing in the fields; they never have to work or spin; yet I assure you that not even Solomon in all his regalia was robed like one of these . . . . So do not worry about tomorrow; tomorrow will take care of itself. Each day has enough trouble of its own (Matthew 6:26-29, 34).

Jesus' understanding of love for people.

Again, it is unfair to stereotype the Jewish notion of morality as one based upon strict justice and even revenge, commonly expressed with the phrase "an eye for an eye and a tooth for a tooth." **The Jews, in fact, had such a sense of communal love, of concern for the poor, and of generosity that these attitudes became their identifying traits to the other cultures that surrounded them.** The Ten Commandments, the cornerstone of Jewish Law, include seven commandments directly related to relationships between people. And the rabbis even went beyond these basic commandments to insist on attitudes of kindness and gentleness. For example, the giving of alms or contributions to the poor was *required,* not simply suggested, by Jewish Law. And, in a touching example of Jewish generosity, the Law forbade the harvesting of corn on the outer edges of the fields so that the poor people would have easier access to it!

The problem that gradually developed among the Jews, however, was an excessive sense of nationalism, a sense of separation from all other cultures which led to the belief by some Jews that "brotherly love" meant Jewish brothers and sisters only. Some—though certainly not all—even felt that one was called to "love his neighbor but hate his enemies," a belief referred to by Jesus in Matthew 5:43 but one never actually stated in the Hebrew Scriptures or in the writings of the rabbis.

Another problem encountered by Jesus was the tendency among his people to become overly legalistic. This was particularly true of the Pharisees. Minute rules and regulations had developed through the years which governed virtually every aspect of Jewish life. The combination of the Torah (the written version of the Law contained in the Hebrew Scriptures) and the oral teachings of the rabbis which grew up over the years led to an extensive system of laws. The Pharisees were the ones most committed to upholding these. There were over six hundred such laws in the Torah alone, governing everything from the Sabbath rest to ritual cleanliness, food and meal preparation, circumcision, and so on. What was a basic and decent moral foundation, in other words, had become overly legalistic and was no longer just guiding the people but actually oppressing them.

Love without limits.

Jesus went beyond these limitations of the Law, shattering any sense of narrow nationalism and breaking down the barriers of legalism. There is a particularly marvelous gospel incident that captures this well. In Luke 10:25-37, we find two scenes combined to express a powerful message about love of neighbor. In the first scene, Jesus asks a lawyer to define what the Law requires for salvation. The lawyer responds, as every good Jew would, with the dual commandment to love God and neighbor, and Jesus approves. But then the lawyer presses the question by asking, "But who is my neighbor?" Jesus responds with the thought-provoking story of the Good Samaritan. We have discussed the Samaritans before—how they were deeply despised by mainline Jews. **By telling the story here, Jesus is clearly telling his listeners that they are called beyond the limits of their own Judaism to love *all* people, even their enemies!** As it is stated in Matthew, "But I say this to you: love your enemies and pray for those who persecute you; in this way you will be sons of your Father in heaven, for he causes the sun to rise on bad men as well as good, and his rain to fall on honest and dishonest men alike. For if you love those who love you, what right have you to claim any credit? Even the tax collectors do as much, do they not? And if you save your greetings for your brothers, are you doing anything exceptional? Even the pagans do as much, do they not? You must therefore be perfect just as your heavenly Father is perfect" (Matthew 5:44-48). Jesus' call to love enemies was unique to him with no parallel in either the Hebrew Scriptures or in other writings of the rabbis.

Jesus actually did not use the word *love* all that much. He spoke more often of the results or expressions of love: forgiveness, compassion, and reconciliation. He claimed that the call to love was a call to unlimited forgiveness, and that God's willingness to forgive us is very much related to our willingness to forgive one another (Matthew 6:14-15). We pray in the Our Father, "forgive us our trespasses *as we forgive those who trespass against us.*" Perhaps if we were more conscious of what we are saying here, the words would not come so easily to us! (For a powerful summary of Jesus' teaching on the Law of love, read the last judgment story in Matthew 25:31-46.)

So we see that Jesus did not believe that the Law was bad in itself but that the many spin-offs and additions to it created by the rabbis and others had actually crippled the believers' ability to respond to people with compassion and love. His challenging of certain dimensions of the Law (for example, the Sabbath laws in Mark 23-28 and the laws on ritual cleanliness in Mark 7:14-23) could not help but alienate many who based their lives on such laws, and these actions put Jesus on a direct and unavoidable collision course with them.

The key to understanding Jesus' teaching about the Kingdom of God, therefore, is his conviction of the passionate, unrestricted, and unconditional love of God which is always and everywhere available to all people, and the power of that love to release and free people to love one another unconditionally, without restrictions. The kingship of God becomes real when God reigns over the hearts of people, and God rules our hearts when we are in tune with his will. It has been said that "the will of God is the good of people." Therefore, when people conform their lives to God's will there will be peace, joy, and love for all—that is, the Kingdom of God will be fully realized.

The "reign of God" versus "the reign of sin."

In praying the Our Father, we ask God to "lead us not into temptation, but deliver us from evil." As the prayer is found in Matthew, it reads, "And do not put us to the test, but save us from the evil one" (Matthew 6:13). Our common word for evil is *sin,* and we all know in our hearts what it means to "be put to the test," to be tempted. In one sense or another all religions acknowledge the experience of sin and evil in life and offer some response to it. Sometimes the source of evil is personified, or given almost human characteristics, as in those cases when evil is represented as a devil or as Satan. At times Jesus uses such language in the gospels, reflecting the common expressions of the Jews of his day. **The chief point to recognize here, however, is that a very real clash exists in the world between God and the power of evil, and that conflict takes place both in the hearts of individual people and in their relationships with one another.**

There are several ways in which sin can be defined, understood, and experienced. We commonly think of sin as personal, freely chosen actions or attitudes which have negative effects on us as individuals and on our relationships with others. But sin can also be understood as a kind of communal social evil that affects all of us simply because we live in community with one another. This kind of sin can be experienced in the sense of isolation and alienation that afflicts so many people today, and it is expressed most dramatically and painfully in war and poverty. And there is still another expression of sin or evil that seems so often to challenge our basic conviction about the goodness of our God— the physical pain and suffering of the helpless and innocent, the awesome destructive power of hurricanes and earthquakes, the jarring experience of an adolescent death, or the birth of a severely retarded child. There is no question about it: Each of us is confronted in countless ways by the problems of sin and evil in life. **If the message of Jesus is to be truly heard as Good News, it clearly must say something about both the personal and social realities of sin and evil and about the power of God in Jesus to ultimately overcome them.**

Throughout the gospels we see Jesus and, in him, the Kingdom of God encountering the power of evil in life. As we will see in our discussion of the miracles, God in Jesus ultimately does conquer evil in all its manifestations. This does not mean, however, that Jesus himself was immune to the temptations we all face or that he was not subject to the effects of sin. On the contrary, in his acceptance of the cross he demonstrated his willingness to submit to evil and the effects of sin in their most brutal forms. But God conquers even death by raising Jesus to life in the Resurrection. That is precisely what the Good News is all about—that God ultimately wins the battle and evil is conquered!

Hard to understand.

In reading the gospels we encounter a repeated tension, if not complete contradiction, between claims made about the Kingdom of God. For example, at one point it seems that the Kingdom is very close to us, right around the corner, so to speak (Mark 1:15). At another time it seems that the Kingdom is a reality to be achieved only at the end of time, as in the last judgment scene in Matthew 25 referred to earlier. Jesus at one time will state that "the Kingdom is among you" (Luke 17:21), but on another occasion he will tell people to pray for it to come (Matthew 6:10). There are several points to make here:

1) Jesus believed that the very nature and foundation of the Kingdom was being revealed in his own life and in his work.

2) God's reign was recognized by the early community of faith—and naturally by the evangelists—not only in the life and message of Jesus but most fully in his death, Resurrection, and the gift of the Holy Spirit at Pentecost. This recognition on the part of the gospel authors comes into play often as they write of Jesus' words and actions when he lived among them.

3) One possible explanation of this tension between the "already" and the "not yet" of the Kingdom is that the power of God was fully present in Jesus and then released to us through his death, Resurrection, and gift of the Spirit. Therefore, the Kingdom of God *is* "close at hand," it *is* already here in the sense that all the power we need to conquer evil is already available to us. But God has chosen to give people freedom, and we individually and collectively have not yet fully accepted the responsibility that is ours to participate in making the Kingdom real by living compassionate and forgiving lives. Until we do accept the challenge to love as Jesus did, the Kingdom in its richest sense will not be fully realized.

Conclusion.

Ultimately we must confront the sense of mystery which accompanies the coming of the Kingdom, God's reign over the world. There is so much variety in the gospel language about the Kingdom that it is impossible to describe it fully. For example, it can come suddenly, like the unexpected return of a traveler (Mark 13:33-37), or very slowly and secretly, like leaven working in bread dough (Matthew 13:33). **All of this variety of language is an expression of a truly wonderful reality: What God can do for people is far greater than anything we can imagine or understand.** The vision of the Kingdom is magnificent beyond understanding, yet somehow simple enough that all can respond to its challenge and invitation.

This complex nature of the Kingdom explains at least to some degree Jesus' unique use of parables—stories which allow us to catch glimpses of a reality that is simply too big for words. We turn now to a discussion of the words and special stories of Jesus.

Review questions and activities:

1) In what ways did Jews recognize the kingship of God prior to Jesus' new insights into the nature of the Kingdom?

2) Why is it improper to speak of Jewish notions about God and human relationships as if their attitudes and beliefs about these matters are directly opposite those of Jesus?

3) What was unique about Jesus' understanding of the nature of God compared to traditional Jewish teaching and belief?

4) The author mentions two major problems encountered by Jesus in the traditional Jewish teaching about the need to love people. What are these two problems, and how did Jesus try to overcome these problems in his own teaching?

5) Try to find one sentence in this chapter that accurately defines and describes Jesus' understanding of the Kingdom of God.

6) The author mentions three different definitions or understandings of sin. What are they? In what ways was Jesus subject to the effects of sin while not actually sinning himself?

7) What does the author mean when he discusses the tension between the "already" and the "not yet" of the Kingdom of God?

Terms to identify and remember:

Abba
Kingdom of God
sin

Exercise for personal reflection:

The vision of the Kingdom of God as proclaimed by Jesus is a joyous one. But the pain and evil we witness and experience in our lives make it clear that the Kingdom has not become a complete reality. Why doesn't God just "make it happen," take away all suffering, hatred, loneliness, and evil?

To grapple creatively with this basic question, do the following exercise: Imagine that you have all of God's power for one day, but that you must "play with his rules," that is, accept the same limitations and restrictions that God has placed upon himself. The challenge is this: Can you think of one major change you would like to make in the lives of people that would not violate their own freedom of choice or that of any other people involved?

You may want to discuss the results of your reflection with other students or with your teacher.

8
Jesus Speaks: Sayings and Stories of the Kingdom

Again he began to teach by the lakeside. . . . He taught them many things in parables, and in the course of his teaching he said to them, "Listen! Imagine a sower going out to sow. Now it happened that, as he sowed, some of the seed fell on the edge of the path, and the birds came and ate it up. Some seed fell on rocky ground where it found little soil and sprang up straightaway, because there was no depth of earth; and when the sun came up it was scorched and, not having any roots, it withered away. Some seed fell into thorns, and the thorns grew and choked it, and it produced no crop. And some seeds fell into rich soil and, growing tall and strong, produced crop; and yielded thirty, sixty, even a hundredfold." And he said, "Listen, anyone who has ears to hear" . . . .

Using many parables like these, he spoke the word to them, so far as they were capable of understanding it. He would not speak to them except in parables, but he explained everything to his disciples when they were alone (Mark 4:1-9, 33-34).

1) No Ordinary Teacher

In previous chapters we briefly discussed Jesus' public life in terms of his role as a teacher. As a matter of fact, the title of "teacher" was a common one given Jesus in the gospels, appearing at least thirty times in direct reference to him. We have also mentioned ways in which Jesus' "style" as a teacher differed from the traditional one played by the rabbis of his day:

1) Jesus "spoke with authority, not as the scribes do," relying on himself alone as the judge of the truths he shared rather than depending on the teaching of other rabbis to support his ideas.

2) He had a unique relationship with his disciples, whom he called into a lifelong relationship of love with him and then commissioned to share in his ministry of spreading the Good News.

3) Jesus referred to his Father as *Abba,* the equivalent of our word *Daddy,* a unique kind of intimacy found in no other biblical or rabbinic writings.

In this chapter we want to pursue this discussion a bit further, looking at the words and sayings of Jesus and particularly reflecting on his special form of story-telling, the parables.

Do we know what Jesus really said?

When reading the gospels we are struck by the fact that the words of Jesus often seem stark, blunt, sometimes even cruel. When calling his first disciples, for example, he simply walks up to them and says, " 'Follow me and I will make you fishers of men.' And at once they left their nets and followed him" (Mark 1:18). It seems difficult to understand how he could get such an immediate response with so little explanation of what he was calling them to. And on another occasion: ". . . anyone who is an obstacle to bring down one of these little ones who have faith, would be better thrown into the sea with a great millstone round his neck. And if your hand should cause you to sin, cut if off; it is better for you to enter into life crippled, than to have two hands and go to hell, into the fire that cannot be put out" (Mark 9:42-43). Jesus clearly could "talk tough" when he wanted to!

In order to understand the words, sayings, and stories of Jesus, we must remember that the gospels are the early faith community's reflections upon and expression of Jesus' life and message as understood in the light of his Resurrection. We therefore don't find his everyday casual conversation in the gospels. **We have, rather, his key thoughts, ideas, and most significant statements expressed through the hearts and minds of those who heard him.** And, in most cases, even these statements had been passed on orally for many years before finally being recorded in the gospels.

Does this mean that we don't know what Jesus actually said while preaching? In one sense we do not. We rarely if ever know his words with the exactness of a tape recording of them. Scholars do agree, however, that the reference to God as "Abba" clearly originated with Jesus. And he also demonstrated a unique use of the word *amen* in his teaching. The word normally was used in his day much as we use it today, as a statement of agreement or affirmation at the conclusion of a prayer. But Jesus *begins* many sayings with the word, saying "Amen, amen, I say to you . . ." followed by a statement of some kind. In this case the word becomes a confirmation of his own teaching, giving a weight to what he was saying that was simply unheard of in his time. Scholars agree that this use, too, reflects Jesus' unique style. So whenever we see such statements, we are probably hearing something at least close to his original words. But beyond these relatively rare occasions, we are not quite sure which words of Jesus recorded in the gospels are directly his own or interpretations by the early faith community.

As we have stated repeatedly, however, this does not mean that we cannot find truth in the gospels. **What we find, rather, is *more than* just what Jesus said, for in the gospels we find not only his words but also the *meaning* the words had for his followers.** That is, we have Jesus' words *plus,* not *just* his words. And, because we have the assurance that the gospels were written with the guidance of the Holy Spirit, we know with certainty that the words and sayings of Jesus as recorded in the gospels reveal truth, even if not in the exact words that Jesus used to share that truth originally.

A Jew speaking to fellow Jews.

We must remember as well that Jesus was thoroughly Jewish, as were most of his followers. He naturally spoke to them with their imagery, speech patterns, and within the context of their way of experiencing and understanding the world. Our own approach to reality has been heavily influenced by the Greek way of thinking. We need and expect the orderly arrangement of ideas and arguments, and we expect—even demand—logical proofs for things. But all of this was completely foreign to the Jewish mind of Jesus' day. **For Jesus, the art of speaking was not so much a matter of convincing people through reason, but rather one of establishing contact with the *total person,* with their emotions and feelings as well as with their intellects.** The Jewish manner of speaking was far more poetic than our own, filled with a heavy use of symbol, figures of speech, exaggeration, and so on. For example, "If your hand should cause you to sin, cut it off." Surely Jesus did not mean this literally, but rather was using exaggeration to make a point as strongly as possible. This was a common Jewish characteristic in speaking.

In the Jewish tradition, the master of public speaking also filled his presentations with imagery from the Hebrew Scriptures. Virtually every statement had to be supported with the word of God as preserved in their Bible. Jesus demonstrated a total familiarity with these sacred writings, and his teachings were filled with references to them. In fact, some of his most striking statements were actually biblical quotes with his own "touch" added. For example, most of us are familiar with his statement that we are called to "turn the other cheek" if someone strikes us. But this statement is actually based on one already contained in the book of Lamentations 3:30. Jesus was clearly following a very common practice when he taught in this way, though he often gave his own special "twist" or insight when doing so.

2) Three Kinds of Sayings

There are three basic kinds of "sayings" or "stories" of Jesus found in the gospels:

1) Pronouncement stories: These are actually short, concise statements that are preceded by a story. The whole intent of the story is to get to the "punch line." For example, in Mark 2:23-28 Jesus and his disciples are seen walking through cornfields on the Sabbath. As they walk along, the disciples begin picking ears of corn, a direct violation of the laws restricting work on the Sabbath. The Pharisees confront Jesus, and he responds with a story about David and his followers. The scene closes with Jesus saying, "The Sabbath was made for man, not man for the Sabbath." The whole point of the entire episode is to get to the final "clincher," a direct and powerfully simple statement about the relationship of the Law to the needs of people. This is the nature of many of the gospel stories.

2) Short sayings: The Jews were very fond of "proverbs," short statements that are very much like "words to the wise." These were offered without any story leading up to them. For example in Mark 8:35 and verses following, Jesus is seen offering a series of short but highly thought-provoking statements: "For anyone who wants to save his life will lose it; but anyone who loses his life for my sake, and the sake of the gospel, will save it. What gain, then, is it for a man to win the whole world and ruin his life?" There is no scene-setting, no story introducing the statements—just the stark and challenging words of Jesus. Matthew, in writing his gospel, used an interesting method for collecting these sayings of Jesus. He developed a scene in which Jesus is seen instructing his disciples on a hill, offering them a series of these short sayings or proverbs. We have come to call this "the Sermon on the Mount," surely one of the most popular sections of the gospels (Matthew 5:1 to 7:29). An example of this use of short sayings in our day might be the religious posters that have become so popular, usually combining beautiful photography with short, insightful statements which catch our attention and cause us to think.

3) Parables: The use of parables is one of the most significant characteristics of Jesus' teaching style. The word *parable* comes from a word meaning "comparison." The term has been used by some for a variety of Jesus' sayings, stories, riddles, and so on, but it is probably most helpful to reserve the title for his special stories. A parable usually builds from a literary device called a simile (sim'-eh-lee). In a simile one thing is compared to another thing of a different kind in order to illustrate a point by comparing the two. The word *like* or *as* usually joins the two, as in those cases when Jesus would say that "the Kingdom of heaven is like . . ." and then compare it to a mustard seed, yeast in

A shepherd with flock before what some scholars believe to be Mount Sinai

bread, or a sower in a field (Matthew 13:24-33). In concluding the Sermon on the Mount, Matthew closes the long scene with a parable that sums up the purpose of the entire sermon: "Therefore, everyone who listens to these words of mine and acts on them will be *like* a sensible man who built his house on rock. Rain came down, floods rose, gales blew and hurled themselves against that house, and it did not fall: it was founded on rock" (Matthew 7:24-25). Because the parables form such a central part of the gospels, we will discuss them at some length here.

Parables based on everyday life.

In developing a parable, Jesus would take a common occurrence of the day and give it a twist, a surprise ending. These clever endings were typical of his style and would keep his listeners alert, even off-guard. The basic stories would grow out of the land, culture, and family life of his people: scenes of farming or shepherding, household lamps and wineskins that break, children playing and adults working at their trades and crafts. Naturally much of this can seem strange to the modern reader. That is precisely why we spent so much time early in this book discussing the land and daily life of the Jewish people. In fact, you may find a quick rereading of chapter 4 particularly helpful in your own study of the parables.

Making the parables even more challenging to us, however, are the surprise comments that Jesus would include in the telling of them—comments that at least would have surprised his Jewish listeners but which we may overlook. For

3) Themes of the Parables

example, in Matthew 18:12-14 and in Luke 15:1-10 we find the story of the lost sheep. In the story a shepherd leaves ninety-nine sheep in search of one that is lost, and then he rejoices almost beyond belief over finding the lost one. Jesus' listeners would have been taken aback by this, because no ordinary shepherd would have considered risking his entire flock for one sheep. Or consider the very popular parable of the prodigal son (Luke 15:11-32). A man's younger son leaves home to go off and spend his inheritance in a wild spree while his older brother remains loyal to their father and continues to fulfill his responsibilities. When the younger son goes broke, he comes back home begging for mercy. What does the father do? He doesn't just reluctantly agree to accept the wayward son. Nor does he start comparing the younger boy to the older one who remained loyal. Instead he throws a magnificent party for the one who had been such a disappointment to him. Now, one would have to be awfully sympathetic with the older son's anger about the situation. In his stories Jesus is using a surprise twist to make people think, to stop them in their tracks, to force them to reflect on the lessons he was trying to teach. In these cases, for instance, Jesus was reflecting upon the boundless and forgiving love of God for those who have strayed from him, a love so profound it literally seems to defy common sense.

Not surprisingly, given our discussion of the central significance of the Kingdom of God in the message of Jesus discussed in the last chapter, many of the sayings and stories of Jesus either relate directly to his proclamation of the Kingdom or flow out of his own awareness of the complex nature of the Kingdom. It's very hard to arrive at a clear-cut breakdown of all the parables, but the following organization by some scholars is helpful. The parables can be organized around four themes or purposes:

1) Some parables *describe the king* of the Kingdom, namely God. That is, these parables deal primarily with the nature of God—his qualities, his attitudes in dealing with people, and so on.

- **The story of the lost sheep (Luke 15:4-7) demonstrates God's gracious love. It is God who takes the initiative and seeks out those who stray.**

- **The stories of the lost coin and the lost son (Luke 15:8-32) illustrate that God will do almost anything to find us and then will rejoice when we are finally found.**

- **The parable of the workers in the vineyard (Matthew 20:1-16), in which a landowner apparently pays some workers more than they deserve, illustrates the almost overwhelming generosity of God, the fact that he operates out of a completely different "economic system" than the one used by people.**

All of these parables, in other words, reflect that wonderful image of the Father presented by Jesus, the image of a God we can call "Abba."

2) Some of the parables emphasize *what our response should be* if we hope to "enter the Kingdom":

- For example, the parable of the Pharisee and the tax collector in Luke 18:9-14 suggests the basic attitude of humility we should have. The Pharisee is very self-righteous, congratulating himself on his strict religious practices, while the tax collector or publican feels deep sadness for his sinfulness. Jesus says the publican is the more righteous of the two because he recognizes, as we must, that there is a real need for repentance in life.

- In the parable of the rich fool in Luke 12:16-21, we find a man who felt very self-satisfied and secure because he had stored up a barnful of grain. Jesus uses the parable to illustrate the need to be open to God's goodness rather than relying on our own resources.

- In the parable of the talents (Matthew 25:14-30), a man gives three servants different amounts of "talents," or weights of silver, and then leaves them to their own resources as to how they will manage it. Two of the men work to turn a profit with their amounts, but one man fearfully hides his, afraid that he will lose what he has. The master angrily rebukes the man for not doing something beneficial with what he had been given. The lesson to Jesus' listeners—and to us—is to make use of the gifts and talents we have if we hope to be part of the Kingdom.

3) Other parables deal with *the relationship of people to one another and to the world at large:*

- The parable of the unforgiving servant (Matthew 18:23-25) tells the story of a master whose slave (the meaning of the word *servant*) begs to be relieved of a debt. The master, moved with pity, completely cancels the debt only to find later that the slave went out and had a fellow slave thrown into prison for not paying a debt owed him. In great anger the master has the unforgiving servant tortured. The lesson of the parable is that God will treat us just as we treat others.

- We have alluded several times in this book to the popular parable of the Good Samaritan in Luke 10:25-37. The lesson, though perhaps only fairly clear to us today, was shockingly clear to Jesus' listeners: If we want to be part of the Kingdom of God, we must open our hearts to *all* people, even to the outcasts of society.

4) Finally, some of the parables refer to the *future coming of God's Kingdom* in its fullness:

- In the story found in Matthew 22:1-14, a king is preparing a feast for his son's wedding. The king's servants are sent out to invite selected guests, all of whom reject his invitation. Some of the invited guests even go so far as to kill the servants who deliver the invitation. The furious king has the murderers killed and then sends other servants out to invite everyone they can find to the wedding. The parable symbolically tells the story of the Jews, who were the first invited to God's Kingdom, but some of whom not only reject the invitation but actually kill God's servant, Jesus. The "heavenly banquet"—which is the Kingdom—is then offered to everyone, Jews and Gentiles alike. The parable clearly points to the future establishment of the Kingdom in its fullness.

• Other parables that seem to have this sense of the future establishment of the Kingdom are those of the bridesmaids (Matthew 25:1-13), who get locked out of the wedding hall because they were unprepared, and of the good wheat seeds and the weeds (Matthew 13:24-30), which must be allowed to grow together but will be separated at the harvest. Both of these parables point to the "end time" or the future day of judgment by God.

It should be noted here that occasionally a parable will be used to teach two different lessons in different gospels. At times they may even be given different locations or settings by the authors. This could be explained in two ways: First, it is quite possible that Jesus used the same story more than once to illustrate different points, and the gospel authors simply differed on which version they selected. A more likely explanation, however, is that the author simply provided a setting for the parable which helped to illustrate the point *he* wished to make to his readers. This does not, of course, deny the truth or lesson of the parables themselves. If anything, this multiple use by the authors just serves to demonstrate how rich and full of meaning each of these marvelous stories of Jesus truly is.

Jesus' Parables in the Synoptic Gospels

	Matthew	Mark	Luke
The house on the rock	7:24-25		
The sower	13:1-23	4:1-20	8:4-15
The weeds in the field	13:24-43		
The mustard seed	13:31-32	4:30-32	13:18-19
The hidden treasure	13:44-46		
The unforgiving servant	18:23-35		
The good Samaritan			10:25-37
The rich fool			12:16-21
The great feast			14:15-24
The lost sheep	18:12-24		15:1-7
The lost coin			15:8-10
The prodigal son			15:11-32
The unjust servant			16:1-13
The rich man and Lazarus			16:19-31
The unjust judge			18:1-8
The Pharisee and the tax collector			18:9-14
The workers in the vineyard	20:1-16		
The pounds			19:11-27
The wicked tenants	21:33-46	12:1-12	20:9-19
The wedding feast	22:1-14		
The faithful servant	24:45-51		
The ten bridesmaids	25:1-13		
The talents	25:14-30		

4) Understanding the Parables

We can see that the parables in a sense give us a picture of the Kingdom, and they challenge us to commit ourselves to accepting it, that is, to accepting the will of God. *We,* as individuals, are called to identify with the lost sheep, with the wicked tenants, with the Good Samaritan, and so on, just as were Jesus' original listeners. We must let these stories speak to our own life situations. How do we do that? Here are a few suggestions that might make the reading of the parables more enjoyable and enlightening for us:

1) **We should generally look for the central message of the parables.** The details which accompany some parables can make them more interesting, perhaps, but we should not try to read too much into the stories. The message of Jesus is often far more direct and to the point than we might expect or recognize.

2) **It is helpful to look for questions that are posed in the parables.** Jesus at times asks his listeners to offer their own response to a parable before he gives his intended message. For example, in the parable of the Good Samaritan, he first asks his listeners, "Which of these three men, *do you think,* proved himself to be a neighbor?" Whenever such questions are posed directly or indirectly in the parables, we should pause and attempt to answer the questions ourselves. In this way we begin to look toward the implications of the parables in our own lives as we experience them today.

3) **Finally, the sayings and interpretations that often conclude the parables are many times the early faith community's reflections on how *it* answered Jesus' questions.** It is possible, in other words, that Jesus may have not actually answered some of his own questions or interpreted the parables for the people, but rather allowed them to gain all the insights they could on their own. As we read the parables, then, we should compare the answers *we* would give to those eventually given by the early Church and recorded in the gospels. This sets up a kind of dialogue or discussion between ourselves and the gospel writers, precisely the kind of interaction and exchange that can make the gospels come alive for us today.

Putting his words into actions.

When trapped by a contradiction between what they say or profess to believe and the way they actually live their lives, some people are inclined to fall back on the old saying, "Don't do what I do. Do what I say." A somewhat related proverb states, "What you are speaks so loudly I can't hear what you are saying." In the case of Jesus, there were no contradictions between what he said and the way he acted. All that he said and did combined to reveal his tremendous vision of the Kingdom of God, the reign of the Father over all creation and in the hearts of people. In this chapter we have discussed the words and sayings of Jesus. But Jesus not only spoke, he also acted, and no thorough study of him and his message can avoid a discussion of some of his most challenging and perhaps confusing actions—his miracles. We will discuss these marvelous actions of Jesus in the next chapter.

Review questions and activities:

1) Do we know what Jesus actually said while preaching in Palestine? Explain your answer.

2) Give brief definitions or descriptions of the three basic kinds of sayings and stories contained in the gospel accounts of Jesus' preaching.

3) Why do we need a good understanding of the world and daily life of the Jews in order to understand Jesus' parables?

4) Some scholars feel the parables can be categorized according to their relationship to Jesus' proclamation of the Kingdom of God. Give the four categories presented by the author, and give one example for each category.

5) Why does the author suggest we pay particular attention to the questions Jesus asks in his preaching and, in particular, in his parables?

Terms to identify and remember:

pronouncement story	parable
amen	simile

Exercise for personal reflection:

To try to gain a clearer sense of the nature and meaning of Jesus' parables, try writing one of your own. Remember, Jesus used common, everyday experiences as the basis of much of his teaching, but he always added his own unique twists and insights. Try to follow his style. Take a subject you are very familiar with as a basis, and then simply allow your imagination to guide you. For example, "The Kingdom of God is like a basketball game . . ." or, "The wise person is like the student preparing for an exam . . ." or, "Discovering God is like a chemistry experiment . . ." This exercise, combined with your background on the daily life of the Jews from chapter 4, can lead to a deeper appreciation for Jesus' teaching and its impact on people.

9
Jesus Heals: Signs of the Kingdom

Now John in his prison had heard what Christ was doing and he sent his disciples to ask him, "Are you the one who is to come, or have we got to wait for someone else?" Jesus answered, "Go back and tell John what you hear and see; the blind see again, and the lame walk, lepers are cleansed, and the deaf hear, the dead are raised to life and the Good News is proclaimed to the poor; and happy is the man who does not lose faith in me" (Matthew 11:2-5).

1) Marvelous Deeds... and a Few Doubts

Perhaps no image of Jesus both captures our imaginations and challenges our minds more than does that of Jesus as "the miracle worker." Our imaginations are caught up with scenes of power and awe—people raised to life with a simple word, blindness cured with a touch, sickness and disease rendered powerless in the presence of Jesus' dominating personality. And yet the scenes that have moved millions to faith throughout the history of the Church often confront the logical and scientific minds of today as serious questions which disturb them rather than as signs of hope which strengthen their faith. It is a question we cannot avoid: What are we to make of the miracles of Jesus? The gospels are filled with several kinds of these "works of wonder":

- *healing miracles,* in which Jesus relieves the physical suffering of people afflicted with fever, paralysis, deafness and dumbness, blindness, and "leprosy"—a general name given many kinds of skin diseases of his day;

- *exorcisms,* in which "evil spirits" or demons are driven out of people at the command of Jesus;

• *restorations of life,* three occasions on which Jesus apparently conquers death itself by "raising people from the dead";

• and *nature miracles,* perhaps the most confusing actions of all, in which Jesus demonstrates apparent control over the natural world by walking on water, calming a storm, feeding thousands with just a few loaves and fishes, and so on.

Why are the miracles so challenging?

It was mentioned in the last chapter that there is a major difference between the way we view the world today and the way in which the Jews of Jesus' day viewed it. We expect and need proofs, evidence, and logical explanations for virtually everything we encounter in life. Many people today, therefore, tend to reject miracles automatically because they are by definition unexplainable exceptions to or contradictions of the laws of nature. There almost seems to be a "take it or leave it" attitude about the gospel miracles among today's Christians. Some simply accept all of the gospel miracles at face value and therefore feel forced to reject many of our modern scientific and even biblical findings. These people are often referred to as "fundamentalists," and it is said that they opt for a literal interpretation of the Bible. That is, these people refuse to accept any part of the Scriptures as symbolic or open to various interpretations. At the other extreme there are those who reject any possibility at all of miracles, people who consider such accounts as illusions of a backward people or as fables of some kind.

It seems to us, however, that there can and should be some kind of middle ground between these two extreme positions. It does not seem right or necessary, for example, to lump all of the miracle accounts together and to treat them all the same way, giving one as much historical validity or importance as another. Certainly all of these marvelous stories have something very true and valid to teach us about Jesus and about his proclamation of the Kingdom. But if we get too bound up with questions about whether an individual event occurred exactly the way the gospels describe it, we will risk completely missing the truth that the story can reveal to us.

Jesus did work some miracles.

We have to be very clear on what we are claiming in our discussion of the miracles. **We are *not* saying that Jesus did not work any miracles. On the contrary, all of the available evidence and even common sense demonstrates that he did in fact work many "wonders."** Consider the following points:

1) In discussing non-Christian sources of information about Jesus in chapter 2, we mentioned that Jesus was referred to by non-Christian historians of his time as a "wonder worker," and it is evident from these historical records that he clearly impressed the crowds a great deal with his actions.

2) Even the Pharisees in the gospels don't deny that Jesus actually worked many wonders. Instead they charge him with doing so through the power of the devil (Matthew 12:24; Luke 11:16). Scripture scholars claim that this charge by the Pharisees is too unusual, too unexpected, to be included in the gospels if it were not based on an actual incident.

3) The undeniable historical fact is that many eyewitnesses of the works of Jesus—many of whom would still be alive when the gospels were written—believed so firmly in him and his message that they became committed followers, even to the point of freely dying rather than denying faith in him. What can account for such devotion other than that his claims—and those made about him—were based on facts? Would there not, for instance, have been real objections by early witnesses to false claims made about Jesus by the writers of the gospels?

So it is apparent that Jesus did in fact work many wonders. Sorting out which of the events included in the gospels occurred just as they are described continues to be a major challenge to biblical schol- ars and certainly beyond the scope of this course. Our major concern here is this: What did the miracles intend to teach about Jesus and his Kingdom or, perhaps more accurately, what did Jesus intend to teach us through his use of miracles?

What's the problem?

There are problems involved in understanding the miracles even for those who accept only a literal interpretation of them. For example, the gospels themselves seem to disagree with each other in some cases, or show definite signs that each evangelist offered his own imaginative details to the miracle accounts. There is a tendency by the authors, for instance, to intensify, magnify, and even multiply the miracles from one gospel tradition to

Jesus' Miracles in the Synoptic Gospels

	Matthew	Mark	Luke		Matthew	Mark	Luke
Cure of a leper	8:1-4	1:40-45	5:12-16	Cure of the son of the widow of Nain			7:11-17
Cure of the centurion's servant	8:5-13		7:1-10	Jesus walks on water	14:22-33	6:45-52	
Cure of Peter's mother-in-law	8:14-15	1:29-31	4:38-39	Cure of the Canaanite woman's daughter	15:21-28	7:24-30	
Calming of the storm	8:23-27	4:35-41	8:22-25	Healing of a deaf man		7:31-37	
The demoniacs of Gadara	8:28-34	5:1-20	8:26-39	Second miracle of the loaves	15:32-39	8:1-10	
Cure of a paralytic	9:1-8	2:1-12	5:17-26	Cure of a blind man at Bethsaida		8:22-26	
The woman with a hemorrhage and the daughter of Jairus	9:18-26	5:21-43	8:40-56	Cure of the epileptic demoniac boy	17:14-20	9:14-29	9:37-43
Cure of two blind men	9:27-31			Healing of the ten lepers			17:11-19
The man with the withered hand	12:9-14	3:1-6	6:6-11	Cure of the two blind men of Jericho	20:29-34	10:46-52	18:35-43
First miracle of the loaves	14:13-21	6:31-44	9:10-17	The barren fig tree	21:18-22		

the next, from the earliest one written by Mark to the later gospels. Consider these examples:

- In Mark, it is said that Jesus "cured *many* who were suffering" (Mark 1:34), while in Matthew it is said that he "cured *all* who were sick" (Matthew 8:16).

- In Mark, a man named Jairus approaches Jesus and pleads, "My little daughter is desperately sick" (Mark 5:23). In a parallel scene in Matthew he says, "My daughter has just died . . ." (Matthew 9:18).

- The healing of one blind man becomes the healing of two, and the healing of one possessed man becomes the healing of two (compare Mark 10:46-52 with Matthew 20:29-34, for instance).

The question raised by these examples is clear: If we can identify this tendency to exaggerate even within the gospels themselves, is it not possible that there could have been such a tendency to exaggerate in the early community of faith *before* the gospels were written, that is, from the death of Jesus in the year 30 to the writing of Mark's gospel in A.D. 70 and beyond? The answer, quite honestly, is yes. Well, if *that's* true, then on what basis can we approach and judge the truth of the miracles? How are we to understand them if they can't always be understood as historical events reported with complete accuracy by the evangelists?

2) The Jews and Miracles

One of our major keys for understanding the miracle stories in the gospels is to recognize that what *we* mean by "miracle" and what the people of Jesus' day understood by "miracle" are not the same things. For us, miracles are exceptions to the laws of nature. To the Jews, on the other hand, they were manifestations of the presence and power of God. And, because God is *always* present and powerful, miracles to the Jews were not exceptions but actually the law of nature itself. In other words, though the Jews would naturally be awed by works of wonder, they were not terribly surprised by them. They simply *expected* God to work this way!

In the Jewish view of the world, everything that existed was a manifestation or expression of either God's creative power or of the power of evil in the world. The rain that fell and the breeze that blew were directly the result of God's activity—the rain released through floodgates that *he* opened, and the breeze recognized as *his* breath passing over the earth. On the other hand, all illnesses, from blindness to leprosy to death itself, were expressions of the power of evil in the world. Any cure, therefore, was by definition an "exorcism" of sorts because it was a sign that evil was being "cast out" or conquered. Given this understanding of the Jewish vision of the world, then, it is not surprising that the Jews would recognize God's "miracles" far more than we do, even though to some degree we might be looking at the same realities. We look for logical explanations for everything. The Jews already had *their* explanation, they already had *their* answer to things they could not understand: They were simply the activities of their God, Yahweh, who was demonstrating his control over the universe.

Therefore, in the Jewish culture of Jesus' day, there were not only more miracles than we would identify in ours, but there were also many more miracle workers, persons who appeared to have strange powers over people and events. We know from sources other than the gospels, for example, that there were other rabbis in the time of Jesus who were also considered wonder workers, able to cure people of their afflictions, and so on. This was also a common belief among many of the Greek religions of the time.

A different kind of world.

It can also be helpful for us to call to mind the rather gruesome world which Jesus encountered, one very different from the one most of us experience. The people of Jesus' day had no hospitals, for example, and no mental institutions for the disturbed or insane. Medicine was very primitive. It may be hard for us to imagine, but it was common for Jesus to see blind and crippled beggars along the roadways and at the gates of the cities. Disease-ridden people like the lepers mentioned in the gospels were forced to roam in bands through the countryside, forbidden to enter the cities. Insane people were chained in caves, where their screams could be heard through the days and nights. And, not surprisingly perhaps, all of these people were banned even from worshipping in the Temple.

Our tendency today might be to condemn the Jewish society for this kind of cruel treatment of the physically and mentally ill. But we must remember *why* they did this. *If* all sickness, insanity, and disease were direct manifestations of the power of evil, then the healthy people would logically be terrified of those who were sick, fearful of being contaminated by them. **It was, in other words, sheer terror, not cruelty, which motivated people to reject and bannish those who were in need.** Some even felt that sickness was a punishment from God for personal sins or the sins of ancestors. This was a terribly difficult belief for those who held it, however, because it was clear that good people seemed to suffer as much, even more, than apparent sinners. (Jesus talked about this in Luke 13:1-5.)

Now, if all illness was the result of the power of evil in the world, then common sense indicated that the true Kingdom or reign of God which the people expected and yearned for would not be truly present until all these manifestations of evil were overcome. **And this is precisely what is demonstrated throughout Jesus' ministry and in a special way in his miracles—that in this man God was destroying evil in all its forms and expressions and that, because of this, Jesus was truly the Messiah, the one sent by God, the one who was establishing the new Kingdom they had been waiting and praying for.**

3) Understanding Jesus' Miracles Today

Given all that we have said so far, we must admit that *some* of the actions that were considered miracles in Jesus' time might not be during ours:

- We understand, for example, the incredible power of the human personality to effect change in our bodies. We talk about "psycho-somatic illnesses" which seem to disappear when the patient's attitudes change, or we know of the remarkable "power of suggestion" that is demonstrated through hypnosis. This understanding may account for *some* of the exorcisms, in which emotionally distraught people would be calmed by the strength of Jesus' character.

- *Some* of Jesus' cures may be explained in part by the use of exaggeration as a characteristic of Jewish writers. They would use this technique to make a strong and *true* point by stretching the historical facts a bit.

But these facts don't explain *all* of the miracles, nor do they negate the solid tradition for accepting miracles throughout the history of the Church, a history which we believe to be guided by "the Spirit of truth." Again, Jesus clearly worked many wonders. Which of his particular actions were most historical continues to be discussed and studied by Scripture scholars and theologians.

Ultimately, of course, we are dealing here with both a faith question and a faith answer. We are not, as Christians, expected to blindly accept irrational claims. Rather we are asked to recognize and accept the true significance of the miracles—their true "sign value"—in the light of our faith in Jesus. We are not dealing here, in other words, with yes or no questions about the historical reality of the miracles. Rather we are dealing with the question we have repeatedly posed for ourselves: What do the miracles *mean*? We can only answer that from the perspective of faith. This was, in fact, as true of the people who actually witnessed these events as it is for us today. It is mentioned over and over again in the gospels that belief in Jesus and faith in God was often demanded *before* one who was ill could experience a cure. Jesus was not in "show business" but, rather, in the "business" of his Father, that is, in the task of revealing God's nature and his relationship with people by revealing and establishing his Kingdom.

Miracles and the Kingdom.

The key to understanding the miracles of Jesus, then, is grasping their relationship to his proclamation of the Kingdom of God—the message of the Father's unconditional love, his offer of complete reconciliation, his commitment to the poor and outcasts of society, and his complete domination over the power of sin and its evil influences. The miracles can, in other words, only be understood in terms of their relationship to the Good News proclaimed by Jesus.

Jesus didn't just speak of his Father's love. He lived out that loving presence of his Father in his actions. It was love that almost forced him to heal and work wonders, not the desire to impress the crowds or to force people to have faith in him. The gospels are very clear on this: Jesus healed quite simply because people needed to be healed. He healed out of profound compassion. In Mark 1:41, for example, Jesus is moved to pity for the leper who begs to be cured. And it is sorrow that touches him in meeting the widow of Naim whose son had died (Luke 7:13).

Kindness is not Jesus' only motive for working wonders, however. The most common word used for miracles and cures in the synoptic gospels is *power,* and in John's gospel the word *sign* is used most often. **Jesus' miracles, therefore, were signs intended to manifest God's power over all creation and, in a special way, over the forces of evil.** This is the chief lesson of the exorcisms, in which Jesus is seen casting out "evil spirits." God in and through Jesus can confront the powers of evil in their most direct manifestations and conquer them. And in the gospels we see that evil is most directly and dramatically manifested in the lives of people—in their suffering, their pain, their death. In all these cases Jesus heals and restores fullness of life.

The so-called nature miracles are perhaps more confusing and difficult to understand, but the same basic message is revealed through them: God's reign over all creation is present in this man, Jesus, and is being revealed to the world through him. Just as Yahweh drew order out of chaos in the creation of the world (Genesis 1:1-2), so God in

Jesus now overcomes all chaos in the world. Just as Yahweh offered the special food, manna, to his people as they roamed in the desert (Exodus 16:12-35), so now God through Jesus multiplies the loaves and fishes to feed the multitudes. Just as Moses parted the waters of the sea to allow the passage of the Israelites (Exodus 14:15-31), so too God in Jesus can calm the storms and walk on water.

Our key point again is this: All miracles are manifestations of the healing and redeeming power of God's love, a loving power present in and revealed by Jesus. No wonder those who walked with him, who watched him touch people, were convinced that he truly was a man of extraordinary power and force!

A concern about our image of Jesus.

If we are to be true to the image of Jesus portrayed in the gospels, we must be very careful to avoid an understanding of him based on the miracles that turns him into a kind of biblical Captain Marvel, a Superman, a magician. Jesus constantly refused any such designation or image. He worked miracles almost reluctantly and, curiously, often told those he had cured to "go and tell no one" what he had done for them (Mark 1:43). Why? Because he didn't want his miracles to cloud or confuse the far greater and more important reality—that "the Kingdom of God is among you!"

The healing of people's hearts was far more important to Jesus than the temporary healing of their bodies. They were, after all, eventually going to die physically. And Jesus even became angry with those who actually expected miracles as proof of his power (Mark 8:12). It is again clear that he never worked wonders just to impress people—then or now.

As we have said, faith was generally demanded before a miracle could be worked. If this were not the case, the miracles would be little more than a magic show. There was a need to believe in Jesus and his message, not just in his miracles. Jesus never forced faith by tricking people or by overwhelming them with displays of his power. He was a man of absolute integrity. And response on the part of people had to be free and genuine.

Once faith is present in people, however, the real miracle has already begun in their hearts. **The physical cure they experience becomes an expression of an interior reality, a conversion, a change of heart.** The cures of their bodies, therefore, manifest a deeper, more profound change within them. It is a liberation not only from lameness but, for example, from legalism as well, not only from a crippling deformity but also from a closed mind, not only from physical blindness but also from the inability to recognize the needs of their neighbors.

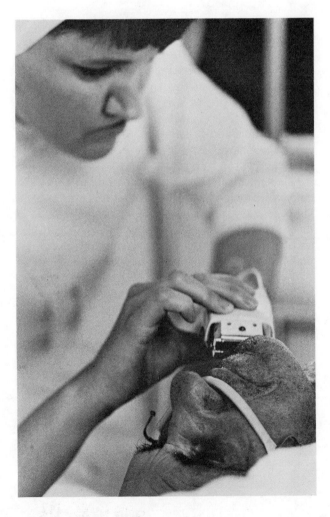

One author has beautifully expressed the meaning of the miracles in Jesus' ministry: "We find in the miracle stories, as in other parts of the gospel heritage, that steady testimony to the absolute wholeness and genuineness of Jesus of Nazareth. He was a man so close to his God that God's own creative power flowed from him in healing waves. He was a man so dedicated to God's work that his own fascinating power seemed to embarrass him; at times it seemed to get in the way of his message. But, most of all, Jesus was a man so charged with God's own compassion and love that any cry of pain or confusion drew from him an instant response of healing and restoration."

A man of compassion on the way to the cross.

It is difficult to comprehend how one as dedicated to works of love and compassion as Jesus could become such a source of conflict, such an object of hatred and fear. And yet surely no single event in the story of Jesus is more etched into the hearts, minds, and emotions of Christians than is his agonizing execution on the cross. How can this be? What can make sense of such a horribly brutal death of such a good man? In the next chapter, we will seek an answer.

1) The author states that "no image of Jesus both captures our imagination and challenges our minds more than does that of Jesus as 'the miracle worker.' " What does he mean by this statement?

2) The author suggests that, in understanding Jesus' miracles, we should seek a "middle ground" between two extreme positions regarding them. Explain.

3) Does the author suggest that Jesus in fact worked no miracles at all? Explain your answer.

4) Explain the major difference between our modern understanding of miracles and that of the Jewish people of Jesus' time. Why is an awareness of this distinction so critical to our understanding the miracles?

5) Why would it be improper to condemn the Jews for their apparently cruel treatment of some physically and mentally ill people?

6) Why was Jesus' overcoming of the power of evil through miracles a necessary part of his revealing and establishing the Kingdom of God?

7) Why did Jesus often tell people who witnessed or experienced his miraculous power to "go and tell no one"?

8) The author states that, once authentic faith is present in people, "the real miracle has already begun in their hearts." Explain.

Terms to identify and remember:

exorcisms	fundamentalists
nature miracles	leprosy

Exercise for personal reflection:

The author indicates that the truly "miraculous" results of Jesus' ministry occurred in peoples' hearts—in the changes he brought about in their values, their lifestyles, and so on. Viewing Jesus' work from this perspective, try to imagine his coming among us today, again bringing his extraordinary message and healing touch to people of the twentieth century. Who are the mentally and physically ill he would meet on our streets today? How would he touch them, and how would they manifest changes in their lives? Where would he find agonizing loneliness, and how would he relieve it? How would he free those "crippled" by alcohol and drug abuse? How would he bring hope to our modern "lepers," those rejected by society because of their appearances? In what ways would he "give sight" to those blind to the needs of others?

10
The Cross: The End or a Beginning?

They came to a small estate called Geth-semane, and Jesus said to his disciples, "Stay here while I pray." Then he took Peter and James and John with him. And a sudden fear came over him, and great distress. And he said to them, "My soul is sorrowful to the point of death. Wait here, and keep awake." And going on a little further he threw himself on the ground and prayed that, if it were possible, this hour might pass him by. "Abba (Father)!" he said, "Everything is possible for you. Take this cup away from me. But let it be as you, not I, would have it." He came back and found them sleeping, and he said to Peter, "Simon, are you asleep? Had you not the strength to keep awake one hour? You should be awake, and praying not to be put to the test. The spirit is willing, but the flesh is weak." Again he went away and prayed, saying the same words. And once more he came back and found them sleeping, their eyes were so heavy; and they could find no answer for him. He came back a third time and said to them, "You can sleep on now and take your rest. It is all over. The hour has come. Now the Son of Man is to be betrayed into the hands of sinners. Get up! Let us go! My betrayer is close at hand already" (Mark 14:32-42).

1) Jesus, a Source of Conflict

"It is all over. The hour has come." With those simple but chilling words of Jesus, the drama that was his earthly life moved toward its horrifying climax. It was probably the year A.D. 30. He was a man of some 35 years, and his life was about to end dramatically and violently. He had preached no more than three years, and perhaps even as little as a few months. He had proclaimed a message of Good News about a Kingdom of love, joy, peace, and harmony. But it had all led to this—the way to the cross. What actually happened and why? Did Jesus know he was going to die when he made that last fateful journey to Jerusalem? And—for Christians especially—what did it all mean? These are the difficult questions we now seek to answer.

Certainly Jesus was a man committed to peace, and Christians are right to remember most strongly his acts of love and compassion. **But we must remember as well that he was a man who seemed to cause conflict and tension wherever he went.** His words were often challenging, even threatening, to his listeners. His behavior often shocked those who witnessed it, running contrary to many of the accepted practices of his day. Consider the following:

- On virtually every important issue of his day—marriage, authority, the role and meaning of the Law, the Temple and its worship—Jesus' opinions conflicted with those of many people, particularly with those of people in positions of power.

- He made the outcasts of society—women, the poor, tax collectors, the physically sick and emotionally disturbed—these he made the very cornerstone of his message about God's Kingdom.

- He claimed a position of authority for himself above that of both the religious and political powers of his day.

The sum total of this and much more brought Jesus to a direct and unavoidable confrontation with the Jews and Romans. He was both a very real religious and political threat to "the way things were," to political stability and religious tradition. As one author put it: "Jesus' violent end was the logical conclusion of his proclamation and his behavior . . . (His) death was the penalty he had to pay for his life."

What actually happened during those last fateful days of Jesus' life? It would be very helpful in preparation for our discussion of these events if you could read at least one, and preferably all, of the synoptic accounts of the passion of Jesus: Matthew 26:1 to 27:66; Mark 14:1 to 15:47; Luke 22:1 to 23:56. We will be discussing a great deal of information here, some of it quite confusing, and a basic familiarity with the main characters and the flow of events will help make the material more understandable.

The nature of the passion accounts.

Before beginning our discussion of the events surrounding Jesus' last days, we should briefly comment on what we might falsely presume everyone accepts as obvious—that Jesus actually did die by crucifixion. This is an absolute historical fact, verified not only by Christian writers but also by the non-Christian historians mentioned earlier in this book. It is important to note as well that the arrest, trial, crucifixion, and death of Jesus are the most extensively reported events in the gospels. It almost seems when reading the gospels that they are keyed to these events, as if everything in them is intended to prepare the reader for Jesus' execution. Even a unique style of writing is evident here, much different from the story-telling, short sayings, and so on that are typical of the rest of the gospel story. There are many more details provided in these accounts, for instance, than are offered in other parts of the gospels. Why should this be so? There seem to be several reasons:

1) **The death and Resurrection of Jesus are at the very heart of the Christian story.** These events had to be very carefully explained to members of the early community of faith.

2) **What happened to Jesus was totally contrary to what the people had been expecting of their Messiah.** Their desire for a great deal of information about these events would have been natural and intense.

3) Remember, the evangelists were writing to and for the early followers of the Risen Jesus. These people would themselves confront almost immediate persecution for their faith in him. **The reminder to them that Jesus himself had suffered persecution and death would be a constant consolation to these people.**

For these and other reasons, the accounts of the passion and death of Jesus were probably among the earliest products of Christian writing, and they may well have been part of the oral worship of the early faith community even before being committed to writing. Though we are given a lot of detail in the accounts, there are also signs of editorial work by the evangelists, who were naturally trying to provide theological insights into the meaning of some of these events. For example, in Matthew's gospel we find mention of the tearing of the Temple cloth, the darkening of the skies, the eruption of graves, and so on. These may well be cases of the addition of symbolic imagery to the basic account of the passion. Nevertheless, by carefully comparing and combining the material expressed in all of the synoptic gospels, we can arrive at a fairly clear idea of the historical facts surrounding the arrest, trial, and brutal execution of Jesus.

2) The Last Supper

The three synoptic gospels give an account of what has come to be known as "the Last Supper." Jesus acted as the host at a meal for his disciples in an "upper room" loaned them by a friend in Jerusalem on the evening before he was crucified. He followed the normal Jewish custom of his day, giving thanks to God for the meal. But then he took the bread on the table, handed it to his disciples, and said:

"This is my body which will be given for you; do this as a memorial of me." He did the same with the cup after supper, and said, "This cup is the new covenant in my blood which will be poured out for you" (Luke 22:19-20).

We talked earlier about the significance of the idea of covenant throughout the history of the Jews. The Last Supper took place near the time when the Jewish people were celebrating one of their greatest religious festivals, Passover. You will remember that, during this time, the people recalled how, many years before, Yahweh had delivered them from slavery in Egypt and how, in gratitude, the people of Israel pledged their loyalty to him. Ever since that time they had been known as "the people of the covenant." When Jesus identified his actions as representing a *new* covenant," therefore, he was speaking of a reality that went to the very heart of Jewish history. What was Jesus saying through his words and actions at that very special meal the night before he died?

The gospel traditions clearly suggest that Jesus had his approaching death in mind as he gathered his disciples for that meal, and that he made a real

connection between the meal itself and his death on the cross. When he stood up to do his customary duty as host in saying the blessing over the cup and bread, he startled his disciples by saying that the cup and bread were now to be recognized as signs of his own death. The disciples—somewhat expectedly but, in this case, perhaps with justification—didn't understand what he was talking about. They believed that he had come to Jerusalem to assume his role as king, not to die! It was only later—after Jesus' actual death and Resurrection—that the early community of faith would recall this meal and begin to use the words and gestures of Jesus as a continuing reminder of his death for generations to come. Nearly two thousand years later, Christians all over the world gather in their communities, solemnly repeating those words and gestures and recalling again in this special way the life, death, and Resurrection of Jesus. They continue to "do this in memory" of him.

What kind of meal?

It should be noted here that there has been a continuing debate among scholars on whether Jesus was actually celebrating the traditional Jewish Passover meal at the Last Supper. Some feel that he was, rather, sharing a more "common" meal to which he added new and profound meaning with his words and gestures. Though the gospel traditions seem to clearly indicate that it was in fact the Passover meal, there seem to be conflicts with calendars, with the accounts of the trial of Jesus, and so on that make scholars seriously question this. The theology involved in this discussion is complex and beyond the purposes of this course. But it is a significant discussion for many reasons. A great deal of our understanding of the death of Jesus and, therefore, of the meaning of Eucharist has been built around the strong notions of sacrifice and atonement that surround the Passover

Jesus and his Apostles may have shared their Last Supper in a setting similar to the one depicted here

meal of the Jews. This religious meal includes the killing and eating of the Passover or paschal lambs which, significantly, are never mentioned in the gospel accounts. In any case, Jesus is spoken of as "the Lamb of God," as the one whose blood was to be "poured out" as a sacrifice for us, and as one who "died for our sins." This understanding of Jesus' death on the cross as a sacrificial offering on our behalf, though very moving, seems to imply some very difficult notions about the nature of God. If, on the other hand, Jesus did not intend to make this strong identification between his actions at the Last Supper and the Passover meal ritual, some of these problems might be more easily resolved. We will return to this difficult but important question in a later discussion of the meaning of Jesus' death.

Judas—betrayer of Jesus?

During the Last Supper Jesus predicted that one of his disciples was about to betray him. All of the disciples were shocked at the thought and vigorously denied the possibility. But among them sat a man, one whose story is probably far more confused, and perhaps touching, than we are normally inclined to believe. The man was Judas. The simple and widely accepted understanding of Judas has been that he was plainly a greedy and very weak man who "sold out" Jesus for thirty pieces of silver. But perhaps it is not quite that easy to assess his motives. Matthew, for instance, is the only synoptic gospel that even bothers to mention the payment of silver. But it is mentioned as well that, even before the official condemnation of Jesus, Judas was "filled with remorse" when he realized what was happening, that he threw the money down before the chief priests and elders, and that he then went out and hanged himself in despair. **It is difficult to mesh the stereotyped image of the greedy Judas with the gospel image of a man filled with sadness, despair, and apparent surprise at what was happening to Jesus.** Some scholars propose that Judas was actually trying to force Jesus to respond to official charges of the chief priests and others, with the assumption that Jesus would do so by revealing his power and by assuming the role of king. In other words, they contend that Judas did not expect or intend Jesus' execution at all, but rather that he was trying to force or pressure him to assume the role of Messiah. This is all guesswork, of course, but it will perhaps keep us from judging Judas—or anyone else for that matter—too quickly or too harshly.

3) Thy Will Be Done

There may be few emotions that are more universally or painfully experienced than loneliness. We have all felt the terrible ache inside us, the feeling that no one understands, that no one cares, that we are left to fend for ourselves in a difficult world all by ourselves, alone. Perhaps it is because we all have shared such pain that the image of Jesus in Gethsemane touches us so personally, so profoundly. Nearly any experience of loneliness we go through, however, must seem at least more bearable if not less agonizing when compared to what he endured.

We cannot allow ourselves to somehow soften the pain of Jesus in Gethsemane with thoughts of how, as the Son of God, he could heroically accept the pain of his impending death with the sure knowledge that his Resurrection awaited him beyond it. **The gospels are clear on this—Jesus' "agony in the garden" was a time of sheer human terror and darkness.** He knew the time was fast approaching when all the conflicts surrounding him would build to the breaking point. Did he know he was going to die? Or, more specifically, did he know he was to die by crucifixion? This was a common form of execution at the time, but one so horrible, so hideous, that it was reserved for non-Roman criminals and slaves. Capital punishment for Roman citizens was the far more "humane" method of beheading. Was Jesus' awareness of his own approaching death the reason for his intense suffering in the garden? **If he *didn't* know he was to die, why was he so terrified and, if he *did* know, why didn't he just run away, escape?** These questions are not simply interesting points for reflection. They deal with issues of tremendous importance if we are to understand the true meaning and significance of Jesus' death as well as of his message of unconditional love.

Reading "the signs of the times."

Did Jesus know he was going to die? It is likely that he did, and also that he knew his death would come, if not within a few days, at least soon. How did he know? We don't have to imagine some interior revelation by God on this, some mysterious inner voice that permitted Jesus to foresee the future. Rather, Jesus could "read the signs of the times," that is, he could look at what was happening about him and "put all the pieces together." This is what he likely recognized:

- He certainly was aware of the building hostility of all the people who opposed him. As we have noted, Jesus was out of step with every faction of Judaism—Pharisees, Sadducees, Zealots. In a rare situation indeed, all of the normally conflicting leaders of his people were united against him. And he was aware as well of the implications of this tension for the Romans who would simply not tolerate the kind of conflicts and displays of high religious and political emotion that seemed to follow Jesus wherever he went.

- He had freely chosen to go to Jerusalem and, at the very least, he must have known that there would be great tension if not violence resulting from his presence there. Even his disciples thought he was going there to proclaim himself king (Luke 18:31-34).

Jerusalem

Herod the Great transformed Jerusalem from a well-populated but unspectacular center of religion to an important provincial city. He built many public amenities, including an amphitheater, and reconstructed the Temple. This is a reconstruction of the city in the first century, based on archaeological excavations.

Herod's Palace

The Hinnom valley, a smouldering rubbish pit which sometimes was featured in Jesus' teaching

The Pool of Siloam. Jesus sent a blind man to wash here after he had been healed

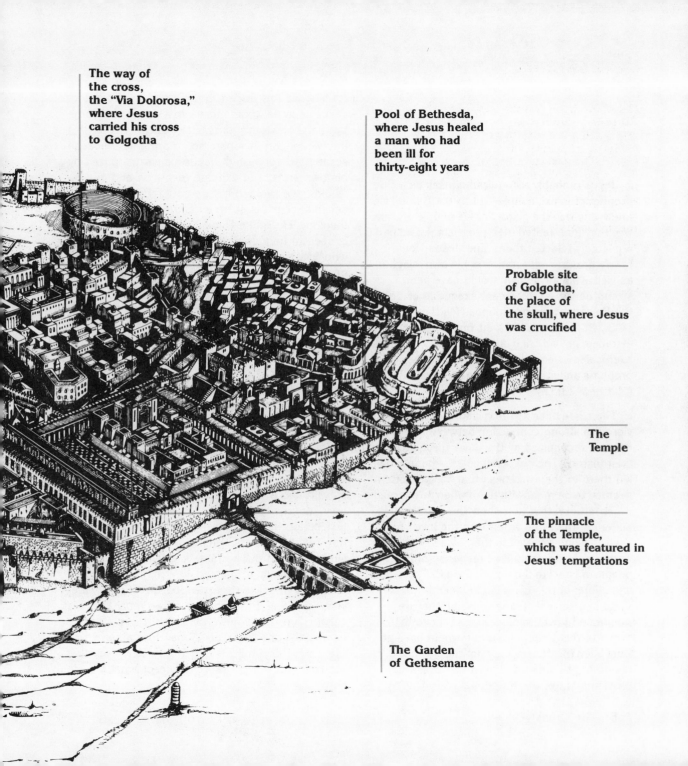

The way of
the cross,
the "Via Dolorosa,"
where Jesus
carried his cross
to Golgotha

Pool of Bethesda,
where Jesus healed
a man who had
been ill for
thirty-eight years

Probable site
of Golgotha,
the place of
the skull, where Jesus
was crucified

The
Temple

The pinnacle
of the Temple,
which was featured in
Jesus' temptations

The Garden
of Gethsemane

• Jesus probably recognized himself as a true prophet of Israel, as one "led by the Spirit." He knew very well the history of his people and the way they had treated their prophets. Israel had repeatedly rejected them, and Jesus would have a growing expectation of his own rejection as well. This awareness would have been strengthened by the recent execution of John the Baptist by Herod Antipas (Matthew 14:3-12; Mark 6:17-29). At one point, for instance, he had cried out over the city of David, "Jerusalem, Jerusalem, you that kill the prophets and stone those who are sent to you!" (Matthew 23:37).

• There had been a strong linking of death and victory, a strong connection between hope and despair, recognized by the Jews throughout their history. Their experience as a people had led them to the awareness that Yahweh often seemed to be most with them when he seemed most remote, that somehow the greater their suffering, the more vividly was the love of Yahweh being revealed to them. We saw this, for example, in the faith-filled response of the people of Israel to their captivity in Babylon, and reflections of this can also be seen in the Suffering Servant theme of Isaiah that we mentioned briefly earlier. Jesus was certainly aware of this tradition, and he would have at least seen the possibility, if not the likelihood, of his having to suffer and even die for his proclamation of the Kingdom.

Given all this evidence, therefore, it is likely that Jesus knew he would meet with a violent end some day—if not at this time, then later. Why is this knowledge on his part so important? Because some have suggested that Jesus was surprised by his own arrest and ultimate execution and that he would have avoided it if he could. But Jesus' free acceptance of his death is central to all of Christian theology. **The entire Good News crumbles if Jesus is seen to be a confused and misguided dreamer who was somehow fooled by circumstances, or as one who would sacrifice his convictions by running away in fear if only he had known what was coming.** This is why, in reflecting upon Jesus in Gethsemane, it is so important to recognize the basic human struggle he was experiencing between fear and the desire to run away and the even stronger commitment to the will of his Father:

"Abba (Father), everything is possible for you. Take this cup [death] away from me. *But let it be as you, not I, would have it*" (Mark 14:36).

This is a very dramatic departure from the other stories of martyrs which were popular in religions even before the time of Jesus. In those stories, as with those of our modern TV and movie "heroes," the martyr faces death with courage and firm resignation, hardly showing a sign of fear. Jesus, however, was no such fictional character, no actor simply playing out a dramatic role. He was a man who was totally immersed in our human experience and who, like us, experienced profound loneliness and fear. But he found, as we must also, his consolation, his source of strength, his ultimate hope in the one he called "Abba," his Father. And it was in his commitment to his Father's will that Jesus found the courage to accept what was to come.

4) Arrest and Trial

Jesus was arrested during that evening in Gethsemane by Jewish officials, by "the chief priests and captains of the Temple guard and elders who had come for him" (Luke 22:52). His Apostles fled in fear. He was led first before the Great Sanhedrin, the official governing body of the Jews. There is some dispute among scholars on whether the meeting between the Sanhedrin and Jesus actually constituted an official trial. It was more likely a kind of "court of inquiry" in which the Jewish aristocracy met to discuss and eventually determine what charge to level against Jesus in a future trial before the Romans. **The Jewish leaders clearly wanted Jesus dead, but they did not have the authority to carry out the death penalty in Judea while under Roman control.** That is why they needed the cooperation of the Romans if they hoped to rid themselves of Jesus for good.

It was during his confrontation with the Sanhedrin that Jesus was asked the fateful question by Caiaphas, the high priest, the question which—along with Jesus' answer—would eventually lead to his execution. Caiaphas, becoming frustrated with Jesus' refusal to answer the questions of the other priests, asks Jesus directly, " 'Are you the Christ, the Son of the Blessed One?' 'I am,' said Jesus, 'and you will see the Son of Man seated at the right hand of the Power and coming from the clouds of heaven' " (Mark 14:61-62). As we have seen, the Jews often substituted words like "Blessed One" or "Power" for God's name. Therefore, in this scene Jesus not only accepts the title of Messiah (Christ) from Caiaphas, but even expands that to include the image of one uniquely in touch with divinity, with God. The accounts of Matthew and Luke are even more direct and clear about this. For example, in Matthew's account the exchange between Jesus and Caiaphas goes this way:

> And the high priest said to him, "I put you on oath by the living God to tell us if you are the Christ, the Son of God." "The words are your own" answered Jesus. "Moreover, I tell you that from this time onward you will see the Son of Man seated at the right hand of the Power and coming on the clouds of heaven." At this the high priest tore his clothes and said, "He has blasphemed. What need of witnesses have we now? There! You have just heard the blasphemy. What is your opinion?" They answered, "He deserves to die" (Matthew 26:63-66).

To "blaspheme" means to show a lack of reverence to God or, more specifically in this case, to claim for oneself a dignity due to God alone. It was *not* Jesus' claim to be the Messiah that caused such a furor among the Jewish leaders. Other men had made that claim before him, and others would make it after his death. According to the gospel accounts, what totally shocked and appalled the members of the Sanhedrin, rather, was Jesus' apparent claim to somehow be divine himself which he expressed through the striking biblical imagery of being "seated at the right hand of Power and coming on the clouds of heaven." By making such a claim, Jesus had clearly gone too far; he had taken the final, fateful step toward virtually guaranteeing his execution. He had almost backed his accusers into a corner by confronting them with a direct statement about his own identity, and they responded with a charge they could make stick—blasphemy.

Pontius Pilate.

So the Jewish leadership now had an official offense with which to charge Jesus. Their problem was how to carry out the death penalty they had determined for that offense. They needed the help of the Romans. So the following morning they took Jesus before the Roman procurator, Pontius Pilate. Pilate appeared somewhat indifferent about the whole affair, even sympathetic to the plight of Jesus. This was, after all, apparently a religious conflict within the ranks of the Jews themselves. Why bother *him* about the matter? Pilate could not accept the charge of blasphemy as a sufficient reason for execution. That was a religious offense, not a political one in any way threatening the Roman state. Claims of messiahship, even claims of divinity, were not enough to bother him. So the Jewish priests and elders offered several alternative charges (see Luke 23:2-7):

1) "We found this man inciting our people to revolt," they said. By this they likely meant that Jesus was challenging their own authority as leaders of the Jews, a charge which would not greatly concern the Romans.

2) "We found this man . . . opposing payment of the tribute to Caesar," they said. Even if this could be demonstrated as true, it was not an offense punishable by death under Roman law.

3) "We found this man . . . claiming to be Christ, a king," they said. Pilate remained unmoved by the charges.

Looking for a way out.

Luke's gospel then includes a scene not contained in Matthew or Mark. The Jewish leaders

persist in their angry accusations about Jesus in front of Pilate: "He is inflaming the people with his teaching all over Judea; it (his teaching) has come all the way from Galilee, where it started, down to here." Pilate sees his opening, his way out. "He asked if (Jesus) was a Galilean; and finding that he came under Herod's jurisdiction, he passed him over to Herod who was also in Jerusalem at that time" (Luke 23:5-7). You might remember from our discussion in chapter 5 that this was Herod Antipas, son of Herod the Great, who had been given authority over the region of Galilee after his father's death. The fact that Jesus was a Galilean, combined with the coincidence that Herod Antipas was in Jerusalem at that time, gave Pilate a possible way out of his dilemma. The importance of this is primarily the demonstration of Pilate's real struggle to avoid condemning Jesus. He was clearly in a bind. Pilate knew that Jesus wasn't guilty of anything deserving death, but it seemed he faced only two choices in the matter. He could release Jesus and further infuriate the Jews who already appeared near rioting during a major religious feast. Such a riot at that time, when the population of Jerusalem swelled with hundreds of thousands of Jewish pilgrims, would have greatly disturbed Pilate's Roman superiors. His other choice was to condemn an innocent man and then live with that fact on his conscience. The presence of Herod had given him an "out."

The problem was that Herod didn't want to condemn Jesus either. Instead, according to Luke, "Herod was delighted to see Jesus; he had heard about him and had been waiting for a long time to set eyes on him; moreover, he was hoping to see some miracle worked by him" (Luke 23:8). Jesus, of course, refuses to respond to such expectations,

and Herod and his guards "treated him with contempt and made fun of him . . . and sent him back to Pilate" (Luke 23:11).

"I am innocent . . ."

Pilate continued to avoid any condemnation of Jesus, but the angry cries of the Jewish leaders became more and more intense. He had one remaining option. It was his practice to release a Jewish prisoner during major religious festivals. He offered the Jewish leaders a choice: He could release either Jesus or another "notorious prisoner" named—perhaps coincidentally—"Barabbas," a name meaning "son of the father." The Jewish leaders made it clear what they wanted. They screamed for Pilate to release Barabbas, and in response to Pilate's inquiry about what to do with Jesus, they cried out, "Let him be crucified!" Pilate realized his situation was apparently hopeless. In a gesture contained only in Matthew, "he took some water, washed his hands in front of the crowd and said, 'I am innocent of this man's blood. It is your concern.' . . . Then he released Barabbas for them. He ordered Jesus to be first scourged and then handed over to be crucified" (Matthew 27:25). **The "official" Roman charge against Jesus was that he had incited a revolt among the Jews.**

The simple washing of his hands, of course, cannot truly cleanse Pilate of the guilt he was to share for the execution of Jesus. Some have tried to minimize his role in the trial, and there is a reasonable chance that the authors of the gospels did so in an attempt to more clearly identify the Jewish leaders as the people chiefly responsible for Jesus' death. But the evidence is that Pilate, under pressure from an angry mob, condemned a man he knew to be innocent to death by crucifixion.

5) Scourging and Crucifixion

Of all the material contained in the gospel accounts of the arrest, trial, and crucifixion of Jesus, the *least* detailed discussion is given to his actual execution. After all the building tension and conflict, the touching and tragic encounter in Gethsemane, the hurried but complex inquiry and eventual trial, the execution of Jesus is described quickly and with near frightening simplicity. He was first ridiculed for his claim to kingship and given a soldier's scarlet cloak as a mocking tribute. A "crown" formed from a thorny plant was pressed onto his head. He was then scourged, a common preliminary beating to the actual crucifixion. During the scourging, Jesus was whipped with leather straps which had either bone or metal chips imbedded in or attached to them. The scourging could be terribly brutal, many times leading to the death of the prisoner as his flesh was literally torn from his body. Jesus survived.

They then gave Jesus the crossbeam to carry—not the entire cross as so many paintings have depicted it—and he was led to a small hill or mound called Golgatha, meaning "the skull" perhaps because of its shape. There he was placed on his back with his arms stretched across the beam he had been carrying. He was nailed through his wrists to the beam which was then "raised up" and attached to an upright beam which was left permanently in the ground. Once elevated, Jesus' body was tied to the cross with ropes around his arms, legs, and stomach in order to keep his body from tearing free of the nails which held it. The cross also had a small "seat" built into the upright beam on which the body could rest to ensure longer life and therefore greater suffering. A placard was nailed to the beam above Jesus' head, bearing not the official charge of *sedition* (the legal term for causing a rebellion or insurrection) for which he was being executed but, rather, the mocking title of "King of the Jews." And he was left to hang there between two thieves until he died.

"Father, into your hands . . ."

Crucifixion was often a brutally long method of execution, sometimes allowing a man to hang for a week or more on the cross until he finally died from either bleeding or choking to death. According to the gospel accounts, Jesus died in six hours or less, surprising both Pilate and the guards. Only John's account mentioned the piercing of his side with a spear to ensure Jesus' death before the Sabbath observance (John 19:31-36). It was against the Jewish religious laws to have a body on the cross during the Sabbath, and the Jews—again according to John alone—requested that the legs of the three crucified men be broken to hasten their death. By the time the soldiers approached Jesus, however, he had already died.

Only Luke of the three synoptic accounts clearly mentions Jesus' last words before he died. In Matthew and Mark, Jesus is said to "cry out in a loud voice" before "yielding up his spirit," that is, before dying. Luke places words on Jesus' lips at that moment, words that, if not spoken by Jesus verbally, no doubt reflect the attitude he carried with him to his death: " 'Father, into your hands I commit my spirit.' With these words he breathed his last" (Luke 23:46).

A mural on the Catholic Worker house in Los Angeles

What does Jesus' death mean?

The struggle to come to terms with the death of Jesus throughout our history as a Church has led to a wide variety of expressions, symbols, and theological interpretations. Certainly the cross has a profound and complex significance for us, one quite literally too great for words. Jesus' death has been referred to as a "sacrifice," perhaps reflecting the Passover themes mentioned earlier. It is said that "Jesus died for our sins," that he "justified us," that he "gave his life as a ransom" for us. **It would be easy but dangerous to settle on any one image to capture the complex meaning of the cross, because in doing so we risk seriously misinterpreting its meaning.** For example, perhaps the most popular statement about the death of Jesus is that "he died for our sins." Unfortunately this terminology is often confusing for the modern reader, because it can imply an image of God that is far removed from that which Jesus revealed to us. Such a statement can give a sense, for instance, that Jesus somehow had to die in our place in order to satisfy an angry God who was demanding his "pound of flesh" in payment for past offenses. In this case, God is given an image directly contrary to the very message of Jesus himself, that of a God who is a totally loving and forgiving Father.

Jesus' death can be understood as a decisive battle in God's war with the forces of evil, a battle that would be proved a victory with Jesus' Resurrection. And in Mark 10:45, Jesus states that "the Son of Man himself did not come to be served but to serve, and to give his life as a ransom for many." When properly understood, this too can be a helpful image for us. In the Roman world a "ransom" was the price paid to release a slave, and it was often paid by a third party. This payment would be made in front of a shrine to a local god to indicate that the slave was now the property of that god and that he or she could no longer be owned by another person. This can be an appropriate image for understanding the cross if we recognize Jesus' death as liberating us from our slavery to sin by demonstrating the incredibly freeing power of a love that knows no limits.

Ultimately it is this—the unconditional love of God for people—that must be the message gained from the death of Jesus. As St. John would say years later:

> Anyone who fails to love can never have known God, for God is love. God's love for us was revealed when God sent into the world his only Son so that we could have life through him; this is the love I mean: not our love for God, but God's love for us when he sent his Son to be the sacrifice that takes our sins away. My dear people, since God has loved us so much, we too should love one another (1 John 4:8-11).

The Resurrection: God's victory over death.

Our major cause of difficulty in understanding Jesus' death at this point in our discussion is that we are, in a sense, asking the question of its meaning too soon. Ultimately we cannot understand the execution of Jesus until we understand what followed it—his being raised from the dead by his Father. None of the gospels ends with the apparent failure of Jesus' passion and death on the cross. Rather we first see Jesus' total trust in God at the moment of his death—"Into your hands, Father, I commit my spirit"—and then the vindication of that trust in the Resurrection. It is to this central and pivotal factor in the Good News that we now turn.

1) Why did Jesus seem to "cause conflict and tension wherever he went," as the author claims?

2) What are the three reasons given for the uniquely detailed and extensive accounts of the arrest, trial, and crucifixion of Jesus provided in the gospels?

3) At the Last Supper, Jesus referred to his execution and spoke about a "new covenant in my blood" which was to be established through his death on the cross. Where did this notion of covenant come from, and in what way was Jesus establishing a "new" one?

4) Why do some scholars think that our common image of Judas is perhaps an unfair one?

5) Give three reasons why Jesus likely knew he was going to die even before his arrest in the garden. In what way does Jesus' terror of his approaching death differ from that of many other martyrs and heroes?

6) The author states that it was *not* Jesus' claim to be the Messiah that prompted the outrage of members of the Sanhedrin. What *did* anger them so? And what was the official charge against Jesus determined by the Sanhedrin?

7) Why did the Jewish leaders have to seek the help of the Romans in order to rid themselves of Jesus for good?

8) Why could Pilate not accept the Jewish charges against Jesus as a reason for executing him? What was the official offense with which Jesus was eventually charged by the Roman authorities?

9) Why is it dangerous to try to settle on just one interpretation of or statement about the death of Jesus? What, according to the author, must ultimately be the message gained from the death of Jesus?

Terms to identify and remember:

Passover meal	Caiaphas
Judas	blasphemy
Gethsemane	sedition

Exercise for personal reflection:

There are many events in Jesus' life that lead us to quiet and reflective prayer rather than to discussion or study. His brutal scourging and execution certainly seem to be such events. Since the fourteenth century, a popular way for the community of faith to reflect on the passion of Jesus has been by following "the Way of the Cross," reflecting on the fourteen "stations" traditionally displayed on the walls of our churches. This is particularly practiced on Fridays during the season of Lent. This devotion can also be a deeply prayerful exercise when practiced by individuals. As a means of reflecting on the contents of this chapter, you are encouraged to meditate on the stations alone at your parish church or in your school chapel, perhaps aided by a guide provided by your teacher.

11
The Resurrection: God Is Victorious! Jesus Is Lord!

When the sabbath was over, Mary of Magdala, Mary the mother of James, and Salome, bought spices with which to go and anoint him [Jesus]. And very early in the morning of the first day of the week they went to the tomb, just as the sun was rising.

They had been saying to one another, "Who will roll away the stone for us from the entrance of the tomb?" But when they looked they could see that the stone—which was very big—had already been rolled back. On entering the tomb they saw a young man in a white robe seated on the right-hand side, and they were struck with amazement. But he said to them, "There is no need for alarm. You are looking for Jesus of Nazareth, who was crucified: he has risen, he is not here. See, here is the place where they laid him. But you must go and tell his disciples and Peter, 'He is going before you to Galilee; it is there you will see him, just as he told you.'" And the women came out and ran away from the tomb because they were frightened out of their wits; and they said nothing to a soul, for they were afraid . . . (Mark 16:1-8).

1) A Few Basic Questions

Anyone trying to understand Christian faith must resolve many questions. Among the most basic are these:

1) How did a world-wide religious movement proclaiming hope and love grow out of the horror which was the crucified Jesus?

2) How did a man like Jesus, condemned in his own time as a teacher of heresy, become recognized by a quarter of the human race as Messiah, Lord, and Savior?

3) How did a man who proclaimed the Kingdom of God as the center of his own life and teaching become himself the apparent center of the religion that today claims him as its founder?

There is ultimately only one answer for such questions: The only reason the story of the passion and death of Jesus discussed in the last chapter has been recalled and passed on for some two thousand years is that it was followed by an event that gave meaning to it—Easter, the raising of Jesus from the dead by his Father.

What happened?

Each of the gospels tells of the Resurrection of Jesus and of some of his appearances to his disciples and others after it: Matthew 28:1-20; Mark 16:1-20; Luke 24:1-53; and John 21:1-29. As we will note in a moment, there are many conflicts in these accounts which are important to recognize, but we can arrive at a basic sense of what occurred that remarkable Sunday morning long ago.

After the death of Jesus, his body was claimed by a Jewish man named Joseph of Arimathaea who had asked Pilate for the right to take the corpse and give it a decent burial. The common practice of the day would have called for the body simply to be thrown into a pit with those of other executed criminals. Joseph took the corpse, wrapped it in a burial cloth called a shroud, and then laid it in a tomb hewn out of stone. A large, round, flat stone was then rolled into place at the entrance of the tomb. Matthew's gospel states that Roman soldiers were assigned to guard the tomb to prevent Jesus' disciples from stealing the body. There was a concern that they would steal the corpse and then claim that Jesus had risen from the dead as he had predicted he would when alive.

From this point on, each of the evangelists offers his own unique version of what happened. The common characteristics of the accounts are that various people go to the tomb and discover that the body of Jesus is no longer there. They find out—either on their own (in John) or through one or more messengers of God (in the synoptics)—that Jesus is no longer dead but alive, and that he will reveal himself to them again soon. The initial reactions of the witnesses are, quite naturally, fear and total disbelief. But soon they actually experience Jesus among them in such clear and striking ways that there can be no doubt it is he—alive again, and yet somehow very different from when he had walked among them before his death. He was risen, and everything he had claimed was proved true by that fact!

We have mentioned that there are many conflicts in the gospel accounts of the Resurrection of Jesus, most of which are easily recognized with just a quick reading of all the accounts. **It is clear that the evangelists were not trying to provide us with an exact historical record of what had happened.** There are too many apparent contradictions in who actually arrived at the tomb first, what they discovered when getting there, how many angels were present, what they looked like, and so on. Some might look at these contradictions as an obvious demonstration of the fictional nature of these accounts, proof that the Resurrection did not actually occur. But the believer can easily offer a different argument: If the evangelists were in fact trying to trick or deceive us, would they not have made sure that all the accounts were in agreement with each other? One of the basic lessons we learn from the gospels is this: The small details involved in the Resurrection accounts are not significant or essential to what is being revealed through them. There are truths being expressed in and through the Resurrection accounts that far surpass any confusion that might be apparent in them.

2) Proclamations of Faith

The gospel accounts, first of all, are not attempts to record the Resurrection as a historical event but, rather, are proclamations or statements of faith about what had happened to Jesus. This does *not* mean that the Resurrection did not happen. On the contrary, the resurrected Jesus is the most consistently proclaimed reality in the entire Christian Scriptures. **But, by acknowledging the gospels as proclamations of faith rather than historical documents, we can avoid much of the confusion that is caused by trying to reconcile the accounts with one another.** The Resurrection of Jesus was simply not a historical event in our usual sense of that term. The passion and death of Jesus was historical in that even nonbelievers would have been able to see Jesus crucified. This was not true with the Resurrection. It is clear that *only* people of faith experienced Jesus risen, and even then sometimes with great difficulty and hesitation. The Risen Jesus could not be scientifically proven to exist. The Resurrection, in other words, is an event that goes beyond history as we know it.

Further evidence for accepting the Resurrection.

St. Paul, in his first letter to the Corinthians, stated, ". . . if Christ has not been raised, then our preaching is useless and your believing is useless . . . If our hope in Christ has been for this life only, we are the most unfortunate of people" (1 Corinthians 15:14, 19). **There is simply no factor in Christian faith that is more central, more important, or more critical to our understanding of the Jesus of History as the Christ of Faith than the Resurrection.** Without trying to overdo our discussion here, there is still more evidence attesting to the reality of the raising of Jesus from the dead by his Father. We offer it not out of a concern that people are filled with doubt about this, but rather in the hope that further discussion will truly impress us with the central importance of the Resurrection in the entire Christian message. Consider the following insights:

1) **The Resurrection was a consistent belief in the early Church.** The early sermons contained in the Acts of the Apostles, the letters of St. Paul, and, of course, all four gospels mention it. In the Acts of the Apostles we see that experiencing the Risen Jesus was even considered a key qualification for being accepted as an Apostle (Acts 1:21-22).

2) **The empty tomb and the appearances of Jesus together testify to the reality of the Resurrection.** Although there is a lot of disagreement among the accounts of the Resurrection, all of them agree on two major points: that the tomb was empty and that Jesus appeared to reliable witnesses.

- **Regarding the fact that the tomb was empty, it is important to point out that the Romans would surely have produced a corpse of Jesus if they could have found one.** Publicly displaying his dead body for all to see would have immediately destroyed any stories of his Resurrection falsely created by his disciples. But, it might be asked, could the disciples have somehow stolen and then either hidden or destroyed the corpse? The problem with this proposition is that many of the disciples would eventually choose to die as martyrs rather than deny their faith in a resurrected Jesus. Would they freely die for a belief in a buried corpse? Moreover, the gospels identify women as major witnesses to the empty tomb. We discussed the role of women earlier in this book, and we know that they were not accepted as legal witnesses in Jewish society. No author would have relied upon them, therefore, unless the incidents described were based on facts.

● What about the appearances, or what we call "apparitions" of Jesus? **Though no one actually witnessed the Resurrection itself, many claimed to have experienced the Risen Jesus later.** The gospels disagree on who saw him where and when and under what circumstances, but there is a common pattern to the appearances: Everyone to whom Jesus appears is downcast, depressed, clearly convinced that he is dead. Jesus then takes the initiative and reveals himself to them, always greeting them with a statement that they should be unafraid and at peace. Finally, he often gives them a command, such as "Go, therefore, and make disciples of all nations" (Matthew 28:19), or "Go out to the whole world; proclaim the Good News to all creation" (Mark 16:16). The knowledge of Jesus risen is not to be kept secret as a kind of private revelation. Those who know him are clearly called to share that knowledge with others.

Both the empty tomb and the appearances of Jesus are important to one another because one firms up and solidifies the other. Without the empty tomb, the appearances of Jesus could be regarded as hallucinations, as the fantasies of depressed people. Without the appearances, on the other hand, the empty tomb could be considered a hoax.

3) Finally, and perhaps most importantly of all, **a thoroughly shattered band of Jesus' followers was transformed into a community of courageous witnesses after the Resurrection.** Their total conviction in what they proclaimed—a Risen Jesus and a

The Three Marys, a miniature from a book of the Psalms, dated about 1200

message of joy and hope—is undeniable. It was, after all, only such a conviction and the commitment to share faith in Jesus motivated by it that can explain the beginning and, indeed, the continuation of the Church. How can such total commitment be explained without a real, rather than an imaginary, Resurrection?

Another theory . . . and a response.

Some have proposed that Jesus was not actually raised from the dead but, rather, that the authors of the Christian Scriptures created a Resurrection story to explain or express an interior experience on the part of the disciples themselves. Unlike the questions posed above, this is neither a matter of doubting the sincerity or honesty of the witnesses nor of suspecting them of hallucinations. Rather, this proposal suggests that the disciples and others

truly experienced the continuing presence of Jesus among them, and that this experience was very much a personal and interior one on their parts. They then—according to this proposal—used the literary techniques of their day and created a story which somehow expressed their interior experience.

This is a serious question to consider, for only if God *actually and truly* conquered death through the Resurrection of Jesus can it be said that God not only glorified Jesus but thereby validated both him and his message. If Jesus did not personally rise from the dead in a very real way, then the gospel proclamation is not Good News but open to rejection as a lie, a hoax, a fantasy, or a dream.

There are many scenes in the gospels that depict Jesus personally encountering people in ways that clearly demonstrate it was he, alive and present, not simply experienced by them in some interior way.

Some ancient tombs
like this one
had many rooms

This seems to be the case in those beautiful scenes in which the Risen Jesus directly touches people (John 20:27), eats with them (Luke 24:41-43), and talks with them (John 21:15-22). At the same time, the gospels indicate that there was clearly something very different about Jesus after his Resurrection. For instance, at times he is not recognized even by his own disciples (Luke 24:15; John 20:14). Some of his closest friends even doubt that it is he (Matthew 28:17; Luke 24:41). And Jesus is shown coming and going freely, completely breaking all restrictions of time and space (Luke 24:31; John 20:19-26).

Jesus is therefore depicted in the gospels as truly transformed through the Resurrection. He was experiencing an utterly new kind of existence. The Risen Jesus was not simply a corpse which had somehow come back to life nor a person asleep who had suddenly been awakened. He was the same Jesus and yet completely different! Resurrected life is neither simply the return to the kind of earthly life we experience nor just the continuation of this life after death. It is, rather, an entirely new way of living, a new relationship in and with God, something completely beyond our imagination. How can we explain this kind of life? The simple answer—we can't! Nor can it be explained how the authors of the Christian Scriptures might somehow imagine or intentionally create such a profound vision. **It would seem that the evidence from the gospels supporting the actual and real Resurrection of Jesus is too complex and too thorough to imagine it being the creation of any one author, let alone of several authors working at least to some degree independently of one another.**

3) What Does the Resurrection Mean?

There are likely some who will read all of the information, evidence, and arguments in defense of belief in the Resurrection of Jesus presented here and conclude it all with a shrug of the shoulders and a yawn. Such a response may simply reflect a persons' honest lack of interest in this discussion at this point in his or her life. Real "life and death issues" do not always seem all that important to us! A perhaps greater possibility, however, is that we have not yet been clear enough in presenting the tremendous significance of the Resurrection of Jesus for us. So let's be very direct about it. Here are some of the implications of the Resurrection:

1) **The Resurrection of Jesus is proof that, in all his claims and teachings about God, Jesus was speaking the truth.**

2) **The Resurrection proves that Jesus was and is the Messiah, the Christ, and Lord of the universe,** not just a good man with a marvelous but mistaken dream.

3) **The Resurrection of Jesus transforms our understanding of all human life.** Because of the Resurrection we realize that "fullness of life" and happiness are not to be achieved merely through

rigid religious practices or through some new self-improvement program. Rather our lives are given a new "center," a new "life force" if you will, a new source of power. That new power in our lives is nothing less than God, the God revealed in and through Jesus Christ. "I live now not with my own life," said St. Paul, "but with the life of Christ who lives in me" (Galatians 2:20).

4) The Resurrection of Jesus promises us a share in "eternal life." What God did in Jesus is made available to each of us as well. This means not only that we can experience God within us now but also that we can do so throughout eternity. The Resurrection of Jesus is nothing less than a pledge and a promise that we too will survive death!

The Resurrection, in other words, affirms that *Jesus was right.* In his claim about God's unconditional love for each of us, *he was right.* In his promise that we can find fulfillment in loving God and one another, *he was right.* In his rejection of empty religious ritual and in his commitment to a prayerful and personal relationship with God, *he was right.* In his conviction that forgiveness of one another will always be more life-giving and enriching than revenge, *he was right.* In his profound respect and special affection for the outcasts of society, *he was right.* In his teaching that the rich must share with the poor, *he was right.* In his absolute refusal to accept anything that would separate people from one another—social status, sexual and racial discrimination, economic standing, political affiliation, even religious beliefs—*he was right.* And ultimately this means that, in accepting Jesus as our Lord and Savior, *we are right!*

Our discussion of the Resurrection has been a challenging one, but necessarily so. Our commitment throughout this book has been to share an understanding of Jesus and the Christian faith that is solidly based and reliable. On no topic we have discussed is it more crucial that we maintain that commitment than in our discussion of the Resurrection of Jesus. Our Christian faith, quite literally, rises or falls with this event. In trying to understand and speak about the Risen Jesus, it is important that we avoid two extremes: We cannot become so philosophical or defensive that we make it seem there was no Resurrection at all, that it is in some way more an idea or myth rather than a reality. But at the same time we cannot be so simplistic, so literal in our understanding of Scripture, and so concrete and physical in our discussion that we make it seem that the Risen Jesus could be experienced even by nonbelievers. That was not the case two thousand years ago, and it is not the case today. Perhaps the greatest lesson to learn from our discussion is this: In discussing the Risen Jesus, we are plunging headlong into a nearly overwhelming mystery, a mystery that can be incredibly exciting and freeing for those who recognize it as truth!

4) The Ascension of Jesus

What happened to Jesus after his Resurrection and his appearances to the disciples and others? Our immediate inclination is to respond that he "went to heaven." But where and what is heaven? And how did he get from here to "there"? These are perhaps obvious and simple questions, but they have anything but simple answers. The Christian Scriptures deal with these issues in the context of what is called the "Ascension" of Jesus into the presence of his Father. It will likely no longer surprise you to learn that there are contradictions and differences evident in the various scriptural references to this "event":

- **Specific mention of the Ascension of Jesus as a historical event is made only in Luke 24:50-53 and in the second part of Luke's work which we call the Acts of the Apostles.** In his gospel account, Luke simply says this: "Then (Jesus) took them out as far as the outskirts of Bethany, and lifting up his hands he blessed them. Now as he blessed them he withdrew from them and was carried up to heaven . . ." In the account of the Ascension given in Acts, Jesus promises his disciples that they "will receive power when the Holy Spirit comes on (them)" and then, "As he said this he was lifted up while they looked on, and a cloud took him from their sight. They were still staring into the sky when suddenly two men in white were standing near them and they said, 'Why are you men from Galilee standing here looking into the sky? Jesus who has been taken up from you into heaven,

this same Jesus will come back in the same way as you have seen him go there' " (Acts 1:6-11).

- **In Luke's gospel it appears that the Resurrection and Ascension of Jesus occur on the same day, while in the Acts of the Apostles it is specifically stated that forty days passed between the Resurrection and Ascension.**

- **Matthew doesn't mention the Ascension at all, and the brief mention of the event in Mark 16:19 may have been added to Mark's original gospel.**

- **There are only two very brief references to the Ascension in all the epistles (1 Timothy 3:16; 1 Peter 3:22).**

It should be noted that there *are* numerous texts in the Christian Scriptures which make reference to Jesus' presence with the Father "in heaven." We have previously mentioned cases when, for instance, Jesus is spoken of as "seated at the right hand of God" or when it is said that "in the end time" Jesus will "come again in glory." But our major point here is to affirm our recognition of the Scriptures as unique kinds of writing that are intended to express *meaning* as much as, and even more than, historical events. The authors of the Scriptures were dealing with realities that simply go beyond our understanding of the world and beyond our ability to express that understanding within the limits of our language.

Right here, right now.

A major limitation experienced by both the evangelists and ourselves is the fact that we are almost forced to deal with images of space and time in our speaking, writing, and even thinking.

For example, when we think of "heaven" we automatically think of "up there." We may well have inherited that tendency from the writers of Scripture, who had a view of the world which to modern eyes may appear very simplistic. The people of Jesus' day viewed the universe as consisting of several "layers": the earth itself, the "heavens" above it which included the sky and stars, and then the "underworld" or the "abode of the dead" which lay beneath the earth. The people imagined the realm or world of God as existing beyond the heavens. It was natural for the authors of Scripture, therefore, to express their recognition of Jesus as the Risen Messiah through these images of time and space, stating that Jesus was "lifted into the heavens" at a particular time and place. But again we must ask our basic and important question: *What does this mean?*

The major lesson of the Ascension is that, following his Resurrection, Jesus passed totally into the presence of his Father, God. In doing so he moved beyond our experience of the limitations of time and space. Though difficult to comprehend, this is a profoundly important reality for us. What this *actually* means—strangely enough—is precisely the opposite of what we often *assume* it to mean. When we speak of the Risen Jesus as "going to his Father," we naturally understand that as a removal of Jesus from our human experience, as a separation of him from us. But we must reflect upon a critical question and its answer: Where is God, the Father of Jesus? Is it right to speak and think of God as "out there" somewhere? It would seem that the entire message of Jesus hinges on precisely the opposite belief—that "the Kingdom of God is among you," that God is not "out there" but rather "right here."

Even as small children we acknowledge God as "being everywhere." But think of what this incredible reality implies. **If God is totally present, if God is "right here and right now," then by "going to the Father" Jesus was actually becoming more fully and truly** *present* **to us than he could possibly be as he walked the roads of Palestine!** Now free of the limitations of time and space which bind us, Jesus can be totally with us. He is no longer tied down to one place at one time talking about one thing to one particular group of people as was true two thousand years ago. Rather he is now free to be everywhere, with everyone, for all time, loving and caring and calling us back to his Father. What a marvelous reality! What incredibly Good News!

But if Jesus has moved beyond our limitations of time and space, how do we find and experience him present among us? We will discuss this question a bit more at the end of this book, but for now we look to the words of Jesus himself for our answer. He said, "Insofar as you did this to one of the least of these brothers of mine, you did it to me" (Matthew 25:40). We discover Jesus in our loving relationships with one another. He said, "Where two or three meet in my name, I shall be there with them" (Matthew 18:20). We discover Jesus in the community of believing Christians, those gathered "in his name," the Church. At the Last Supper Jesus took the bread and cup and said, "This is my body which will be given for you; do this as a memorial of me" (Luke 22:19). We discover Jesus in a special and unique way in the celebration of Eucharist, the Mass. And if, despite his constant presence among us, we feel we cannot find Jesus and we lose our sense of his presence, we must continually call back to mind and acknowledge within our hearts the promise he made to his disciples and, through them, to us: ". . . know that I am with you always; yes, to the end of time" (Matthew 28:20).

5) The Titles of Jesus

It was only after his Resurrection, Ascension, and the gift of the Holy Spirit at the event we call Pentecost (which will be discussed in the next chapter), that Jesus' true identity was recognized by his disciples and others. Even after the experience of him risen, however, the early community of believers did not—in fact, could not—settle on one particular title or expression to capture the meaning Jesus had now taken on for them. The gospels and other writings in the Christian Scriptures include some fifty different titles for Jesus! Some of these—like "teacher" and "the Nazarene"—we have already mentioned. But what about the titles for Jesus that we as contemporary Christians so easily, perhaps even carelessly, use? The key titles of honor given Jesus in the Christian Scriptures are these: Lord, Messiah or Christ, Son of David, Son of Man, Servant of God, Savior, Redeemer, Son of God, and Word of God. It would be possible, quite literally, to write a book on each of these titles and its meaning for the early community of faith and for us. By looking at the frequency with which each title is used in the Scriptures, however, we can gain some sense of the popularity of each in the early Church:

- **"Son of David"** is used about 20 times, and refers to Jesus' roots in the line of David, the most revered king in the kingdom of Israel.

- **"Son of God"** is used some 75 times. As we will see below, this did not seem to mean to the early community of faith exactly what it means to us today.

- **"Son of Man"** occurs about 80 times. This is a very complex title carrying several meanings. It seems to refer at times simply to Jesus' humanity, and at other times it clearly refers to his role as Messiah.

- The title **"Lord,"** which we will discuss below, is used about 350 times in the Christian Scriptures.

- And, finally, the title **"Christ"** or **"the Christ"** is used a remarkable 500 times!

Jesus the Christ.

As we discussed earlier, the word *Christ* is based on the Greek translation of the Hebrew word *messiah,* and it means "the anointed one." Because of its roots in Jewish history, it is not too surprising that this title would be so popular among the writers of the Scriptures. It was initially used as a kind of adjective to describe Jesus after his Resurrection, so that he would be referred to by believers as "Jesus *the* Christ." This quickly, but perhaps unfortunately, became shortened to become almost a surname or family name for Jesus, so that he eventually was referred to as "Jesus Christ," the title we so commonly use for him today.

"Son of God" was a title that had been used in reference to the kings of the Israelite nation, and it was not unheard of for the Jews to refer to any particularly good or great man as *a* son of God. The writers of the Christian Scriptures, however—though occasionally using the title in this broad sense—often fundamentally changed the significance of the term by referring to Jesus as *the* Son of God, indicating his very special relationship to the Father. Jesus' unique relationship to God was often expressed in the Scriptures in the way he would refer to "my Father and your Father," indicating a radically different sense in which he was *the* Son of God and the way in which we might speak of ourselves—with justification and great joy!—as "sons and daughters of God." We will discuss the way in which this title took on greater significance through the history of the Church in the next chapter.

For the early community of believers, however, no phrase quite so fully and beautifully summed up all of Christian faith as did the powerful proclamation, "Jesus is Lord!" We discussed earlier the way in which the Jewish people avoided speaking the name of God, Yahweh, by substituting the word *Lord* and other expressions or words for God's name. This use of the word is common in many parts of the Christian Scriptures as well, and there are many times in which the title is used by Jesus himself in speaking to or about Yahweh, his Father. But rather quickly after his death and Resurrection, Jesus became popularly referred to by believers as "the Lord" or "our Lord." By giving Jesus this title, they were taking an almost unbelievably radical step, particularly for loyal and faithful Jews. For by calling him Lord they were proclaiming for Jesus a divine identity, a unity with Yahweh that was then—

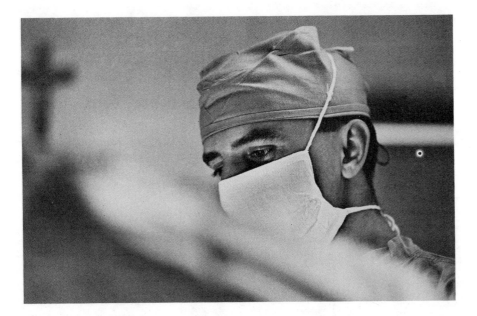

and in a very real sense, remains—absolutely beyond understanding. It must have erupted out of their hearts with profound joy and overwhelming awe: "Jesus is Lord . . . My God, he's God!" So thoroughly did this title sum up all that faith in Jesus implies that it was used as both a great Christian prayer of hope and as the closing words of the entire Bible. "The one who guarantees these revelations repeats his promise: I shall indeed be with you soon. Amen; come Lord Jesus! May the grace of the Lord Jesus be with you all. Amen" (Revelation 22:20-21). Amen, indeed!

Recognizing the Risen Jesus today.

For Christians today, the same depth of faith is required which was demanded of the first disciples if we are to "see" Jesus and to recognize him as Lord. Ultimately there is nothing to *force* us to believe, nothing which compels us to accept him

as Lord and Christ. There is, however, a great deal about Jesus that *invites* us to freely accept him and his message—his words, his actions, the values he professed and lived, the challenges he presented—all of which were proven worthy of our trust by the raising of Jesus from the dead by God. **The key criterion for judging or deciding if one is a Christian is this: whether one is willing to let one's life be shaped and led by the power of the life and message of Jesus.** This openness to a faith that is lived is of far greater importance than one's intellectual grasp of the kinds of difficult ideas we have shared in this chapter. The Risen Christ is revealed in and through loving Christians. "I live not now with my own life, but with the life of Christ who lives in me." This is, after all is said and done, what it means to discover and know the Risen Jesus and to meet God in and through him. And it is only then that the gospel becomes what we profess it to be—the Good News of salvation in Jesus Christ!

On the journey through history.

Throughout our long discussion of Jesus in this book, we have rarely if ever mentioned the words, teachings, and issues which we might most readily think of in contemporary discussions of him. During your education you have likely encountered many doctrines or Church teachings about Jesus: teachings about the Incarnation, discussions about his relationship to the Father and the Holy Spirit in the Trinity, the fact that he is "true God from true God, one in being with the Father," and so on. The reason we have delayed any discussion of these matters is that they can only reasonably be presented and understood in the context of the Church and its history. It is the Church which through the years developed the doctrines, traditions, and practices which are so familiar to most Christians. These realities cannot be effectively discussed solely in terms of the gospel proclamations of Jesus simply because they do not even appear in those sacred writings—at least not in the same sense and clear terminology with which we are familiar today. The official teachings of the Church about Jesus were developed over hundreds of years of reflection on his life, death, and Resurrection. We turn now to a discussion of that development.

Review questions and activities:

1) What, according to the author, is "the only reason the story of the passion and death of Jesus . . . has been recalled and passed on for some two thousand years"?

2) Why is it clear that the evangelists were not trying to provide us with an exact historical record of the Resurrection of Jesus?

3) The author provides many insights which lend support or evidence for belief in the Resurrection of Jesus. Give four reasons for accepting the truth of the Resurrection which most impressed you in your study of this material.

4) Is it accurate to think of the Resurrection as similar to a corpse being brought back to life, or like a sleeping person being awakened? Explain your answer.

5) What are four major implications of the Resurrection presented by the author? Which of the four impressed you most and why?

6) What, according to the author, is the major lesson of the Ascension of Jesus? In what ways do our limitations of time and space make it difficult to discuss and understand the meaning of the Ascension?

7) In what ways are we able to experience the Risen Jesus among us today?

8) What are the key titles of honor given Jesus in the Christian Scriptures? Which two were by far the most popular titles given him?

9) What short proclamation summed up all of Christian faith for the early community of believers? What incredible reality did this statement represent for them?

10) What, according to the author, is the criterion for deciding if one is Christian?

Terms to identify and remember:

Resurrection	Son of David
shroud	Son of God
apparitions	Son of Man
Ascension	Lord

Exercise for personal reflection:

The author writes in this chapter that we can encounter the Risen Jesus in many ways today: in our loving relationships with others; in the community of faith we call the Church; in the celebration of the Eucharist. Certainly there are many other ways as well in which we can get in touch with the living presence of Christ among us. Reflect on your own experience of faith to this point in your life. Can you identify an event or experience in your life when you felt particularly close to God or "in touch" with Christ? What circumstances may have helped to make that possible—attitudes or factors both within yourself and present in the situation as a whole? Can you learn anything from that experience that may indicate things you can do in your life now to make your awareness of God's presence more "real" and more constant for you?

12
Jesus Christ and the Church Through History

That very same day, two of them [the disciples] were on their way to a village called Emmaus, seven miles from Jerusalem, and they were talking together about all that had happened. Now as they talked this over, Jesus himself came up and walked by their side; but something prevented them from recognising him. He said to them, "What matters are you discussing as you walk along?" They stopped short, their faces downcast.

Then one of them, called Cleopas, answered him, "You must be the only person staying in Jerusalem who does not know the things that have been happening there these last few days." "What things?" he asked. "All about Jesus of Nazareth" they answered, "who proved he was a great prophet by the things he said and did in the sight of God and of the whole people; and how our chief priests and our leaders handed him over to be sentenced to death, and had him crucified. Our own hope had been that he would be the one to set Israel free. And this is not all: two whole days have gone by since it all happened; and some women from our group have astounded us: they went to the tomb in the early morning, and when they did not find the body, they came back to tell us they had seen a vision of angels who declared he was alive. Some of our friends went to the tomb and found everything exactly as the women had reported, but of him they saw nothing."

Then he said to them, "You foolish men! So slow to believe the full message of the prophets! Was it not ordained that the Christ should suffer and so enter into his glory?" Then, starting with Moses and going through all the prophets, he explained to them the passages throughout the scriptures that were about himself.

When they drew near to the village to which they were going, he made as if to go on; but they pressed him to stay with them. "It is nearly evening," they said, "and the day is almost over." So he went in to stay with them. Now while he was with them at table, he took the bread and said the blessing; then he broke it and handed it to them. And their eyes were opened and they recognised him; but he had vanished from their sight. Then they said to each other, "Did not our hearts burn within us as he talked to us on the road and explained the scriptures to us?"

They set out that instant and returned to Jerusalem. There they found the Eleven assembled together with their companions, who said to them, "Yes, it is true. The Lord has risen and has appeared to Simon." Then they told their story of what had happened on the road and how they recognised him at the breaking of the bread (Luke 24:13-35).

1) "Did Not Our Hearts Burn Within Us?"

The evangelist Luke was, among other things, a masterful story-teller. In this apparently simple but truly captivating story of two disciples on the road to Emmaus, he manages to sum up the entire Good News of Jesus. But Luke's story also provides us with insights into what it means to be a follower of Jesus as well as a member of the community which professes faith in him. Two confused and depressed disciples are joined by the Risen Jesus, but they are so wrapped up in their own grief about his recent crucifixion that they cannot recognize him. Jesus does not force himself upon them, nor does he dramatically reveal his identity in some miraculous way. Rather he simply walks with them, sharing their journey and listening to their story. They tell him of all the things we have discussed in this book to this point: of Jesus of Nazareth "who proved he was a great prophet by the things he said and did"; of how they had hoped that he would be the one who would set Israel free from its oppressors; of how he had been crucified; and of the stories they had just heard about his now being alive. And Jesus listens. "Then starting with Moses and going through all the prophets, he explain(s) to them the passages throughout the scriptures that were about himself." Still they do not recognize him, though they will recall later that their hearts "burned within them" as they listened to him speak.

As they approach the town of Emmaus, Jesus begins to move on. But now it is the disciples' turn to take the initiative, to show at least some degree of openness to what he can offer them. And they do so with the simple request that Jesus stay with them. Jesus, of course, accepts their invitation, and as they gather that evening for a simple meal, he again takes bread and wine as he had just a few days earlier, and again he blesses the bread, breaks it, and hands it to them. "And their eyes were opened . . . and they recognized him at the breaking of the bread."

Remember, sometimes believing is "seeing."

This is a story about what it means to "recognize the Risen Jesus," a task which ultimately confronts all who would choose to be his followers. The very word *recognition* is significant. It is based on two words: *re-*, meaning to do something again, and *cognoscere,* a Latin word meaning "to know." So in the act of recognition we come to know something or someone again, we experience a rediscovery or renewed awareness of a reality which we had already experienced before. This is what happened to the disciples on the road to Emmaus. In the simple act of blessing and breaking bread, Jesus is recognized. Suddenly the disciples rediscover him, and all the memories of what they had shared before his death flood back upon them. They come to the overwhelming realization that Jesus is alive, present, with them. And what is their response to that realization, to their recognition of Jesus? "They set out that instant" to share the news with other disciples, and together they all celebrate their shared experience of the Risen Jesus.

This is precisely, though somewhat poetically, what the Church is all about. The Church is a community of persons who have come to some personal recognition of the Risen Jesus in their lives and who are almost driven by that experience to gather with others to share and celebrate and deepen that awareness. **They do so in several ways: (1) by recalling their past experiences of Jesus; (2) by celebrating his risen and living presence among them through signs and symbols such as the "breaking of the bread" which we know as Eucharist; and (3) by then going out as a renewed people to share the Good News of Jesus with others.** To fully participate in that community of faith, each Christian must somehow arrive at a moment of personal "recognition of Jesus," a point at which he or she becomes personally aware of his risen presence and open to the guidance of the Spirit which he shared through his death and Resurrection. The Church in its fullest and most beautiful sense is that community of believers who share a most remarkable treasure—the recognition of Jesus present and a commitment to the truth of his message about a God whose love is infinite. It is a reality which, once experienced, can truly make one's heart "burn" with joy, hope, peace, and love.

The road
from Jerusalem
to Emmaus

2) The Church in History

Another scriptural incident which illustrates the meaning of the Church is related in the Acts of the Apostles 2:1-13. This is the account of the event we call Pentecost, when the gift of the Holy Spirit was poured out upon the frightened disciples and suddenly transformed them into courageous witnesses of the Risen Jesus. This incident is often referred to as "the birthday of the Church," because in it we encounter that initial gathering of disciples who begin a whole new way of living in communion with one another after experiencing the presence of Christ in a particularly powerful way. The story is filled with marvelous imagery—a powerful wind, tongues of fire, people moved to speak in foreign languages and, perhaps most significantly, nearly uproarious joy. But the message is essentially the same as that of the Emmaus story: Disheartened and frightened people are encountered by the Spirit of the Risen Jesus, they arrive at a profound recognition of him, and they are so moved by the experience that they go out with joy to share the Good News with others. A shattered band of disciples who had followed Jesus during his lifetime is therefore transformed into a community of faith through his death, Resurrection, Ascension, and gift of the Spirit. **So it is that the Church is born, and it is from this small but striking beginning in the religious experience of a handful of Jewish people some two thousand years ago that the Church has grown to a world-wide community today numbering a quarter of the human race.**

In this chapter we want to trace briefly the gradual development of the Church's understanding of Jesus Christ along its long and complicated journey through history. In our previous discussion of the development of the gospels, we noted that the early community of faith gradually grew in its understanding of Jesus following his death and Resurrection. So, too, the Church has gone through constant change, growth, and development through the centuries from its early days until now. Not surprisingly the history of that development has been extremely complex, filled with moments of great hope and profound tragedy, distinguished by moments of truly heroic dedication to the gospel of Jesus, but tainted as well by moments when it seemed to lose all sense of its true mission in the world.

Throughout its history the Church has inevitably been affected by the cultures and times in which it has found itself. What was initially a very loose fellowship consisting of just a small sect of Jews in Palestine gradually spread out into the world. **As it did so, it developed more stability as a community by placing increasing emphasis upon maintaining certain traditions, preserving right teachings, evolving lines of authority, developing various roles for Church leaders, and so on.** All of this was necessary if the Church were to survive in a very hostile world. But some have rightly claimed that the Church occasionally—though perhaps unavoidably—seemed to lose its direction and sense of purpose in its struggle for survival. There have no doubt been times in our history when we have lost touch with the gospel of Jesus, when our faith has been deeply affected by superstition, misunderstanding, and poor leadership. But through it all the Church has survived, and it has done so primarily because of the deep and constant faith of so many of its members, people influenced, guided, and supported by the ever-present Spirit of God.

It's not over yet.

We should note also that our development as a Church continues on to this day, and that recent developments in our understanding of Jesus have radically affected our Church structures, forms of piety, sacramental worship—virtually every facet of our life as a community of faith. **This is due to the fact that our understanding of Jesus is always at the very center of our identity as a Christian community.** When we gain a new insight into him and his message, it has the effect of throwing a stone into a calm pool of water. The new insight strikes with various degrees of intensity, but it always results in a ripple effect of steadily expanding changes. We change the ways in which we express our beliefs, perhaps, or in the manner in which we celebrate our sacramental life as a community. We might gain a new understanding of our roles and responsibilities in a wounded world that yearns for the healing touch of Jesus and his message. We

can only determine what we are to do and believe as Christians today by reflecting on what Jesus and his vision would demand of us. That is the central purpose of getting in touch with our history, of reflecting on our evolving sense of Jesus and his message. Our goal and challenge is to more perfectly attune ourselves to that gospel understanding of him which we have repeatedly stated must be our touchstone, our compass, and our foundation for understanding our identity as Christians and as Church.

As we begin our review of the Church's understanding of Jesus through history, we must affirm again a central conviction we hold as Christians. We believe that our history as a Church has been guided by the presence of God's Spirit, a Spirit Jesus promised would lead us to all truth (John 16:7-15). We are a free people capable of making many mistakes, but ultimately we are also a people loved profoundly and providentially by our God. With a sensitivity and commitment to that reality, let's begin our review of the Church's developing understanding of Jesus Christ.

Did Jesus intend to "found a Church"?

We begin our discussion with a fundamental and critical question: Did Jesus ever intend to form a community of faith at all, much less one like the Church as we experience it today? If our answer to that question is yes, then it would seem that Jesus intended us to discover him and preserve his teaching in union with one another. This would of course imply the need, or at the very least the desirability, for believers to gather with other Christians or, to use more customary language, to "join a church." If Jesus had no such intention, however, then it would seem that individuals have a perfect right to "do their own thing" in regard to their response to Jesus rather than having that response to some degree determined, governed, or in some way subject to evaluation by a broader community of people.

The question of Jesus' intentions regarding the establishment of a Church is not as easy to answer as one might think. There are several gospel references that seem to indicate clearly that he did intend such a community. In Matthew 16:18-20, for example, Jesus says to Peter, "You are Peter and on this rock I will build my Church. And the gates of the underworld can never hold out against it. I will give you the keys of the kingdom: whatever you bind on earth shall be considered bound in heaven; whatever you loose on earth shall be considered loosed in heaven." And in a later comment on the need for people to correct the wrong behavior of others, Jesus says, ". . . if (the wrongdoer) refuses to listen to (his fellow Christians), report it to the community; and if he refuses to listen to the community, treat him like a pagan or a tax collector." One difficulty with these statements, however, is that scholars think they may have been added by Matthew himself as he tried to give direction to the community for which he was writing his gospel.

Some scholars feel that Jesus would not have seen any need for a structured institution, believing along with many of his followers that the Kingdom of God would be fully realized very soon. Others feel that Jesus only intended a renewed and revitalized *Jewish* community, not the creation or development of an entirely new one. Such views would indicate that the Church only developed slowly out of the lived experience of the believers, not as a reality preached and promoted by Jesus himself.

While admitting the confusion which surrounds these questions, it seems reasonable to state the following:

- **If Jesus ever directly preached or implied the concept of a "church," he would likely not have had in mind the kind of structured institution that is a part of our understanding and experience of Church today.**

- **Nevertheless, many of the gospel images of Jesus do seem to indicate or imply some kind of communal experience by his followers. Parables like those of the shepherd and his flock (John 10:11-18) and the vine and the branches (John 15:1-11) seem to point to this, and the gospels include many sayings about the Kingdom which seem to have this communal sense.**

- **The moral or ethical teaching of Jesus also shows a real concern for the communal nature of our actions (Matthew 5:23; 7:3-5).**

- **Jesus' relationship with and training of his Apostles seems to indicate an ongoing role for them as the foundation of some sort of gathering or fellowship of those who believed in and followed him.**

3) From Proclamation to Explanation

After the death of the Apostles, the Church's teachings about Jesus broke from the kind of joyous *proclaiming* of the Good News that is typical of the gospels and entered upon a course of *explaining* Jesus and his message to peoples outside the Jewish communities of Palestine. As the Church spread out beyond the small geographic area in which it was born, it inevitably encountered different cultures, lifestyles, philosophies, and beliefs. Toward the end of the second century, a new group of thinkers steeped in the Greek philosophy of the time entered the Church. These people tried to translate the experience of the Apostles into a philosophical framework that made sense to them and suited their audiences. These men—whom we today refer to as "the Fathers of the Church"—tried to think through the experience of the early Christian community and reevaluate the Christian Scriptures in terms of their own way of thinking about and understanding the world. This seems to have been a reasonable, even a necessary, step to take if people from various cultures were to understand Jesus at all. But some historians of the Church feel this development was a major setback for authentic Christianity and that it represented a radical break from the true message and meaning of Jesus.

What essentially happened was that people stopped talking about the simple but moving gospel proclamation of "Jesus is Lord!" and began talking in terms that perhaps you, and certainly

So it would seem that Jesus did intend some kind of continuing community or fellowship of believers following his death, but this was perhaps not an organized religious community in our sense of that term. It would be up to the early followers of Jesus themselves, under the guidance of the Spirit of God, to give that initial community its form and direction, and these would in turn be directly affected by each succeeding generation of Christians as it struggled to pass on the faith. As we discussed in some detail earlier, this notion of "passing on the faith" was a major cause and purpose for the development of the Christian Scriptures. **It was also this desire to preserve the core teachings of Jesus, to keep the community from error, and to help hand on the faith from generation to generation which led to the gradual development of Church teachings and doctrines.**

your parents, would find familiar. Words like *God-man, substance, person,* and *nature* entered into the discussions about Jesus and his identity. These were Greek philosophical terms of the time, and their use amounted to a major shift in the Church's way of thinking about Jesus—a shift from a human, tangible, and somewhat simple approach to a more abstract, philosophical, and technical approach. Jesus and his message seemed to become a mystery to be explained rather than a relationship and vision to be lived. Instead of the joyous proclamation of the gospels, a whole new language began to develop, and the Church began to speak of Jesus as "one person with two natures sharing one substance."

The development of "heresies."

This shift in the Church's way of viewing, understanding, and discussing Jesus opened up all kinds of problems and arguments. Three major "heresies" or false teachings arose out of the debate, and each one of them resulted in the calling of a Church "council" or official gathering of Church leaders to try to resolve the issues:

1) About the year A.D. 300, a priest named Arius made a daring pronouncement that Jesus was not one with God but rather just a special creature of God, a being of a very high order created by God at a particular point in time. In other words, Jesus was viewed as more than a human being but less than God as the early Church claimed him to be. This teaching led to the calling of the first great council of the Church, the Council of Nicea (ny-seé -ah) in the year 325. **This council solemnly declared that,**

The ruins of an ancient Greek temple

Jesus Christ and the Church   185

in Jesus, God had truly appeared on earth in the person of his own Son. The profession of faith drawn up by this council is one which is likely very familiar to you. It states that Jesus is ". . . God from God, Light from Light, true God from true God, begotten, not made, one in being with the Father . . . For us men and for our salvation he came down and became flesh, was made man, suffered, and rose again on the third day. . . ."

2) About the year A.D. 400, a theory was proposed that the divine person who was acknowledged as "one in being with the Father" and the man Jesus of Nazareth who walked the face of the earth were in fact two different persons rather than one and the same. This was an attempt by some to guard what was a false notion of God's "purity" by attempting to establish a complete separation of God from the sinfulness of humanity. A debate also flared up at this time about the mother of Jesus, Mary, and her role in God's plan of salvation. One side argued that Mary could not be given the title "Mother of God" because, among other reasons, a human mother could not be said to give

birth to a divine being who already existed from eternity. On the other side were those who argued that, if Jesus were truly to be recognized as *both* God and man and yet one person, then Mary could rightly be called the "Mother of God" simply because she gave birth to the Jesus of History. In response to these disagreements, the Council of Ephesus (eh'-feh-sus) was convened in 431. **This council proclaimed that, despite the differences between his divine and human *natures*, there is but one *person* in Jesus. The council also formally and officially gave Mary the title of "Mother of God,"** though it is important for our discussion to note that this title was more of an attempt to make a statement about Jesus than it was about the nature of Mary herself.

3) At about the same time, another group of devout people proposed that Jesus possessed a divine nature only, and that despite all the apparent indications of his humanity while on earth, he was not truly a human person. Jesus, according to this belief, only *acted* human for our benefit. In the year 451, the Council of Chalcedon (kal'-seh-don) was called to deal with this heresy. **This council solemnly declared that Jesus was not only divine but also fully human.**

The Nicene Creed.

Though there were other Church councils which dealt with the identity of Jesus, the three councils we have discussed are often referred to as "the Great Christological Councils" of the Church. **Nicea defended Jesus' divinity as the Christ, Ephesus defended his unity as both God and man, and Chalcedon defended his full humanity.** Out of this complex history evolved one of the great creeds of the Church, an official statement of belief issued by the Church which attempted to find words to express realities that are truly beyond words. We have briefly referred to this creed above, but because of its central significance for us as Catholic Christians, we will now state it in full. This creed was initially promulgated by the Council of Nicea and then later reaffirmed by a council convened in Constantinople. Since the seventh century it has been officially known as the Nicene-Constantinopolitan Creed, but this is often shortened in common usage to simply the Nicene Creed. We often repeat this creed together as a community of faith during our liturgies—so much so, perhaps, that we begin to say the words quickly and without thought. But here we ask you to read the creed slowly, reflectively, prayerfully, recalling the hundreds of years of Church history, nearly endless argument and discussion by devout Christians, and profound expressions of faith and prayer which led to its development. And recall as well not only the historical situation which gave birth to this statement of our faith as Catholic Christians but also the gospel portrait of Jesus as it has been presented in this book. In doing so you will recognize here the basic gospel proclamation of Jesus and also the effects of our history as a community of faith trying to come to terms with the man and his message.

We believe in one God, the Father, the Almighty, maker of heaven and earth, of all that is seen and unseen. We believe in one Lord, Jesus Christ, the only Son of God, eternally begotten of the Father, God from God, Light from Light, true God from true God, begotten, not made, one in Being with the Father. Through him all things were made.

For us men and for our salvation he came down from heaven: by the power of the Holy Spirit he was born of the Virgin Mary, and became man. For our sake he was crucified under Pontius Pilate; he suffered, he died and was buried. On the third day he rose again in fulfillment of the Scriptures; he ascended into heaven and is seated at the right hand of the Father.

He will come again in glory to judge the living and the dead, and his Kingdom will have no end.

We believe in the Holy Spirit, the Lord, the giver of life, who proceeds from the Father and the Son. With the Father and the Son he is worshipped and glorified. He has spoken through the Prophets. We believe in one holy catholic and apostolic Church. We acknowledge one baptism for the forgiveness of sins. We look for the resurrection of the dead, and the life of the world to come. Amen.

4) A New Way of Thinking

The line of thought and approach to understanding Jesus which we have been discussing continued through the centuries and reached its peak in the Middle Ages with the rise of scholasticism. **This was a form of philosophy based heavily on the concepts of the Greek philosopher Aristotle, and it relied to a great extent on order and logic as its foundation.** As a philosophy or way of understanding reality, it has endured to this day. Its greatest proponent in the Church was St. Thomas Aquinas (1225-1274), almost without question the greatest and most influential theologian in the entire history of the Church. The scholastic philosophy as applied to Christian faith by Thomas and others became *the* foundation for thinking and teaching employed by the Church for nearly seven hundred years. It was almost certainly the approach used in the educating of your parents if they were formally taught in either Catholic schools or parish religious education programs. This approach involves an extremely ordered and organized approach to reality which, when abused, can lead to an overly strict commitment to certain forms or ways of stating things and to a high degree of rigidity and resistance to change and new ideas. As we will see later, this tendency would be deepened in the eighteenth and nineteenth centuries.

The major problem with this approach to understanding Jesus is that he and his message can quickly become almost cold and calculated realities, more like logical problems to be solved than the Good News of a loving God announced by Jesus. People can become so bound up with learning and remembering philosophical arguments in defense of teachings about Jesus that they can lose a clear sense of his humanness. And the qualities which so characterized the members of the early community of faith—sheer excitement and unbridled joy, deep conviction, raw courage, compassion and love, and a real exuberance about the Good News of Jesus—can be lost as well.

It seems that whenever the Church begins to lose its bearings, however, the Spirit of God leads us back to a balanced view of Jesus. In the Middle Ages this happened through a strong reaction by "the common folk" against the image of Jesus presented by the philosophers. People like St. Francis of Assisi (1182-1226) in the thirteenth century recognized the people's need for a more personal and human understanding of Jesus, and a popular movement based on devotion to Jesus and acts of piety developed. But, despite the great benefits of this development, a new problem gradually evolved. **There is a danger in oversimplifying the person of Jesus and his message that is perhaps just as real as that of overcomplicating him.** When our approach to Jesus becomes governed by our need for emotional experiences, or when we begin to seek artificial experiences of the sacred or mysterious dimensions in life, we can become open to superstition, fables, and even magical understandings of Jesus. This happened in the Middle Ages and, to one degree or another, among some elements in the Church even to the present. Legends about Jesus began to develop, art forms began to reflect false notions about him, and popular practices were initiated that were out of touch with the Jesus of the gospels.

One of these expressions is the celebration of Christmas that developed in the medieval period and which remains very much with us today. For most Christians today, the Christmas celebration of the birth of Jesus is *the* central religious feast of the year. This was certainly not the case in the early Church in which the emphasis—very properly—was not on the birth of Jesus but rather on his Resurrection, on Easter. This is surely not to suggest that it is wrong to celebrate Christmas. But it is clearly true that the event in the entire life of Jesus which gives meaning and power to all he said and did was his Resurrection from the dead by his Father. And it is the belief in this event, and the deep joy which accompanies it, that should most strongly mark and identify those who would be his followers. As some have stated it, we as Christians are above all else "an Easter people."

The Reformation.

After awhile the kind of philosophical analysis and discussion of Jesus that had characterized the Church for centuries began to fade a bit. The Church became increasingly concerned about itself, about its own identity, purpose, and role in the world. Conflicts regarding the pope and his role arose, and in the thirteenth century there were actually two and then even three men who claimed that they were the duly elected leader of the Church. New teachings and ideas challenged accepted traditions, and scandalous behavior among the clergy became commonplace. All of this, combined with a rise in an awareness of Scripture and a heightened personal spirituality among some

A typical fifteenth-century interpretation of the Nativity, by Botticelli

Jesus Christ and the Church   189

5) Into the Modern Age

During the eighteenth and nineteenth centuries, the studies of science and technology increased dramatically. And a whole new field of study—psychology—was born. A completely new set of problems, therefore, confronted the Church. Some people tried to prove that Jesus never even existed or, more commonly, that he was just an ordinary person with no special relationship to the divine. The Resurrection and the Apostles' reaction to it were explained away by some as symptoms of psychological disorders. Human beings were increasingly viewed as self-sufficient, and God was explained by some to be a "projection of people's minds," as a kind of psychological "father figure" created by people through the years to explain the mysteries of the world. Atheism, or the rejection of a belief in God, was proposed as an acceptable philosophical position.

The Catholic Church was already in a defensive posture from its experience with the Reformation. The increasingly scientific mentality, with all the doubts and questions it raised, only deepened the Church's commitment to "defend the faith" against all attacks. Christian education, for example, became recognized as the process for preparing Catholics to be "soldiers of Christ," ready to stand in defense of the faith. To prepare them for that role, students were expected to memorize very rigidly defined answers to basic questions about Catholic belief. The sense that the average Catholic had of Jesus often consisted of remembering key teachings about him—about his relationship to God and

members of the Church, led many to yearn for a renewal of the Church. **Out of this climate of great tension and desire for change the Reformation was born in the sixteenth century, and Protestant churches (the name given those who "protested" against the Roman Church) gradually developed.**

In terms of our discussion of Jesus, it is interesting to note that, during this period, ideas and teachings about Jesus were considered more as arguments in defense of certain beliefs about *the nature of the Church* than as points of contention or disagreement in themselves. Martin Luther, for example, revolted not against the teachings about Jesus of his day but, rather, against the Roman understanding of the Church, the papacy, and the practice of selling indulgences.

For the next three centuries, Catholics and Protestants became caught up in debates about who was right and wrong in the Church, about proper forms of Church government, about the number and nature of the sacraments, and so on. Jesus and the God he revealed were no longer the focal points of the Church and its members. We were dangerously close to losing touch with the Jesus of the gospels.

the Spirit in the Trinity, about his presence in the sacraments, and so on—rather than of entering into a developing love relationship with God in and through Jesus. This was the case as recently as twenty years ago in the Church, but it is clearly not so today. What happened to change things so much?

The contemporary Church: A return to the Jesus of the gospels.

The Church of today, particularly since Vatican Council II in the early 1960s, has reacted and responded to its long history in a variety of ways, many of them dramatic, and nearly all of them touching upon our understanding of Jesus:

- **There has been, perhaps most importantly, a tremendous renewal in our interest in and study of the Scriptures. Literally tens of thousands, even hundreds of thousands, of Catholics are reading and studying the gospels today who would not have even considered doing so just twenty years ago.**

- **There is a completely different perception of the Church itself, a movement away from the sense of it as a defensive protector of the faith and toward an image of a faith-filled "people of God," a "pilgrim community" in touch with its roots in the faith experience of the early Christian community of the gospels.**

- **There is a new awareness of the relationship between science and religion and a decreased tension between the two. It is to a great extent the breaking down of this division that has made our renewed understanding of the Scriptures possible by opening us to the real contributions which can be made by archeology, the study of languages, and so on.**

All of these developments to greater or lesser degrees relate to our changing understanding of Jesus. And with this developing understanding of the meaning of both Jesus and the Church, we have witnessed a dramatic change in all the expressions of faith we experience as Catholics—in our sacramental worship, in our discussions of theology and the meaning of Jesus, and in our relationships with our fellow Christians in other churches and denominations. To use our earlier image of the stone hitting the calm pool of water, with Vatican Council II and the increase in biblical scholarship that was so much a part of it, the deceptively calm and controlled body of water that was the Church of the eighteenth and nineteenth centuries was struck, not by a pebble, but by a boulder of great proportions. The resulting waves of change have amounted to a tidal wave to some Catholics, at times completely shaking them from their roots in the past. But for many others, the effects of that monumental period in the Church have only served to cleanse and purify us as a community of faith, thrusting us not into chaos but back to our deepest roots in the gospel proclamation of the early community of faith.

Pope John Paul II greets Mother Teresa following a Mass honoring her for her work among the poor of India

A shift from "Jesus from above" to "Jesus from below."

The central change we have experienced in our understanding of Jesus is one which has been reflected throughout this book. Scholars today talk about the shift of emphasis in our way of thinking about Jesus (what we call our "Christology" or study of Jesus) as a move away from primarily a "Christology from above" to a new emphasis on a "Christology from below." This is somewhat technical language, certainly, but its central meaning is quite clear and extremely important. In an approach to Jesus "from above," we *begin* our discussion and understanding of Jesus with a recognition of his special relationship with his Father from the beginning of time. In this view, Jesus is seen as the divine Son of God who comes from heaven to take on our humanity in order to save us from our sins and lead us to salvation. By starting from this

point of view, great weight is logically given to Jesus' *Incarnation*, the formal term for the teaching that the Son of God took on human nature in Jesus. This led to the strong emphasis on Christmas which we discussed briefly earlier. In this approach to understanding Jesus, his divinity is strongly stressed, and there is a sense that he is more a Superman of sorts than a person like us. He is very much removed from our human experience, one who at all times was aware of his divine origin and therefore not truly in touch with life as we experience it. Jesus is seen, in this view, as freely accepting death as a perfect offering to his Father, thereby satisfying our debts to God and opening the gates of heaven to us once again. It is this understanding of Jesus "from above" that for the most part characterized the Catholic education of our parents and preceding generations for centuries.

Today scholars speak about an understanding of

Jesus that starts "at the other end" so to speak, a "Christology from below." In this approach to understanding Jesus, we *begin* not with his divinity but rather with his humanity, with his historical life as a faith-filled Jewish preacher of first century Palestine. Through our study of and reflection upon the gospels primarily, we gradually come to terms with his message about the Kingdom of God and its profound implications for our understanding of both God and our relationship to him. We consider the ways in which the disciples only slowly grew in their full awareness of his identity, and we reflect upon the ways in which we as Christians today must perhaps follow their lead. We see Jesus, not as a Superman, but as a marvelous person who truly shared our own humanity, with all its fear and loneliness, its confusion, its pain, and we discover deep consolation in that knowledge. In this view of Jesus, everything about him comes together and makes sense, not just in the experience of his death on the cross, but even more so in the event which followed it—the Resurrection of Jesus from the dead by God.

This book has been clearly based on an understanding of Jesus "from below." It is possible, perhaps even likely, that your parents might be initially surprised and even confused by this approach, simply because it is so foreign to the educational experience of most adult Catholics. You are encouraged to share what you have learned here with them in whatever way you can, perhaps most effectively by suggesting they read this book and then discussing it with them. Many adult Catholics have been greatly freed and even relieved by this understanding of Jesus and his message. This reaction is not necessarily caused by a discovery of truths that they did not know before. On the contrary, what an understanding of Jesus which begins with his humanity can offer is another path to precisely the same essential truths we have always professed as a community of faith. But this approach follows our own journey as human persons more closely. Therefore, what were before perhaps only mysterious teachings to be memorized and accepted as truth now become far more understandable realities that can touch our hearts as well as our minds. And the gospel of Jesus Christ can more fully be realized as the wonderful reality the Church has always proclaimed it to be—the Good News of salvation that can bring joy, peace, and love to our lives.

6) The Journey of Faith in Jesus

Our study of Jesus has been a long, occasionally difficult, but hopefully rewarding and enriching one. As a young person in today's Church, you are heir to a profoundly rich history of some two thousand years of struggle in our attempts as a Christian community to come to terms with the historical Jesus we recognize as the Christ, our Lord and Savior. But you are even more than that. You are also privileged to be a witness of and a participant in one of the most incredibly exciting eras in that long history, a time in which our knowledge and understanding of Jesus has nearly exploded with insights, questions, and the search for answers which satisfy the needs of contemporary Christians. It has always been a marvelous gift to be a follower of Jesus, but at no time in our history as a Church has it been more exhilarating, challenging, and gratifying to be one.

The invitation and the challenge offered you to come to your own "recognition" of Jesus is an intensely personal one, and it is not our right nor our desire here to compel you to make a decision about faith in him. What we *can* and *must* urge you to do, however, is to take the person and message of Jesus seriously, to recognize the questions he posed about the meaning of life as central to your struggle to become a mature person. *What* you ultimately decide about him is for you to determine with honesty, openness, and integrity. *That* you must decide is a reality that can be postponed but not permanently avoided.

We opened this chapter with Luke's beautiful story about the two disciples on the road to Emmaus. That story has tremendous insights to offer each of us in our personal struggles to come to terms with Jesus. The story tells us that God always meets us on our own terms, that he "walks with us" in our journey through life, and that he is sensitive to our own story and our unique needs. If our need as young people is to question, to doubt, and to search, it is our responsibility to do that honestly and without guilt. Jesus and his message can offer each of us an understanding of life that can "burn within our hearts" if we choose to accept it. But each of us, like the two disciples on that dusty road long ago, needs to open our hearts to God, just as those two men invited Jesus into their home. Once that openness on our part is present, we can be sure that God will reveal himself to us and that we will truly recognize him.

Our history as a Church has taught us that such recognition seems only to come fully in the company of others, in community, and in communion with other believers. The questions presented in the gospels nineteen hundred years ago are put to each of us today. As you search out your own answers to those questions posed by Jesus and his message, we urge you to do so in the company of others who can share that search with you.

It is truly a marvelous journey, the journey of a life lived with faith in the God revealed by Jesus. Our prayer for you as we end this book is the beautiful one attributed to St. Paul and contained in his letter to the Ephesians:

That is why I kneel before the Father from whom every family in heaven and on earth takes its name; and I pray that he will bestow on you gifts in keeping with the riches of his glory. May he strengthen you inwardly through the working of his Spirit. May Christ dwell in your hearts through faith, and may charity be the root and foundation of your life. Thus you will be able to grasp fully, with all the holy ones, the breadth and length and height and depth of Christ's love, and experience this love which surpasses all knowledge, so that you may attain to the fullness of God himself.

To him whose power now at work in us can do immeasurably more than we ask or imagine—to him be glory in the church and in Christ Jesus through all generations, world without end. Amen (Ephesians 3:14-21).

Review questions and activities:

1) In what three ways mentioned by the author does the Church celebrate and deepen its awareness of the Risen Jesus?

2) How did the very loose fellowship of a small Jewish sect in Palestine that was the early Church develop more stability as a community and therefore survive in a hostile world?

3) In what sense is our understanding of Jesus "at the very center of our identity as a Christian community"?

4) According to the author, did Jesus ever intend to "found a Church," given our common understanding and experience of what the Church is today? Explain your answer.

5) The author describes a shift from "proclamation" to "explanation" of the Good News early in the Church's history. Explain what this means, and state some of the implications of this development for later generations and their understanding of Jesus.

6) What three major heresies about Jesus Christ came to the fore in the fourth and fifth centuries, and in what ways did the Church respond to each? What major communal statement of belief evolved out of those developments?

7) What is scholasticism? What are its major characteristics, and what are its weaknesses when applied too rigidly to the sharing of faith in Jesus?

8) How did some elements of the Church in the Middle Ages react against the rigidity of scholasticism? Do you see any parallels to this in our modern Church?

9) How did Protestant churches develop? What is the name given the general movement which gave birth to them, and when did it occur? What role did discussion of Jesus play in this development?

10) What was the Church's response to the increasingly scientific mentality developed during the eighteenth and nineteenth centuries? How was this reflected in the approach to Christian education popular in the Church until the fairly recent past?

11) What major factors led to the development of a new approach in discussing and understanding Jesus today?

12) Describe the shift in the study of Jesus from a "Christology from above" to a "Christology from below."

13) What significant insights about personal faith development can be provided by the Emmaus story which opened this chapter?

Terms to identify and remember:

Pentecost
Fathers of the
  Church
heresies
Council of Nicea
Council of Ephesus
Council of Chalcedon
Nicene Creed

scholasticism
St. Thomas Aquinas
St. Francis of Assisi
Reformation
Protestants
atheism
Christology

Exercise for personal reflection:

As the author suggests near the end of this chapter, we encourage you to share this book with your parents or other adults. Then discuss with them the differences they recognize between the approach to Jesus represented by this text and the one with which they were likely raised. This kind of sharing can lead to better communication and understanding for all concerned, and ultimately to the kind of unity Jesus prayed would be the result of his life and message. (See John 17:20-23.)

Glossary of Key Terms

Abba. Uniquely intimate name used by Jesus for God. An Aramaic word meaning "Daddy."

Apostles. Based on the Greek word for "to send forth," the title primarily given to the twelve men first called by Jesus and through whom the future Church was to be established.

Apparitions. Appearances made by Jesus to various persons after his death and Resurrection.

Ascension. The term given that event in which Jesus passed totally into the presence of his Father after his death and Resurrection.

Baptism. The act of bathing in water as a sign of spiritual purification. A common religious symbol for many religions, including Judaism.

Babylonian Captivity. The period from 587 to 539 B.C. when the people of Israel were carried off into captivity by the Babylonians, then to be freed by the Persians. Also known as "the Exile."

Christ. Based on the Greek word, *Christos,* meaning "the anointed one." A Greek translation of the Hebrew word, *Messiah.* A major title for Jesus *after* his death and Resurrection, when he was referred to as "*the* Christ."

Christian Scriptures. Term preferred for "the New Testament." The collection of the sacred writings of Christians, including the gospels, Acts of the Apostles, various epistles or letters, and the Book of Revelation.

Christology. That branch of theology committed to the study of the person, role, nature, and message of Jesus.

Circumcision. A Jewish religious practice which involves removing the foreskin of the male child's penis as a permanent sign of the child's membership in the covenant community of the Jews.

Covenant. A special relationship established between God and individuals (e.g., Abraham, Jacob) and/or with a people (the Sinai covenant). The Law, and more specifically the Ten Commandments, represented the response required of the Jewish people to the commitment of Yahweh's protective love in the covenant relationship. Christians believe a "new covenant" was established with God through the life, death, and Resurrection of Jesus.

Day of Atonement. A major feast during which the Jewish people solemnly repented of their sins (as they still do today) and the high priest purified the Holy of Holies in the Temple.

Diaspora. The term given all those Jews who settled in regions outside of Palestine during or after the Exile.

Essenes. A small Jewish sect which was so conservative in religious matters that it withdrew from Jewish society in order to maintain strict religious practices.

Evangelist. From the Greek word, *evangelion,* meaning "good news." Name given the editors of the gospels—Matthew, Mark, Luke, and John—who "proclaimed the good news" of Jesus' Gospel.

Exile. See "Babylonian Captivity" above.

Exodus. The name given that event in which Moses led the Israelites out of their slavery in Egypt and into the Promised Land of Canaan.

Exorcism. The act by which an "evil spirit" is driven out of a "possessed" person.

Galilee. The province in the northern region of Palestine in which Jesus was raised and initially shared his message.

Gospel. From the Middle English word, *godspell,* meaning "good news." Name given the major sources of information about Jesus attributed to Matthew, Mark, Luke, and John and contained in the Christian Scriptures.

Hanukkah. Also called "the Feast of Dedication," this feast celebrates the overthrow of the Seleucids by the Jews and the rededication of the Temple in 164 B.C.

Hebrew Scriptures. Term preferred for "the Old Testament." The collection of the sacred writings of the Jewish people which deeply influenced Jesus and remains treasured by both Jews and Christians today.

Heresies. False teachings about matters of faith officially rejected by the Church.

High priest. The head of the priestly class and president of the Sanhedrin. Caiaphas was high priest during Jesus' trial and execution.

Idumea. Southern region of Palestine from which Herod the Great came.

Incarnation. The doctrine or formal teaching that the Son of God took on human nature in Jesus.

Infancy narratives. Special stories offered by Matthew and Luke at the beginning of their gospels to "explain" the origin and meaning of Jesus as understood through the eyes of faith.

Israel. Name given to Jacob after Yahweh made a covenant with him. During the history surrounding him and his sons, the Hebrew people were known as "Israelites." The name Israel was then later given to the northern kingdom.

Jesus. Common Jewish name meaning "Yahweh (God) saves" or "Yahweh (God) is salvation."

Judaism. The official name of the Jewish religion following the return of the remnant to Jerusalem after the Exile in Babylon. Based on Judah, the southern kingdom, from which the remnant came, and the word from which the title "Jew" is derived.

Judea. Region in central Palestine which constituted the geographic and religious center of Judaism. Jerusalem was located there, and the region was settled by "mainline" Jews after their return from the Exile.

Judges. Great warriors who led the people of Israel against their enemies in the period between settlement in Canaan and the establishment of the kingdom.

Kingdom of God. For Jesus, the rule or reign of God's love over the hearts of people, and a new social order based on unconditional love of God and others.

Messiah. The Hebrew word meaning "the anointed one." The title given the saving figure hoped for by the Jews of the Hebrew Scriptures, and later applied to Jesus whom some believed had fulfilled that hope.

Miracles. In relation to Jesus' ministry, signs intended to manifest God's power over all creation and, in a special way, over the forces of evil.

Nicene Creed. An official statement of the basic beliefs of the Church, originally promulgated by the Council of Nicea in A.D. 325, and often shared to this day during Mass and on other occasions.

Palestine. The land on the eastern shore of the Mediterranean Sea which forms the backdrop of the gospel story. Variously referred to in the Bible as "the Land of Israel," "the Land of Canaan," "the Promised Land," or "the Land of Judah."

Parable. A literary or speaking device which teaches a lesson by comparing one reality to another. These short stories often end with a surprising "twist" intended to catch the listener's attention.

Passover. A major Jewish feast based on the Exodus of the Hebrew people from bondage in Egypt.

Patriarchs. The title given to the founding fathers of the Hebrew people, particularly Abraham, Isaac, and Jacob. The history surrounding these men is known as "the patriarchal period."

Pentecost. For the Jews, a major feast celebrating the giving of the Law to Moses. For Christians, often called "the birthday of the Church" when the Holy Spirit "descended upon" the first Christians.

Pharisees. A faction within Judaism that was conservative in politics but liberal in matters of religion, in that they accepted new developments in Jewish thought. Their tendency toward legalism put them in conflict with Jesus.

Pronouncement stories. Stories of Jesus whose intent was to lead to a short, concise "punchline" or direct teaching.

Reformation. Sixteenth-century movement within the Church which resulted in the development of the Protestant churches.

Remnant. The term given those Jews who returned from the Exile in Babylon to resettle in Jerusalem and rebuild the Temple there.

Resurrection. The term given the event in which Jesus was raised from the dead by God.

Sabbath. The weekly day of rest and prayer for the Jews based on the creation story in Genesis. It lasted from what for us would be Friday to Saturday evenings. Sabbath worship was a source of conflict between Jesus and the Pharisees.

Sadducees. A faction within Judaism which was liberal in politics but conservative in religious matters. They constituted the priestly aristocracy of the Jews.

Samaria. Territory in north central Palestine occupied by a remnant of those tribes of the northern kingdom of Israel who had not been sent into Babylon during the Exile. The Samaritans were therefore despised by many mainline Jews from Judea.

Sanhedrin. Literally an "assembly," the official governing body of the Jews. It consisted of seventy members representing the priests, scribes, and elders. It acted like a kind of supreme court during the trial of Jesus.

Scholasticism. An approach to philosophy made popular in the Middle Ages and relying heavily on logic and order of thought.

Scribes. A class within Judaism consisting of writers and jurists. Responsible for studying the Law and ruling on matters regarding it. The most respected scribes were called "doctors of the Law," and when teaching they were called "rabbis."

Synagogue. A building or place used by Jews for worship and religious study. It became the central communal institution of the Jews after the destruction of the Temple in A.D. 70.

Synoptic. From a Greek word meaning a "common view," the term applied to the gospels of Matthew, Mark, and Luke, which share many characteristics and can only be fully understood when looked at together.

Yahweh. The Hebrew symbolic name for God, variously translated as "I am who am," "I am the one who is present," or "I bring into existence all that is."

Zealots. A faction within Judaism committed to a military overthrow of the Romans.

Index

Acknowledgments continued:

Line drawings for maps by Therese A. Gasper. Photos: ABC, page 158; Joel Barry (Nancy Palmer Agency), page 96; The Bettman Archive, Inc., pages 50, 89; CBS, page 29; Cincinnati Art Museum, page 105; Editorial Photocolor Archives, cover, page 110; National Catholic Reporter/Patty Edmonds, page 161; The Genesis Project, pages 151, 168; Joel Gordon, pages 76, 81; The Granger Collection, New York, page 34; Jack Hamilton, pages 12, 16, 20, 23, 146, 175, 176, 194; Susan Lapides (Design Conceptions), page 185; Jean-Claude LeJeune, page 172; Peter M. Lerman (Nancy Palmer Agency), page 121; Matson Photo Service, page 132; Garo Nalbandian/Argus, page 180; Joseph Noble, page 122; Dale Peterson, pages 24, 130; Norman Provost, FSC, pages 2, 8; Religious News Photo Service, pages 63, 79, 189, 192; Marc Riboud (RNS), page 38; Ron Sievert, page 144.